The American History Series

SERIES EDITORS

John Hope Franklin, *Duke University*
A. S. Eisenstadt, *Brooklyn College*

Arthur S. Link
GENERAL EDITOR FOR HISTORY

Steven A. Riess
NORTHEASTERN ILLINOIS UNIVERSITY

Sport in Industrial America
1850–1920

HARLAN DAVIDSON, INC.
WHEELING, ILLINOIS 60090-6000

Library of Congress Cataloging-in-Publication Data

Riess, Steven A.
    Sport in industrial America. 1850–1920 / Steven A. Riess.
        p.   cm. —(The American history series)
    Includes bibliographical references and index.
    ISBN 0-88295-916-6
    1. Sports—United States—Sociological aspects. 2. Sports—United States—History—19th century. 3. Sports—United States—History—20th century. I. Title. II. Series: American history series (Wheeling, Ill.)
GV706.5.R54   1995
306.4'83'0973—dc20   94-43286
                                       CIP

Cover painting: Frank O. Small, *Slide, Kelly, Slide.* Courtesy of the Boston Public Library, Print Department.

Manufactured in the United States of America
99 98 97 96 95 94 1 2 3 4 5 BC

FOREWORD

Every generation writes its own history for the reason that it sees the past in the foreshortened perspective of its own experience. This has surely been true of the writing of American history. The practical aim of our historiography is to give us a more informed sense of where we are going by helping us understand the road we took in getting where we are. As the nature and dimensions of American life are changing, so too are the themes of our historical writing. Today's scholars are hard at work reconsidering every major aspect of the nation's past: its politics, diplomacy, economy, society, recreation, mores and values, as well as status, ethnic, race, sexual, and family relations. The lists of series titles that appear at the back of this book will show at once that our historians are ever broadening the range of their studies.

The aim of this series is to offer our readers a survey of what today's historians are saying about the central themes and aspects of the American past. To do this, we have invited to write for the series only scholars who have made notable contributions to the respective fields in which they are working. Drawing on primary and secondary materials, each volume presents a factual and narrative account of its particular subject, one that affords readers a basis for perceiving its larger dimensions and importance. Conscious that readers respond to the closeness and immediacy of a subject, each of our authors seeks to restore the past as an actual present, to revive it as a living reality. The individuals and groups who figure in the pages of our books appear as real people who once were looking for survival and fulfillment. Aware that historical subjects are often matters of controversy, our authors present their own findings and conclusions. Each volume closes with an extensive critical essay on the writings of the major authorities on its particular theme.

The books in this series are designed for use in both basic and advanced courses in American history, on the undergraduate and graduate levels. Such a series has a particular value these days, when the format of American history courses is being altered to accommodate a greater diversity of reading materials. The series offers a number of distinct advantages. It extends the dimensions of regular course work. Going well beyond the confines of the textbook, it makes clear that the study of our past is, more than the student might otherwise understand, at once complex, profound, and absorbing. It presents that past as a subject of continuing interest and fresh investigation. The work of experts in their respective fields, the series, moreover, puts at the disposal of the reader the rich findings of historical inquiry. It invites the reader to join, in major fields of research, those who are pondering anew the central themes and aspects of our past. And it reminds the reader that in each successive generation of the ever-changing American adventure, men and women and children were attempting, as we are now, to live their lives and to make their way.

John Hope Franklin
A. S. Eisenstadt

CONTENTS

ACKNOWLEDGMENTS

It seems as if I have been preparing to write this book for most of my adult life. I began studying the history of American sport as a graduate student in 1970, and I have continued ever since. I owe a great deal to my colleagues in sport history for their encouragement and criticisms, especially Benjamin Rader and Melvin L. Adelman, who read an earlier draft of this manuscript. Their criticisms were extremely useful and helped make this a better essay. I also would like to thank Abraham S. Eisenstadt, who also went through an earlier draft with a fine-tooth comb, and whose judicious suggestions were both friendly and beneficial. I want to thank the staff at Harlan Davidson, especially Maureen Hewitt, for their patience, since I did not exactly make my deadlines, and my copy editor, Claudia Lamm Wood, for her excellent work. I thank my colleagues at Northeastern Illinois University, especially June Sochen who read a portion of the book. I also want to thank my many students with whom I have tested my ideas on sport history since 1974. I owe a great deal to my wife Tobi, my chief editor and sounding board, for putting up with me while this project was on the boards. And finally, I want to thank Jodi for keeping my PC in operation, and Jamie and Jennie for having patience with their Daddy.

Steven A. Riess
Chicago, Illinois

For Jodi, Jamie, and Jennifer

INTRODUCTION

Sport in modern society is one of the most popular forms of mass entertainment. People all around the world enjoy playing and watching sports. Millions attend soccer matches, horse races, and baseball games, while over a billion watch the Olympics and the World Cup on television. The United States in the late nineteenth century became one of the first countries in which sport was a widespread obsession. England was the first modern nation in which sport was an important institution, and the American fascination with sport began as a product of its colonial English heritage and the nineteenth-century, trans-Atlantic, Anglo-American culture. In the mid-nineteenth century, before the United States became an industrial, urban nation, sport had not yet achieved a high level of prominence or widespread popularity. Sport appealed largely to segments of the economic and social elite and to lower-class subcultures that composed the sporting fraternity. The term "sport" had very negative connotations. It was defined as a mutation, an object of derision, or a person with a flashy lifestyle. As historian Elliott Gorn points out, "sport" intimated boisterousness, defiance of social constraint, and loutish behavior.

Historians today define sport as pastimes, primarily competitive, that require physical dexterity. These contests may be against oneself, another individual, or a rival team. The sporting games of most people around the world in the mid-nineteenth century were premodern traditional village pastimes, such as wrestling, or they were adjuncts to religious ceremonies, such as the Native American games of lacrosse and shinny. Historians Allen Guttmann and Melvin Adelman, authors, respectively, of *From Ritual to Record: The Nature of Modern Sports* (1978), and *A Sporting Time: New York City and the Rise of Modern Athletics, 1820–70* (1986), describe premodern sports as unorganized or informally arranged athletic contests. Rules were simple, unwritten, and based on local customs and traditions; competition was local, and little role differentiation existed among participants. Reports of contests were not widely disseminated or remembered (other than by oral tradition), and no statistics or records were kept. Modern sports, on the other hand, are described as highly organized, secular activities with formal institutions at local, regional, and national levels. Rules are formal, standard, and written, and competition is theoretically open to everyone under the same conditions. Roles are highly differentiated between spectators and players, and among professionals and amateurs who specialize in particular sports and even certain positions. Finally, in modern sports, results are widely publicized and statistics and records are carefully maintained.

American sport in 1850 was substantially premodern and virtually an exclusive male preserve that defined and exemplified manly behavior as aggressive, courageous, vigorous, and unchildlike. Popular sports were primarily participatory and offered athletes an opportunity to demonstrate physical prowess, make money from prizes or bets, and fraternize with their rivals. Mass spectatorship had already become significant, particularly for elite-sponsored thoroughbred racing (harness racing was the first modern sport organized by middle-class Americans), which was attended by large audiences, and pedestrianism (long-distance running races), which matched working-class athletes. These contests provided spectators with entertainment, sociability, and gambling opportunities.

American sportsmen up to the 1850s constituted a sporting fraternity of upper- and working-class men who enjoyed traditional sporting pastimes. They composed an important segment of the male bachelor subculture, which rejected Victorian morality. These men enjoyed camaraderie and sociability in male-only settings where they escaped from women, domesticity, and work. They valued such manly behavior as drinking, frequenting prostitutes, gambling, and demonstrating athletic prowess. However, sport was not yet very popular among future-oriented middle-income men who generally frowned upon it as an immoral, socially debilitating waste of time.

The premodern, mid-nineteenth century sporting culture was heavily influenced by the agrarian character of society. At this time 85 percent of Americans still lived in rural areas, and their favorite sports were contests of strength, skill, and courage that they enjoyed at taverns and in the countryside. Woods and streams were readily accessible to most American sportsmen who fished, hunted, shot at targets, and rode horses. Spectators could watch horse races, combat contests like gouging (rough-and-tumble, no holds-barred frontier matches), prizefighting and wrestling, and such blood sports as animal baiting and cock fighting. Nonetheless as early as the colonial era, cities played an important role in American sport; with their relatively concentrated populations, they provided a site for sports clubs and sports entrepreneurs. Eighteenth-century colonial cities had elite fishing, racing, and fox-hunting clubs, and by the early 1800s cities also had more democratic organizations for rowing, racquets, gymnastics, and target shooting. Colonial publicans were the first sporting entrepreneurs. They sponsored animal baiting, marksmanship contests, billiards, and bowling, all pastimes that involved wagering and attracted thirsty sporting men. Tavern promotion of animal baiting declined in the antebellum era, replaced in part by an occasional illegal prize fight. Boxing demonstrated courage and other manly traits; in 1837 the *New York Herald* argued that this sport was "far preferable to the insidious knife . . . , or the cowardly and brutal practice of biting, kicking or gouging." Other spectator sports were mainly contested in cities that had sufficient gate-paying sportsmen to encourage promoters to arrange matches.

The purpose of this book is to explain how sport in the United States developed from a morally suspect, premodern entertainment in 1850 that did not attract the interest of most Americans into a respectable, modernized national obsession, culminating in the Golden Age of Sports of the 1920s. During this period the variety and number of sports rapidly increased, sporting institutions became modernized, and participatory and spectator sport became popular with men from all social classes and most demographic groups. Cities became responsible for providing public space for their residents to play, sports arenas became prominent semipublic facilities, and star athletes became national heroes. My analysis of the rise of sport and its development focuses both on the internal history of major sports (the rise of leagues, rules, and championships) and the influence of broader societal developments, primarily urbanization (city building) and industrialization and secondarily class, race, ethnicity, and gender, upon sporting institutions. In addition, I will examine the impact of sport upon the broader American culture and society.

The changes in the American sporting scene began at midcentury and then accelerated after the Civil War, primarily as a result of urbanization and industrialization. The greatest relative increase in urban population in American history occurred in the mid-nineteenth century. As a result the proportion of the population that resided in cities quadrupled from 5 percent in 1820 to 20 percent in 1860.

The small, commercial antebellum cities were known as "walking cities" because residents usually walked wherever they had to go. These cities were modest in size, had small populations, and a highly mixed land use. By the 1870s, the accelerated pace of urban growth led to the rise of the industrial radial city. These cities had substantial populations and were physically much larger than walking cities, their size made feasible by the emergence of extensive public transportation systems. Their economies were increasingly based on industry rather than trade. Land uses were highly specialized with distinctive commercial, residential, and industrial areas radiating out in concentric circles from the downtown core (or central business district). Organized sport emerged in the larger walking cities of the mid-nineteenth century, but the great boom in sport took place in the radial industrial cities after the Civil War. Their concentrated populations included a critical mass of potential sports participants and spectators; they provided a ready market for sports entrepreneurs who sold athletic equipment or promoted commercial sports contests.

The role of the city in the rise of modern sport was greater than simply being the site where athletes were drawn from and where sport became organized, commercialized, and professionalized. Cities were organic entities composed of physical structures, social organizations, and value systems that interacted over time to create urban change that itself helped shape the rise of sport. A city's physical structure included its spatial dimensions, demographics, neighborhoods, communication and transportation networks, and economic institutions. Its social organizations included political and governmental structures, social institutions, social classes, and ethnic and racial groups. Value systems comprised individual and group attitudes, ideologies, and behavior. American sport in the era of the industrial radial city was primarily a product of the constant blending of the elements of urbanization with each other and with sport itself.

The late-nineteenth-century sporting boom had its origins in various social forces operating in the antebellum walking city. A major factor was the emergence of a sports creed that changed middle-class attitudes toward sport from negative to positive. This transformation was produced by a broad-based reform movement that sought to ameliorate living conditions for slum dwellers as well as for sedentary white-collar workers by promoting wholesome out-of-door sports. The new sport doctrines demonstrated that athletics could be uplifting and promote public health, improve morality, and build character. It placed sport firmly within the traditional American expectation that leisure-time activities should be useful as well as diverting.

Once sport's popularity began to grow, the rise of industrial capitalism heavily influenced its direction. The shift from an agrarian and commercial economy to an industrial economy re-shaped the urban social structure, the distribution of wealth, and traditional leisure patterns. The industrial age also ushered in remarkable technological innovations. Improved communication networks made possible immediate reports of sporting events by cheap daily newspapers that were widely distributed. New, economic transportation made sport more accessible. Further-more, factories used innovative manufacturing techniques to mass-produce inexpensive sports equipment that increased op-portunities for participation.

The changing spaces of towns that evolved into radial cities had a big impact on sport. Traditional playing areas were often destroyed as land use patterns shifted. Empty lots that once served as cricket pitches were used for housing or factories. Lovely boulevards and quaint rural roads used for trotting be-came busy city streets. Once remote streams and woods were drained and cleared, sportsmen had to travel further to reach timberlands and unpolluted waterways. Some of the problems of accessibility were alleviated by innovations such as railroads and electric trolleys that enabled athletes and spectators who could afford the cost to get to sporting venues.

City governments responded slowly to the growing needs for outdoor space. Social reformers and boosters pressured mu-nicipalities to secure and develop public space for recreation. Led by the example of New York's Central Park in 1858, cities established beautiful suburban public parks after the Civil War. By the early 1900s, municipalities also developed inner-city sites for small parks and playgrounds, baths, recreational piers, and schoolyards. Local governments continued to be responsible for protecting public property, maintaining order, and promoting morality. The authorities kept young ballplayers out of city streets, regulated sports crowds, issued licenses for sports pro-motions, and fought the gambling menace.

Sport in industrial America was substantially influenced by social class, which was itself heavily shaped by industrialization and urbanization. The economic changes that resulted from in-dustrial capitalism greatly benefited the old rich and also created outstanding opportunities for industrial entrepreneurs and financiers. The upper class constituted less than 5 percent of the population, yet by 1890 owned about 30 percent of the national wealth. The elite had considerable leisure time and abundant discretionary income, which society men and women enjoyed in various ways, including exclusive sports. The rich, especially people of new wealth, organized and joined athletic, racing, and country clubs with restricted memberships. They enjoyed sports at these private organizations, and their membership certified their status and separated them from lesser sorts.

Middle-class athletic participation grew markedly in the industrial age. Industrialization altered the antebellum middle class of independent master artisans, farmers, clerks, and shopkeepers into a largely dependent cohort of white-collar clerks, bureaucrats, and professionals who were increasingly employed by business or the growing government. The old middle class remained critical of sport and stressed hard work over leisure. The new middle class, however, was interested in sport because of the influence of the new sports creed, the emergence of upright games such as baseball (nonviolent, not identified with gambling, and potentially character-building), and the positive role models of the British and German sporting subcommunities. Besides having the interest, the new middle class had the time, money, and access to athletic facilities that enabled them to enjoy sport.

On the other hand, blue-collar participation was hindered by industrialization, particularly by factory work schedules, limited leisure time, and low incomes. The shift in workplace from small craft shops to the machine-driven factory system made skills less valuable. Artisans who had considerable control over the antebellum workshop and considerable free time lost most of their independence and control over their labor with the rise of industrialization. Like machine operators and unskilled labor, they worked extremely long hours for modest wages. By 1890 the bottom 90 percent of the population owned only one-fourth of the national wealth. Besides low incomes and limited discretionary time, lower-class sporting opportunities were also hindered by the loss of traditional playing areas to urban development and by the increased size of cities, which made outdoor sporting sites such as rivers, woods, parks, and baseball fields increasingly inaccessible.

Ethnicity and race were also major factors in the emerging American sporting experience. With the exception of the Irish, who readily fit into the male bachelor subculture, immigrants from western Europe brought over with them a sporting heritage that provided a positive role model for middle-class Americans. Voluntary ethnic sports clubs established in urban neighborhoods or rural communities helped these newcomers adjust to American life by sustaining their traditional culture. The new immigrants from eastern and southern Europe came to American cities without a sporting legacy, and they did not become sports-minded. Their sons, however, who wanted to become Americanized, became active in sports, especially those that fit in with their inner-city environment. Ironically, their athletic participation often enhanced their ethnic identity as they emulated ethnic heroes or joined ethnic sports clubs. The immigrants' athletic experience was quite different from that of African Americans, whose participation in the national sporting culture was limited and even barred because of race. Despite their skill in many sports, African Americans in the late nineteenth century were forced out of many amateur organizations as well as most professional sports.

Other major sporting developments in the industrial age were intercollegiate sport and youth sport, the latter closely tied to educational programs. Based on the Oxbridge model, intercollegiate sports provided college men with a chance to demonstrate traits considered to be manly, and men and women an opportunity to display their prowess, organize extracurricular activities, and promote school spirit. Intercollegiate sport emerged primarily at elite eastern institutions whose student bodies were upper or upper-middle class. By the late nineteenth century other schools, including the more democratic state universities, copied the program. While ostensibly an amateur game, college football became highly commercial, and important matches were played in major cities to draw the largest possible audiences. The commercial nature encouraged the rise of the professional coach, who often violated the ethics of amateurism and sportsmanship to win.

High-school students appropriated the collegiate paradigm, creating student-run interscholastic athletic associations that provided a focal point for the student body and the surrounding neighborhood. Sports programs were also developed by physical educators for elementary-school students, and by boys' workers at settlement houses, YMCAs, and inner-city parks to acculturate inner-city second-generation youth, improve their health, and train them to become productive, law-abiding citizens.

The final theme to be considered is the boom in commercial spectator sports made possible by the great increase in the number of cities and in the size of cities. By 1920, when half (51.4 percent) of the national population lived in cities, sixty-eight cities housed over one hundred thousand residents, led by New York with 5.6 million. Growing populations in the industrial era provided the potential audience needed to encourage a boom in sport. The three leading professional sports were prizefighting and horse racing, which appealed to gamblers, and baseball, which appealed to everyone. Prizefighting was widely banned in industrial America because of its violence, the low-life origins of fighters and spectators, and the gambling nexus. Horse racing was also often proscribed because of the wagering. Baseball, on the other hand, was the national pastime, and its popularity was unrivaled. Professional baseball appealed to all classes, but especially catered to middle-class audiences. A popular baseball creed developed in the early 1900s that epitomized the finest American values, such as self-reliance, respect for authority, and teamwork. Professional teams, usually locally owned, became public symbols of their hometowns. The players then were themselves mainly drawn from cities and came from lower middle-class backgrounds.

The preeminent sports promoters were typically professional politicians or close associates whose connections provided sports entrepreneurs with protection for their investments, inside information (regarding property for arenas and transportation, as well as warnings about gambling raids), and preferential treatment from City Hall. The promoters built spectator sports facilities that were originally flimsy and dangerous edifices, but as sport became more commercialized, the structures became larger, more modern, safer, and costlier. They included large, multifunctional downtown arenas and enormous outdoor structures such as baseball parks and racetracks built on the outskirts of town or in nearby suburbs. Facilities such as Madison Square Garden, Belmont Park, and the Polo Grounds were among the most prominent semipublic edifices in the industrial radial city.

By 1920, sport was one of the most prominent popular institutions in America. During the decade of the 1920s, the Golden Age of Sport, men of all social and ethnic backgrounds played and watched sport, as did many middle- and upper-class women. Attendance and rates of participation were at record highs, reflecting the decade's higher standard of living, greater discretionary income, and increased leisure time. Once-shunned gambling sports such as thoroughbred racing and boxing enjoyed great revivals. In 1927, a record 104,000 fans at Chicago's Soldier Field saw Gene Tunney earn $990,000 when he successfully defended his heavyweight title against Jack Dempsey.

Every major sport had its great heroes: Babe Ruth (baseball), Red Grange (football), Jack Dempsey (boxing), Bill Tilden (tennis), Bobby Jones (golf), and Charles Lindbergh (aviation). There were even a few heroines, most notably Gertrude Ederle (swimming) and Helen Wills (tennis). In an increasingly bureaucratic and urban society, their achievements demonstrated the continuing merit of traditional, small-town American values such as hard work and self-reliance. Team sports heroes also epitomized more modern values, such as cooperation and teamwork. Idols such as Grange and Lindbergh combined the best of both worlds, the qualities of both the pioneer and the organization man of the modern industrial society.

CHAPTER ONE

Urbanization, the Technological Revolution, and the Rise of Sport

Sport in the industrial United States was dramatically shaped by urbanization and technological innovation. In cities, major amateur and professional sports as well as many popular recreational sports achieved their modern form. Most top athletes were born and reared in cities, and they played at urban sports facilities ranging from billiard parlors and bowling alleys to parks and baseball fields. Yet the city was more than a place with a large population that provided players, spectators, and playing sites. Cities played an active role in the evolution of athletic institutions and sporting cultures that developed in interaction with the principal elements of urbanization.

The city's influence on sport dated back to the colonial era when 5 percent of the population lived in urban sites. In towns such as New York, Philadelphia, and Charleston, the relatively concentrated populations provided tavern owners sponsoring sports events with a potential market and facilitated the formation of mid-eighteenth-century sports clubs. Residents relied on their municipal governments to regulate semipublic institutions (particularly taverns), public space (parks and streets), and Sabbath behavior to protect community norms and morality when threatened by the growing sporting interest.

Urbanization did not proceed very rapidly in the early-nineteenth-century walking city. Settled areas in commercial antebellum cities seldom extended much beyond two miles from their center. Land use in these compact communities was unspecialized, and people from different social classes and backgrounds lived in close proximity. The countryside was nearby, and cities often had vacant lots that could be used for outdoor sports.

Beginning in the 1830s the pace of urbanization accelerated greatly. During that decade the urban population increased 63.7 percent; 92.1 percent in the 1840s, the highest in American history; and 75.4 percent in the 1850s. Population increased dramatically in established cities, accompanied by physical expansion and the appearance of hundreds of new cities. Between 1830 and 1860, New York, the nation's largest city, grew from 202,000 to 814,000; Philadelphia from 161,000 to 566,000; and Brooklyn from 15,000 to 267,000. Chicago in 1830 had merely 50 inhabitants but grew to 109,000 in 1860, when it was the ninth largest city in the United States. By 1870 one-fourth of the national population was urban, and fifty years later, most Americans were living in cities.

The industrial radial cities of the late nineteenth century grew through annexing outlying communities, made possible by rapid mass transit systems that enabled residents to live far further than walking distance from their jobs. The central business district (CBD) formed the nucleus of this city. Its property became extremely expensive, shaping the CBD into a highly specialized center of business, culture, and entertainment, housing corporations, banks, and professional people as well as department stores, hotels, museums, theaters, and railroad stations. The high cost of land pushed heavy industry out toward cheaper peripheral areas and satellite cities and dispersed city dwellers into concentric residential zones surrounding the downtown. The first residential belt was the slum, a heterogeneous, impoverished area filled with the latest arrivals to the city. It had poor quality housing, inadequate urban services, and high mortality and crime rates. Next came the zone of emergence, an area of upper-lower-class neighborhoods, often of second-generation Americans, that was safer and healthier than the slums. Families lived in modest homes on small lots. The third residential region was at the suburban fringe. These homogeneous, middle-class, white Anglo-Saxon Protestant (WASP) localities had large, single-family homes on substantial, grassy, tree-lined lots.

The rapid pace of urbanization influenced the rise of sport in several ways. The problems created by urbanization, such as rapid social change, growing social divisions, sedentary middle-class lifestyles, and the expansion of crowded, disease-ridden slums led Jacksonian reformers in the 1830s and 1840s to develop a positive sporting ideology. The new sports creed portrayed humane, nongambling athletics (clean sport) as socially useful recreations that would improve the health, morality, and character of alienated poor inner-city residents and revitalize the hard-working middle class who spent little time in the fresh air engaged in exercise or physical labor. These beliefs also prompted a park movement to preserve and create public park space for outdoor recreation, especially crucial in slum neighborhoods where residents had no access to open space and fresh air. Empty lots, formerly used for playing areas, were lost to urban development, significantly limiting outdoor space for sport and hindering participation. By the turn of the century, reformers used sports to teach immigrant children traditional American values and to promote hometown pride among rootless urbanites.

Urbanization also had an important impact on the rise of spectator sports. The growing populations of cities created potential markets for spectator sports, although the expanding size of cities made accessibility to arenas and sports fields problematic. Along with public parks, these semipublic facilities became important city institutions that contributed to the urban booster spirit and publicized that town's progressive qualities.

The industrial revolution contributed to the rise of sport in many ways, most directly through technological innovations. The three main contributions of modern technology to the sports of the post–1870s were improved communications that provided fans with information quickly about sporting events; transportation innovations that reduced the cost of travel to contests by participants and spectators; and the mass production of inexpensive sporting equipment, which encouraged participatory sport.

Urban Reform and the Ideology of Sport

The emergence of a sports ideology justifying athletic participation as a positive force led to sport becoming one of the most popular American amusements. The idea that sport needed to be a beneficial and uplifting institution was rooted in Puritan values that required all pastimes to be moral, revitalizing recreations. The new positive sports creed that emerged in the Jacksonian era was closely tied to other reform movements that promoted political democracy, social justice, and economic opportunity to address the problems created by the rapid rate of urbanization. Class conflict was threatened by growing extremes of wealth and poverty. The urban population was becoming far more heterogeneous because of Irish and German immigration (in 1850 half of Boston's heads of households were immigrants). Traditional values and norms seemed to be breaking down, reflected by skyrocketing crime rates because of widespread poverty and transiency, especially among unsupervised young men. Urban riots became commonplace, often a result of racism and nativism. Disastrous public health problems characterized city life. Impoverished, overcrowded slums with inadequate sanitation and polluted water resulted in terrible epidemics and high mortality rates. Thus it was hardly surprising that social critics compared city life unfavorably to rural society, whose homogeneous residents presumably enjoyed closer interpersonal ties. Farmers were portrayed as healthy, honest, self-reliant, hardworking, and nonmaterialistic.

Reformers sought to improve urban life for civil and religious reasons. Secular reformers were prompted by unsettling urban conditions, their social conscience, and a desire to implement republican virtues, such as self-improvement and good character. Religious reformers, inspired by the Second Great Awakening, sought to fight sin and to prepare a more perfect society for the impending Second Coming of Christ by promoting order, building character, encouraging Victorian morality, and improving public health. Reformers also sought to alleviate social problems through voluntaristic drives against such sinful behavior as intemperance and prostitution, and by pressuring municipalities to provide such basic services as water, sanitation, compulsory education, and police and fire protection.

Many reformers identified physical fitness as a potential instrument of positive social change, and they developed the positive sports creed. This ideology evolved slowly from the rhetoric of eighteenth-century Enlightenment philosophers such as Benjamin Rush; the sporting traditions of ancient Greece, where fitness and education went hand-in-hand; and the ideas of early-nineteenth-century European educators such as Pestalozzi and Guts Muths, who emphasized physical activity in their new model schools. The American fitness movement began in the 1840s under the leadership of liberal clergymen such as William Ellery Channing, a Boston Unitarian; scientists such as Lemuel Shattuck, the founder of statistics; journalists such as William Cullen Bryant of the *New York Evening Post*; physicians such as Bronson Alcott; and health faddists such as Sylvester Graham, inventor of the Graham cracker.

Proponents of the sports creed described urban males as unhealthy, unproductive, and often absent from work. They were particularly critical of money-hungry, middle-class office workers who spent the entire day huddled over their desks. Fresh-air sports were recommended as a substitute for the healthier lifestyle of the yeoman farmer, serving the dual purpose of providing exercise and teaching urbanites the traditional moral values of idealized American farmers. Oliver Wendell Holmes, a Boston fitness advocate, who ran and rowed for his health, criticized the inactive, middle-class lifestyle in his column "The Autocrat of the Breakfast Table" in the inaugural volume of the prestigious *Atlantic Monthly* (1858). He pointed out that the contemporary social elite found sports and exercise socially unacceptable. The doctor disparaged "the vegetative life of the American" compared to the robust life of the English gentry. Holmes foresaw the impending rapid demise of his countrymen, certain that "such a set of black-coated, stiff-jointed, soft-muscled, paste-complexioned youth as we can boast in our Atlantic cities never before sprang from loins of Anglo-Saxon lineage." He recommended participation in sports that sustained Victorian values such as hard work and sobriety.

Holmes's concerns were seconded by fellow Boston Brahmin Thomas Wentworth Higginson, a Unitarian minister and prominent abolitionist and feminist. In "Saints and Their Bodies," which also appeared in the initial volume of the *Atlantic Monthly*, he reproached unfit bourgeois Americans for being too concerned with making money and not enough with their mental and physical well-being. Higginson recommended enjoyable and health-enhancing outdoor activities and exercises. He wanted required exercise in schools, and he urged men to leave their office woes behind them and meet him at the local gymnasium for a good workout.

Jacksonian reformers, particularly Catherine Beecher, a leading advocate of domesticity and author of *Course of Calisthenics for Young Ladies* (1832), pointed out that women also needed physical fitness, perhaps even more than men. Reformers argued that athletic participation could prevent or cure chronic frailty and illnesses such as nervousness, indigestion, palpitations, and headaches. In 1830, for instance, the *Journal of Health* recommended horseback riding and dancing as a panacea for "women's ailments." By the 1850s, physicians and editors of popular periodicals such as *Harper's Weekly* and *Godey's Lady's Book and Magazine* were recommending gymnastics and moderate exercise to promote femininity, beauty, and grace.

Concerns over the health needs of urban residents led to the public health movement. Physicians believed that sound diets, fresh air, and moderate exercise could build up resistance to potentially fatal diseases. As urban space became more precious, reformers turned to parks for breathing space, especially for the urban poor. Dr. Shattuck proposed in 1850 that since "intellectual culture has received too much and physical training too little attention," governments should appropriate funds for "open space [that] would afford to the artizan [*sic*] and the poorer classes the advantages of fresh air and exercise, in their occasional hours of leisure."

Participation in sports would benefit society by promoting traditional American values, teaching valuable new virtues, and developing higher standards of character. By the 1850s certain social critics, frightened by the growth of urban anomie, identified sport as an institution (along with the family, police, and asylums) that would protect communities and alleviate the urban crisis. Exercise would promote manly qualities, especially courage and self-discipline. It would also help bring families closer together because fathers would make time to play and communicate with their sons.

The sports creed offered a solution for the problem of vile slum amusements. Cities were perceived as cesspools of depravity where unsupervised young farmers had gone for work and excitement. Freed from the traditional customs and social control mechanisms that regulated small-town life, they were attracted to such pleasures of the male bachelor subculture as music halls, saloons, brothels, gambling houses, and blood sports. Perhaps the most famous locale in the Civil War era for such ignoble sports was Kit Burns's Sportsman's Hall, a popular barroom frequented by New York City's best-known rogues. The arena could hold up to four hundred at its center pit. One of its strangest attractions was Jack the Rat, who bit off the heads of mice for ten cents, and the heads of rats for twenty-five cents.

Degenerative diversions were criticized for hardening men's souls toward brutality and offering instant gratification through gambling. Reformers wanted to shelter urban youth from such loathsome pleasures. By the 1830s reformers believed wholesome sport could substitute for ignoble amusements; they could restore the individual and prepare him for greater usefulness. Reformers such as Reverend Channing recognized that lower-class urbanites had a great need for leisure, and he promoted such moral entertainments as the legitimate theater, classical music, and exercise as alternatives to vile diversions.

Noted Unitarian social reformer Rev. Edward Everett Hale was the foremost advocate of rational recreation (useful and moral entertainment). He knew that city dwellers could not readily go fishing, hunting, or enjoy other traditional uplifting rustic pleasures, and he advocated wholesome alternatives. Hale had no confidence in commercial entertainments that catered to the lowest tastes to secure the largest possible audiences, and he sought church-state cooperation to promote wholesome recreation. He advocated muscular Christianity, recommending that clergymen promote ameliorative sports such as cricket and football to improve health, develop courage, and build character.

Muscular Christianity was a mid-nineteenth-century English philosophy that focused on harmonizing mental, physical, and spiritual dimensions. It advocated clean sport and exercise to develop moral, devout, and physically fit men. Muscular Christians such as Higginson repudiated the conventional wisdom that "physical vigor and spiritual sanctity are incompatible." The connection between morality and exercise was popularized by Thomas Hughes's best-seller *Tom Brown's School Days* (1857), a fictional account of Rugby, an English private school that emphasized athletics to build character.

Muscular Christianity fit in well with the Victorian disdain of libertine behavior. Its alleged benefits, which included an increased potency, assuaged upper-class New Englanders' fears of depleting their sexual energies. This was particularly important in the late nineteenth century, when it seemed to old-stock Americans that their race was declining in numbers in comparison to the population of immigrant groups. Muscular Christians saw sport as a promoter of manliness, a check on effeminacy, and an alternative to sexual expenditures of energy. Moral men would earn their manhood on the playing fields, not in the bedroom. As historian Charles Rosenberg points out, "The manly Christian gentleman was the athlete of continence, not coitus, continuously testing his manliness in the fires of self-denial." Sport would enable sedentary middle-class men to maintain such "manly" physical characteristics as ruggedness, robustness, strength, and vigor rather than degenerating into foolish fops.

The muscular Christian philosophy was a cornerstone of the Young Men's Christian Association (YMCA), an evangelical organization founded in London in 1844. The YMCA was brought to the United States seven years later to help farm youth adjust to urban life in a moral milieu. By 1860 the YMCA movement supported moral athletics and gymnastics as "a safeguard against the allurement of objectional places of resort," and soon established facilities where white-collar males could enjoy exercise with their peers in a pleasant environment. In 1869, for instance, the New York YMCA opened a gymnasium, bowling alley, and baths. The YMCA soon expanded its mission to reach more men and older boys through gymnastics and calisthenics classes.

The YMCA was the primary institutional supporter of muscular Christianity. It sought to develop Christian gentlemen through its philosophy that a strong mind and healthy body supported the spirit. The Christian gentleman was honorable, exercised self-control, avoided sentimentality or yielding to pain, abstained from sex outside of marriage, and, like Frank Merriwell, the hero of late-nineteenth-century juvenile literature, used his strength to protect others. The YMCA's work was supplemented in the late nineteenth century by institutional churches that sought to bring the social gospel of Christ to alienated and impoverished inner-city parishioners by providing various social services, including gymnasiums and athletic programs. These churches used sport as a carrot to attract male parishioners at a time when Protestantism was often perceived to have been feminized.

By 1892 there were 348 YMCA gyms, 144 full-time physical education leaders, and about 250,000 members. The fitness program's emphasis shifted from gymnastics to team sports, reflecting a growing interest in athletic competition, and led to the invention of basketball in 1891 and of volleyball four years later at the YMCA training college in Springfield, Massachusetts. Basketball was invented by thirty-year-old James Naismith as a class project to develop an indoor, nonviolent winter game. The YMCA established the Amateur League of North America in 1895, and its teams competed with colleges and athletic clubs in basketball, swimming, and track and field. Top players were recruited by free memberships, room and board, and travel allowances. The most outstanding YMCA team was the Buffalo German YMCA basketball team that captured the gold medal at the 1904 Olympics. By 1911, however, the YMCA deemphasized competition among top athletes to focus on serving the greatest number of participants.

The Young Women's Christian Association (YWCA) lagged behind the YMCA in sport but nonetheless was a leader in promoting women's athletics. The YWCA was founded to protect middle-class young women from the contaminating effects of city life by educating and housing them in dormitories. Historian John R. Betts found that by 1890 physical education had become a crucial part of the YWCA movement. The Boston YWCA, at the forefront of women's sports, first held athletic games in 1882. Two years later it constructed a new building that included a well-equipped gymnasium. YWCAs emphasized gymnastics and dance, along with other feminine sports such as swimming, golf, and tennis. By 1916 YWCAs enrolled over fifty-eight thousand girls in physical training programs.

Sport and Urban Space

The changing spatial patterns that accompanied urbanization had an enormous impact upon athletic participation. Overpopulation, urban development, and municipal codes that regulated streets, roads, and docks made it harder to find a place to play ball, ride horses, or swim. Furthermore, the pristine countryside became more and more distant, lessening opportunities for traditional field and stream sports. These trends first appeared in New York, and soon thereafter in other crowded cities such as Jersey City and Newark. By the mid-nineteenth century New York had already lost traditional sporting sites, where cricket had been played and trotting horses raced, to new buildings, streets, and railroad tracks. Local sportsmen moved their outdoor contests to the nearby cities of Brooklyn and Hoboken. These trends occurred later in less densely populated cities like Chicago, which in 1870 still had ample baseball fields in open prairies a mile from the town center.

One example of the impact of changing land use patterns on New York's sporting activities can be seen in the history of a single block at Twenty-seventh Street and Fourth Avenue in the Madison Square neighborhood. In 1842, it was a vacant lot where respectable middle-class young men played a ball game for exercise and fun. Three years later, Alexander Cartwright, Jr., organized them into a permanent society called the Knickerbocker Base Ball Club, and drew up formal rules of play for baseball. Later that year, compelled to move from their old location by the northward expansion of New York's residential and commercial properties, the Knickerbockers rented space at Hoboken's Elysian Fields.

Madison Square became the site of prestigious hotels and luxurious town houses, and the old ball field became the site of Cornelius Vanderbilt's train station, freight shed, and stable. In 1871 Vanderbilt relocated to the new Grand Central Station, and leased the site two years later to impresario P. T. Barnum. In 1874 Barnum opened the thirty-five thousand dollar Great Roman Hippodrome for his circus. After just one season he leased his structure to bandmaster Patrick Gilmore, composer of "When Johnny Comes Marching Home." Gilmore staged various events including religious revivals, the first Westminster Kennel Show in 1877, long-distance races, and boxing matches. In 1878 an executive of the dog show operated the facility, and one year later, William Vanderbilt, heir to the family empire, took over the building and renamed it Madison Square Garden. He emphasized sports promotion, especially boxing. By then the neighborhood was the center of the city's social and sporting life, with elegant theaters, shops, and restaurants.

The growth of cities also created a crying need for public play space. This need became an important municipal problem, especially in rapidly growing older and densely populated north-eastern cities. Even Boston Common, the finest northern public park at midcentury, rapidly became inadequate as the metropolitan area's population quadrupled between 1830 and 1870. By the 1840s a municipal park movement was underway in over-crowded New York, led by journalist William Cullen Bryant and landscape architect Andrew Jackson Downing. In the 1850s the New York park movement comprised a broad-based coalition of social reformers, physicians, labor leaders, urban boosters, businesspeople, and professional politicians. Advocates claimed that public parks would improve public health and cut down on sick days by increasing access to fresh air. They hoped to allevi-ate class conflict and improve order by enabling social classes to mingle. Members of the lower classes could then learn from their betters. Proponents also anticipated that public parks would encourage citizens to support their municipality on other issues in return for providing them with an important service. Park sup-porters further asserted that parks would aid the local economy by providing jobs, raising property values and taxes on adjacent land, and boosting New York's public image. The Tammany Hall machine, which controlled a major segment of the Democratic party, anticipated gaining patronage jobs, especially crucial dur-ing the depression of 1857.

The park movement scored a signal success with the con-struction of 843-acre Central Park in 1857–58 at the outskirts of New York's residential sections. The Park Board held an open competition for the park's design, which required a wooded area, a formal English garden, and a parade ground for cricket. Frederick L. Olmsted's and Calvert Vaux's sketches were cho-sen, and Olmsted was hired to supervise construction. Olmsted never built the cricket field because he believed the park should be reserved for receptive (pleasure derived from enjoying beau-tiful scenery) versus active, recreation. Active recreation be-longed elsewhere, not on Central Park's green grass. "Keep Off the Grass" signs became ubiquitous. The Park Board did permit ice skating and boating, which did not mar the park's natural beauty. Central Park was considered an "elite park" during its first decade because of Olmsted's recreational philosophy and because it was mainly accessible to wealthy owners of horses or carriages.

The completion of Central Park demonstrated how an independent government agency could administer projects, and it encouraged municipalities to use urban planning to protect the environment. Most important, Central Park became the model for the many large suburban parks built after the Civil War. Olmsted went on to become America's greatest landscape architect, designing parks for Boston, Brooklyn, Chicago, Philadelphia, and San Francisco.

The suburban parks were mainly middle-class resorts during the nineteenth century, despite the democratic ideology of park reformers and Olmsted's own expectations that they would be used by everyone as urban populations expanded toward the outskirts of town. Upper- and middle-class residents either lived near these parks, or they could afford the cost of traveling to them. Because the parks were several miles from inner-city neighborhoods, inadequate mass transit made them inaccessible to poorer residents. If the truth be told, middle- and upper-class citizens preferred that the "riff-raff" stay out of the parks, particularly when lower-class individuals sought to use them for vigorous sports contests and rowdy parties. In such cases, historian Roy Rosenzweig notes, "Parks were providing a setting for precisely the sort of behavior they were supposed to inhibit."

Speedy electrified trolley systems developed in the late 1880s and 1890s did not help the poor use parks; the five-cent fare was too steep. An 1890s survey of Lower East Side New York youth discovered few of them had ever been to Central Park because of its inaccessibility even though their own neighborhoods had no parks. Furthermore, the enforcement of blue laws that proscribed many popular amusements on Sunday, the one day working men and women were off from work, and the presence of unfriendly police at the parks, also discouraged the working class from visiting city parks. In addition, as upper-lower-class neighborhoods expanded in the direction of suburban parks, sections of the parks were often considered home turf by the dominant local ethnic group, typically the Irish, who would intimidate interlopers.

In the mid-1880s, pressure from park users for more active recreation led to their greater use for baseball and other sports. Tennis courts were among the first innovations because they occupied little space and required limited maintenance. By 1885, Central Park had 30 tennis courts, with 125 courts seven years later. Chicago's South Park system had 100 courts by 1905, and over 300 ten years later. Public golf courses, which required a lot more land and expensive upkeep, were introduced in Boston in 1898, and twenty years later about fifty public courses in the United States catered mainly to the middle class.

At the same time that suburban parks were under pressure for more active use, a small park and playground movement emerged to complement them. Reformers hoped these innovations would serve inner-city residents in their neighborhoods. Modest facilities would provide fresh air, uplift children, and keep the poor out of middle-class parks. Park development, especially in the Northeast and Midwest, had fallen behind the growing needs of the slums, where nearly every lot was used for residential, commercial, or industrial purposes. For instance, Chicago's world-renowned suburban park system had fifteen hundred acres, second only to Philadelphia. Poor neighborhoods, however, were largely ignored. Three of Chicago's largest communities did not have a single park in 1900, despite a combined population of 360,000 and a high rate of disease and crime.

The use of public parks became a class issue in the 1880s, particularly since the suburban parks were not very accessible and inner-city boys had few places to play. Working-class residents of Boston and Worcester, Massachusetts, became increasingly resentful of limited access to their cities' beautiful middle-class parks and of restrictions placed upon park use. As historians Stephen Hardy and Roy Rosenzweig pointed out, the working-class residents of those two cities responded by actively fighting for small neighborhood parks. Community organizations lobbied their ward committeemen and councilmen to seek appropriations for neighborhood parks and to pass laws permitting their use for athletic fields and children's playgrounds. They used their influence with Democratic Irish machine politicians to build modest neighborhood parks that fulfilled their needs for breathing space and recreation.

Despite the determination exercised by Boston's and Worcester's working class, the impetus for the small park movement in the 1880s came mostly from middle- and upper-class outsiders. Support came from mugwump politicians such as Mayor Abram Hewitt of New York (1886–87), charity organizations such as the Children's Aid Society, social gospel ministers who wanted to bring Christ's message to the unchurched, crusading journalists, and landscape architects. The movement came to fruition around the turn of the century, led on the local level by progressive middle- and upper-class organizations such as New York's Outdoor Recreation League (1898), and nationally by the Playground Association of America (1906). The association was a coalition of progressives, particularly businessmen, settlement-house workers, and community leaders. There was some opposition to small parks from machine bosses who preferred larger projects with more patronage, from slum dwellers who wanted any available land reserved for cheap housing rather than baseball diamonds, and especially from proponents of cheap and weak government.

Small-park advocates believed that playgrounds should be more than merely safe places for inner-city children to play. Reformers believed that they knew what was best for inner-city youths. They would use the parks to uplift or control second-generation kids. Slum children would be protected from their neighborhood's deleterious influences and gain a positive alternative to the vile amusements of the streets. Reformers were convinced by sociological evidence that adult-directed team games were more effective than independent play in teaching important values such as obedience, self-sacrifice, and hard work. Playing sports like baseball and basketball would improve morals, fight juvenile delinquency, and Americanize recent immigrants.

Under the prodding of settlement-house leader Jane Addams, Chicago became the national model for small parks. The city established a special commission in 1899 that in five years opened nine small parks, all less than five acres. Thereafter the city's three park boards were empowered by the legislature to issue bonds for recreation centers as large as sixty acres, complete with field houses, swimming pools, and athletic fields. These new facilities helped increase Chicago's park use fivefold between 1905 and 1916. President Theodore Roosevelt, honorary president of the Playground Association, described these new parks as the greatest municipal accomplishment of his day. The number of cities with supervised recreation programs rose from fewer than 10 in 1900 to 41 in 1906 and 504 by 1917. City parks became an enormously popular progressive reform that promised a relatively inexpensive way to assimilate children of the immigrants and to promote order in the inner city.

Sport and the Promotion of Public Pride

Another function of sport was to engender pride in one's hometown (boosterism) and country (nationalism). According to conventional wisdom, people could more easily identify with their neighborhood, city, region, or nation when they cheered for athletes or teams who represented them in sporting competition. Any leading late-nineteenth-century metropolis was expected to have such cultural institutions as art museums, symphonies, and universities, as well as public parks and major league baseball teams. No large eastern or midwestern city was truly "major league" unless it had a major league franchise and a first-class baseball field. The absence of a major league team in Buffalo in the early 1900s reflected poorly on the eighth largest city in America, especially since Boston, Chicago, Philadelphia, and St. Louis had two teams each. Only New York, the nation's leading city, had three major league teams in 1903. Local boosters in smaller cities had more modest ambitions. They regarded their baseball team's minor league level and the extent of hometown support at the box office as an index of the community's progressive character. Thus Atlantans were proud to be in the Southern League with New Orleans, which had three times the population. Atlantans demonstrated their hometown spirit with large turnouts on opening day often greater than that of New Orleans. Befitting New York's status as the nation's leading metropolis, it usually hosted the most important sporting events, including amateur track-and-field championships, boxing, Ivy League football title matches in the 1890s, and, beginning in 1915, the men's national tennis tournaments. Other cities staged an occasional special event, such as an automobile race, to boost their reputations. In 1904, for instance, St. Louis hosted the third modern Olympic Games in conjunction with its world's fair. Although the games brought some prestige to the host city, the Olympics were still a relatively minor festival, attracted limited publicity, and drew modest crowds. Only twelve countries participated because of the high costs of trans-Atlantic travel. On the other hand, the promotion of disreputable sports such as prizefighting, illegal well into the twentieth century, was not encouraged by most urban boosters. Small, obscure cities such as Reno, Nevada, relied on boxing championships to advertise themselves.

In the 1920s municipalities and other local governments began building public stadiums to provide facilities for sporting events, promote tourism, and bolster their civic image. The first important facility was the Rose Bowl in Pasadena (1922), which eventually seated over one hundred thousand. It was followed the next year by the Los Angeles Coliseum, and then Baltimore's Municipal Stadium and Chicago's Soldier Field in 1924.

Along with fostering local pride, sport also provided a valuable means to demonstrate national self-esteem. Nineteenth-century American sportsmen measured themselves against British standards and made a giant leap forward with *America*'s victory in 1851 over the finest British yachts. Nine years later, Americans took great pride when champion John C. Heenan earned a draw in his fight against English titlist Tom Sayers for the world championship. International baseball tours by professional teams in 1874 and 1889 promoted baseball and spread American culture around the world. Baseball soon became a popular sport in Japan, where it represented modern western culture. Japanese college teams in the early 1900s played teams of American sailors and touring teams from schools such as the University of Chicago. Baseball also became enormously popular among the Latin countries of the Caribbean basin. In late-nineteenth-century Cuba, for instance, baseball symbolized liberty, progress, modernization, and opposition to the Spanish colonial regime.

The modern Olympics was inaugurated in 1896 with competitors originally participating as individuals. Ten years later the United States Olympic Committee sent its first official, publicly financed, uniformed team to the unofficial interim games in Athens. Almost from the start, journalists kept careful account of American medal victories, particularly in track-and-field events. American achievement in this sport became an excellent vehicle for demonstrating the American social system's presumed superiority.

Americans completely dominated the St. Louis games where 432 of the 554 competitors were from the USA. They won seventy of seventy-four track-and-field medals, twenty-nine of thirty in rowing, and all the medals in boxing, cycling, wrestling, and women's archery. Four years later at the 1908 London games, where national teams were employed, chauvinism became a dominant factor. By mistake, the host nation failed to display the American flag at the opening ceremonies. In response, several Americans carried their own U.S. flags in the opening parade and were the only athletes who did not dip their flags in respect when marching before King Edward VII. This gesture was seen as an affront to Great Britain, and British judges seemed to retaliate by cheating American athletes. Judges interrupted the four hundred meters race in which two Americans were leading an Englishman, declaring a foul on one of the Americans and disqualifying him. They ordered a rerun, but the remaining Americans refused to run, leaving Britain's Wyndham Halswelle to win in the only walkover in Olympic history. Then in the marathon the Italian Dorando Pietri collapsed three hundred meters from the finish line and was dragged across by British judges.

Hours later an American protest was upheld and Johnny Hayes was awarded the victory. In the future Olympics, host countries were barred from judging and supervising the contests.

The Technological Revolution and the Rise of Sport

Sport and the Communications Revolution

Sports journalism played a key role in generating and sustaining popular interest in sport. Without television, Americans depended on daily newspapers for their sporting news. In a nation of seventy-five million people in 1899, the average daily newspaper circulation was fifteen million. The *New York World* was in the forefront with a circulation of six hundred thousand. Much of the local news was devoted to sports. In the 1920s, for instance, 40 percent of local news in the *World*, and 60 percent in the *New York Tribune*, was sporting news.

Antebellum newspapers were usually expensive and primarily served readers who were interested in business and politics. By the 1830s, however, penny newspapers written for the masses, such as the *New York Sun* and the *Philadelphia Ledger*, began reporting horse races and prizefights, along with crime and gossip. In the 1840s, James G. Bennett's *New York Herald* emphasized sport and other popular subjects to build circulation, sending up to eight reporters to cover a sporting event. On May 5, 1845, its entire front page was devoted to the Fashion-Peytona match, one of the five great North-South horse races of the antebellum era. Readers were informed not only about the outcome of the race, but also about crowd composition, wagering, and track ambience. Bennett made excellent use of the latest technological innovations, such as telegraphy, which helped journalists quickly report major events at distant sites, and the speedy rotary press (1846) that printed twenty thousand sheets an hour. As a result, Bennett built the *Herald* into America's most popular paper by the Civil War with a circulation of sixty thousand.

Subsequent inventions further speeded mass production of newspapers and cut costs. Improved presses printed on a continuous roll of cheap pulp-based paper, cut it into sheets, and folded it, while the Merganthaler linotype machine (1886) mechanized typesetting. Along with excellent distribution systems and the rise of yellow journalism, these inventions facilitated a boom in the penny press that resulted in huge circulations. Yellow journalism emphasized sensational and popular topics such as crime, sports, and sex. In the 1880s the number of New York dailies rose from thirty-three to fifty-five, and circulation almost doubled to nearly 1.8 million. The *New York World*, purchased in 1883 by Joseph Pulitzer, became the model. Pulitzer drastically cut production costs, used lots of illustrations, and stressed yellow journalism. Pulitzer raised the *World*'s circulation from 15,000 to 250,000 in just four years.

The *World* established the first sports department and, according to literary critic Michael Oriard, the first distinctive sports page (1896), which other papers quickly emulated. Pulitzer also pioneered sensationalist evening editions aimed at working men as well as entertainment-oriented Sunday editions with special sports coverage. He and his competitors enhanced the sports section with expensive engravings that by themselves told complete stories independent of any reporter's narrative. Halftone photographs were added in the late 1890s to further lighten up the printed page and to bring readers some of the excitement of the playing field.

The baseball writer was the star of the sports page. He helped popularize the sport and linked the home team to fans who followed professional baseball in the media even if they seldom attended games. English immigrant Henry Chadwick, originally a cricket expert, was the first baseball journalist and the inventor of the all-important statistic, the batting average. Chadwick started covering baseball for the *Herald* in 1862; he wrote for other newspapers and sports weeklies, especially the *Sporting News*, which began in 1886. He edited the first baseball guide, the *Beadle Base-Ball Player* (1860–81), and then the *Spalding Official Baseball Guide* until his death in 1908. He was a staunch proponent of sportsmanship and rule reforms. As a member of the rules committee of the amateur National Association of Base

Ball Players, founded in 1858, Chadwick led the effort to make baseball more manly by advocating the fly-out rule, adopted in 1864, which required a fielder to catch a batted ball without a bounce to record an out. He established a widely emulated, straightforward manner of reporting a game's major events, but in the late 1880s a more entertaining and creative style was developed in the competitive Chicago newspaper market. Leonard Washburn began the trend in 1886 by spicing up his stories with an appealing light and breezy tone soon adopted by Finley Peter Dunne ("Mr. Dooley") and Charles Seymour, who employed slang, metaphors, and similes instead of dry and formal reporting.

The first major sports weeklies were John Stuart Skinner's rurally oriented *American Turf Register and Sporting Magazine* (1829), which emphasized horse racing, and William T. Porter's more urbane *Spirit of the Times* (1831), which promoted angling and horse racing and also covered cricket, rowing, and yachting. Porter aimed his weekly, which cost ten dollars for a one-year subscription, at gentlemen of property and standing. By the mid-1850s the *Spirit* had a weekly circulation of forty thousand copies. Other urban periodicals included George Wilkes's sensationalist *National Police Gazette* (1845) and Frank Queen's *New York Clipper* (1853), a popular advocate of baseball and a leading defender of prizefighting. In 1856 Wilkes sold the plebeian *Police Gazette* and bought the *Spirit*, which in a slightly altered form remained in business through 1902. The *Spirit* covered track and field better than any other magazine and was the preeminent horse-racing weekly of its day. The *Police Gazette* fell on hard times until Irish immigrant Richard Kyle Fox took it over in 1877. Fox emphasized crime, sex, and working-class sports, primarily boxing. He made the *Police Gazette* the bible of boxing and promoted several major matches. He donated jeweled belts for boxing's weight divisions, as well as medals and trophies for other sports, such as pedestrianism and weight lifting, that were popular with the male bachelor subculture.

The *Gazette* was printed on garish red-tinted paper and amply illustrated with sketches of scantily clad women. Its average weekly circulation was 150,000, one of the highest in the United States, topped by a 400,000 run following the Paddy Ryan–Joe Goss boxing championship in 1880. By comparison, the circulation of *Harper's Weekly*, a prestigious middle-class opinion maker, was only 85,000. The *Police Gazette* was extremely influential among working-class sports fans whose interests it irreverently and constantly defended. The magazine was ubiquitous in saloons, barbershops, hotels, and other centers of the male bachelor subculture, where each edition passed through dozens of hands.

Popular general-interest periodicals provided considerable sports coverage as well. By the 1890s these magazines were second to the daily press in the coverage of football, but they mainly emphasized baseball. The more high-brow weeklies and monthlies were much more critical of sports than the hugely successful middle-brow magazines such as *Colliers* or the *Saturday Evening Post*. A remarkable surge in readership of these types of periodicals occurred in the early 1900s. The *Post* alone had one million subscribers by 1913.

Communication innovations not only speeded up sports reportage and made it more accessible, but it also had a big impact on illegal gambling. Western Union sold information on sporting events in the late nineteenth century to poolrooms (illegal offtrack betting parlors), billiard halls, and saloons where a lot of betting on sports occurred. The bet takers needed instant reports about baseball games, boxing matches, and especially horse races to prevent cheating by their clients. By 1891 the racing department was Western Union's most profitable, earning eighteen thousand dollars a week just from New York City poolrooms. In the early 1890s New York tracks temporarily barred Western Union because they were losing too much of the betting business to offtrack sites. The wire-service employees responded by initiating several imaginative schemes to secure racing news. These included sending in female agents with carrier pigeons hidden under their dresses to forward the results. In 1904, the racing bureau was bringing in five million dollars a year, but the moral opposition of Helen Gould, daughter of robber baron Jay Gould, and other major stockholders forced the telegraph company out of the racing business. A new racing wire was established that ended up seven years later in the hands of Chicago bookmaker Mont Tennes, who thereafter monopolized racing news for sixteen years. By the 1890s some use was made by gambling syndicates of Alexander Graham Bell's telephone (1876) to warn poolrooms about impending raids, and later to distribute race results from a central office to neighborhood bookmakers. Bookmakers did not take bets by telephone, however, until the 1920s.

The Transportation Revolution and Sport

Transportation innovations, especially the railroad and the trolley car, were crucial in facilitating the rise of sport. The railroad substantially shortened long-distance travel, making it easier for top athletes to compete, outdoorsmen to reach distant hunting and fishing sites, and the rich to enjoy their exclusive resorts. Within cities, mass transit greatly increased access to sporting facilities.

As early as the 1840s, racing fans used railroads to reach distant racecourses. The railroad's potential to stimulate long-distance trips for sport was initially demonstrated in 1852 when the Boston, Concord, and Montreal Railroad sponsored the first American intercollegiate athletic contest, a Harvard-Yale crew race to promote rail travel to Lake Winnipesaukee, New Hampshire. The competitors were given a free vacation for their efforts. Shortly after the Civil War, trains played an important role in the growth of baseball. The 1869 national tour by the undefeated Cincinnati Reds, the first all-salaried team, was made feasible by railroads, and one year later, Harvard's team toured by rail as far west as Milwaukee. The new professional leagues, beginning with the National Association of Professional Baseball Players in 1871, depended on trains to complete long-distance trips that might start in Boston and end in St. Louis. Rail lines competed for the baseball trade by offering teams special rates and proudly advertising their patronage. Local lines solicited business by selling reduced-rate tickets to fans or by running special trains to the ballparks.

Railroads contributed significantly to the survival of prize-fighting, a sport that was universally banned until the 1890s. Even major bouts, including heavyweight-champion John L. Sullivan's title defense against Jake Kilrain in 1889 for a record twenty thousand dollar purse, had to be clandestinely staged. The sporting fraternity gathered for the bout in New Orleans, and on July 7, two thousand boxing fans who had paid ten to fifteen dollars for excursion tickets were whisked out of town on three trains on an unannounced route. The trains stopped after crossing the state line into Richburg, Mississippi, where a ring was laid out the next morning. This was the last heavyweight championship fought under the London Prize Ring rules of 1838. Pugilists brawled bare-knuckled and were permitted to tackle their opponents, but hair-pulling and head-butting were forbidden. Rounds were unlimited and lasted until one fighter was downed. He then had thirty seconds to come to the middle of the ring and resume fighting. The Sullivan-Kilrain bout lasted for about two hours until the challenger failed to appear for the seventy-sixth round.

Railroads had a major impact on horse racing by transporting horses across the country to compete at various racecourses. Trains also brought spectators to suburban racetracks as well as to more distant, out-of-town tracks. In 1870, for instance, the Harlem, Rensselaer and Saratoga Railroad shipped thoroughbreds from New York City to Saratoga Springs at cost. The line's purpose was to promote the resort and thereby increase future ridership. Railroads also provided a means to ship horses over long distances, which made trotting's Grand Circuit, a regular schedule of racing dates at major eastern and midwestern tracks, feasible.

The railroads recognized that racing was good for business, and they used their political influence on its behalf. The Pennsylvania Railroad, for example, did considerable business in the late nineteenth century carrying New York and Philadelphia bettors to neighboring New Jersey tracks. Its lobbyists in Trenton were among the strongest supporters of racing from the mid-1880s until the state banned horse-race gambling in 1894. Railroads also catered to cyclists, anglers, hunters, and other sportsmen by offering special rates or free baggage. Touring cyclists off to rustic destinations were not charged for their bicycles, while the Chesapeake and Ohio Railroad, known as "the Route of the Sportsman and Angler to the Best Hunting and Fishing Grounds of Virginia and West Virginia," proclaimed, "Guns, fishing tackle, and one dog for each sportsman carried free."

The emergence of mass transit in antebellum New York and Philadelphia, the nation's most populated cities, was tied to the physical growth of the walking city. The horsedrawn carriage (omnibus) and the horsedrawn streetcar that rode over rails were mainly used between 1850 and 1880 for shopping or recreation. New Yorkers, for instance, used streetcars to reach Central Park, which was several miles north of the principal residential areas. They also commuted by ferry to popular Brooklyn and Hoboken athletic fields.

As walking cities grew into radial cities, urbanites increasingly had to travel farther than they could comfortably walk. Technological innovations after the Civil War greatly improved the speed and comfort of mass transit. Horsedrawn vehicles in the largest cities were soon supplanted by machine-powered transit. Cleaner and faster cable cars were the first big improvement in 1873, but they were expensive and often broke down. Far more important was the electrified streetcar (1887); within a few years it virtually eliminated all competition. In addition, subways were introduced in 1897 in Boston and in New York seven years later, circumventing the dilemma of overcrowded downtown streets. The principal transit routes extended outward from the central business district toward middle-class residential neighborhoods and anticipated sites of development at the urban periphery. Lines often terminated at a distant suburban park. Trolleys made sports facilities and municipal parks very accessible to middle- and upper-lower-class urbanites.

Traction companies frequently encouraged traffic by developing recreational sites near their terminals. Over one hundred lines sponsored amusement parks that included roller-skating rinks, shooting galleries, and arenas for bicycle, dog, and foot racing. Their success encouraged traction interests to support professional baseball. Streetcar companies subsidized clubs, owned teams, and built ballparks at the end of their routes. Historian Ted Vincent found that in the late nineteenth century, transit firms in seventy-eight cities were financially involved in professional baseball. Streetcar interests even owned or sponsored major-league teams. Cleveland fans in the late 1890s could buy a round-trip ticket and admission to the ballpark right on the trolley, both of which were owned by the Robison family. The close ties between rapid transit and baseball provided a nickname for Brooklyn's team in the 1890s when they played in Brownsville at Eastern Park. The club became known as the "Trolley Dodgers," or Dodgers for short, because fans walking to the field had to be careful to avoid getting struck by passing trolley cars.

Lights, Camera, Action

Certain technological innovations contributed to sports development by recording achievements and preserving great athletic moments. Measurement and evaluation of athletic achievements was greatly enhanced by the stopwatch, which originally recorded times in fifths of seconds, and the camera, which helped determine winners of close horse races. Motion pictures provided a means to keep a permanent visual record of a sporting event in action. In 1889 Thomas A. Edison invented the kinetoscope, the first practical motion picture camera. In 1894, one of his first subjects were boxing matches, because he felt there was a market for fight films. Three years later the James Corbett–Bob Fitzsimmons heavyweight championship fight was filmed, grossing seventy-five thousand dollars.

The introduction of electric lights had an important impact on the viewing of indoor sports. Indoor arenas were originally poorly lit by dull, flickering, and dangerous gas lamps. Edison's incandescent light bulb, invented in 1879, was a superior alternative, emitting an adjustable and consistent illumination that used independently operated outlets. In 1880 William K.

Vanderbilt's Madison Square Garden became one of the first semipublic buildings to use electric lighting. Vanderbilt admired the quality of incandescent lighting, and he also wanted to advertise Edison's Electric Light Company, which his family helped to finance. Athletes complained, however, that the lights were too bright, and the Garden returned to gas until 1885. By 1890, electric lighting was commonplace at leading indoor sports facilities. Historian John R. Betts believed that the improved illumination helped draw athletes and spectators to athletic clubs, armories, and sports arenas.

Artificial lighting was seldom used out-of-doors, although the first night baseball game was played in Fort Wayne, Indiana, in 1883. The illumination was originally inadequate for baseball, but the technological problems were apparently resolved by 1909, when an amateur game was played under artificial lighting at Cincinnati's Palace of the Fans. One year later a semipro night game at Chicago's Comiskey Park drew twenty thousand spectators. Conservative baseball owners did not implement night baseball until the Depression, however.

Technological Innovations and Sports Equipment

One of industrialization's principal influences on sport was the fabrication of cheap sporting goods and the invention of new and superior equipment. Mass production techniques in factories that used the American system of manufacturing, which involved strict division of labor and standardization of parts, sharply lowered consumers' costs. By 1892, a cheap Spalding baseball cost five cents. The top-of-the-line major-league model cost $1.25. Consumers could purchase sports equipment in the late nineteenth century at specialized sporting goods stores and from mail-order catalogues. The great demand for athletic equipment was reflected by Sears, Roebuck catalogues; the 1895 edition had over eighty pages devoted to sporting goods. In the early 1900s Macy's tried to capitalize on the trade by establishing the first sporting-goods section in a department store.

A. G. Spalding was the preeminent manufacturer of sporting goods. Spalding pitched for the Boston Red Stockings of the

National Association of Professional Base Ball Players from 1871 to 1875, and he was the league's premier pitcher with a 207–56 record, over fifty more victories than anyone else. In 1876 he became player-manager of the Chicago White Stockings of the new National League, and he played two more seasons. When he came to Chicago he opened a sporting-goods store and a publishing company that printed a full line of sports guidebooks. These books sought to instruct the public how to play each sport, to provide them with its rules, histories, and records, and to advertise Spalding's products. Spalding expanded his firm into a well-integrated and efficient sporting-goods company that manufactured athletic equipment. By the 1890s Spalding nearly monopolized all aspects of the sporting-goods industry. He increased market share by advertising heavily in sporting magazines and sponsoring sports tournaments to promote his merchandise. The company became closely identified with the governing agencies of various sports by publishing their rules and guidebooks and becoming their official supplier of equipment, a status that seemingly certified the quality of Spalding's products. Spalding employed the same business methods as other captains of industry who structured their businesses to control the distribution of finished goods and the supply of raw materials (Spalding bought his own lumber mills to guarantee a supply of wood for manufacturing bats).

Entrepreneurs developed new products that improved performance for sandlot and professional athletes. The speed of racing crews was enhanced in 1870 by the introduction of sliding seats, and subsequent innovations such as swivel oarlocks, and smooth, lacquered, lightweight racing shells. Harness racing was dramatically enhanced by streamlined sulkies with pneumatic tires (1888) that cut the mile record by about five seconds. Baseball was improved by the introduction of the catcher's mask and chest protector, enabling the receiver to move closer to the batter. Ball games were ameliorated by the use of vulcanized rubber that produced more elastic and resilient balls. The rubber-cored golf ball of the early 1900s enabled players to hit up to seventy-five yards further than with the old gutta-percha ball, a development that required architects to design larger courses.

The bicycle was one of the most important new sporting goods, providing urbanites with personal transportation to go wherever and whenever they wanted. A "machine in the garden," the bicycle enabled millions of men and women, especially those of the middle class (who could afford the cost), to escape modernity and the crowded industrial city for pastoral landscapes and a slower pace of life on a vehicle that was itself a testament to modern technology. The first bicycle was Pierre Lallement's velocipede, invented in France in 1865. He brought the "boneshaker" (nicknamed for the quality of its ride) to America one year later. A riding fad began in 1868 in eastern cities that caused many municipalities to pass regulations curtailing cyclists who interfered with horseback riders and pedestrians.

The velocipede was superseded by the English ordinary, an odd-looking vehicle first exhibited in 1876 at Philadelphia's Centennial Exposition. It had a large front wheel (sixty inches in diameter) and a tiny rear wheel that lightened the machine's weight. The ordinary cost a steep one hundred dollars; it was hard to master, uncomfortable, and dangerous. Most riders were middle-class daredevils who had conquered the difficult techniques of mounting, riding, and braking, and they traveled at high speeds. Manufacturer Albert A. Pope championed the ordinary by promoting cycling magazines and cycling organizations. In 1878 he established the first cycling club in Boston and also helped organize the League of American Wheelmen. The LAW was a national pressure group with the goal to galvanize riders into a voting bloc to rapidly secure access to city streets and parkways. The league also provided other services such as publishing road maps and evaluating routes to make cycling more enjoyable.

The invention of the English safety bicycle in the late 1880s created a safe, comfortable, easy-to-ride, lightweight vehicle with equal-sized pneumatic tires and efficient coaster brakes. Although it was not cheap—a medium-quality vehicle cost one hundred dollars—cycling rapidly became enormously popular. The new vehicle led to a new bicycle fad in the mid-1890s. By 1896, 1.2 million bicycles were produced annually, and there were 4 million cyclists. At the turn-of-the-century there were 10 million bicycles in the United States.

Manufacturers promoted the safety bicycle by subsidizing professional riders whose victories would ostensibly confirm their machine's high quality. Six-day indoor bicycle races dated back to 1879, and in the 1890s major events at New York's Madison Square Garden (site in 1889 of the first professional women's six-day event) drew up to ten thousand spectators. Professional sprint racing was dominated by African-American Marshall "Major" Taylor, world champion in 1899 and American champion in 1898 and 1900. Amateur racing organizations also sponsored competitions, such as the annual fifteen-mile Chicago-to-Pullman Race that attracted up to four hundred participants. Cycling clubs, which numbered over five hundred by 1895, also sponsored races of up to one hundred miles for their members. Just completing the course was victory enough for most riders.

Cycling was the most popular physical activity for middle-class women. Most health professionals and other advocates applauded cycling for women because it provided exercise, affordable and independent transportation, and an escape to the countryside. Cycling necessitated the wearing of less-restrictive sports clothes that signified women's growing liberation from Victorian patterns of dependence and subservience. Riders discarded corsets and floor-length dresses for slightly scandalous bloomers and split skirts. On the other hand, critics found the sport stressful and feared it might encourage housewives to shun domestic chores. Cycling also threatened respectability by fostering coed activities and making women too independent and visible.

Historian Richard Harmond has pointed out that safety bicycles epitomized progress, symbolized the victory of technology over environment, and provided a means to escape the negative features of urban industrialization. The bicycle was a machine, yet it freed people, albeit temporarily, "from the disruptions and stresses of a machine-based society." Nature became more accessible for riders who exercised while enjoying visions of beauty and peace of mind. These could be brief jaunts or more substantial tours along well-organized routes where riders could stay at LAW-approved inns.

By the turn of the century, well-to-do men seeking a more exciting and prestigious experience turned to the more complex, speedier, and expensive automobile, which originally cost several thousand dollars. The car's early history recapitulated the bicycle's, which it displaced as the primary mode of individual transportation. By World War I the bicycle was mainly a toy for children. The automobile and the internal combustion engine were invented in Germany in the late 1880s, and their cars set the early standard. Several of the first American manufacturers, including Henry Ford, came from the cycling business, and they applied their experience to car production. They tested their vehicles and advertised their quality by participating in car races, starting in 1895 with a fifty-three-mile round-trip contest from the South Side of Chicago to Evanston. Six cars started the race, which was won by automobile manufacturer Charles Duryea. Only one other car finished. Henry Ford got into the racing business seven years later. He originally drove his own cars before turning them over to professionals such as Barney Oldfield. Races in enclosed ovals were sponsored by local boosters in Atlanta, Daytona Beach, and Indianapolis to promote tourism and to bring attention to their cities. The first Indianapolis 500 in 1911 drew eighty thousand spectators. There were also road races that tested endurance and publicized the need for good highways, such as the long-distance Glidden Tours inaugurated in 1904. By the 1920s, cars were readily available mainly because of Henry Ford's innovative production and marketing of the Model T, which brought the cost down to $290, as well as an improved standard of living, installment buying, and the emergence of a second-hand market. Car racing remained a significant sport in the 1920s, but the automobile's primary role in sport was mainly transporting fans to ball games and golfers to the links.

The unparalleled rate of urbanization and industrialization in the nineteenth century and the emergence of a positive new sports creed in response to the problems created by rapid urban growth shaped the emergence of American sport in the period between 1850 and 1920. Justification for widespread sporting interest came from the positive new sporting creed that encouraged physical fitness and athletic competition in nongambling, humane sports as a substitute for traditional vile amusements and the lost pastoral life. Sports were seen as a partial antidote to such urban problems as the antisocial behavior of the male bachelor subculture, unacculturated immigrants, high rates of disease, and the fear of declining vitality and manliness among middle-class urbanites. Yet as cities grew, access to healthful outdoor playing space became more difficult because of competing needs for that valuable space. Urbanites in the industrial city relied heavily on public parks near their homes for sporting opportunities.

Cities provided an ample market in a physically concentrated area to encourage industrialists to manufacture sporting equipment; sufficient numbers of potential ticket buyers stimulated entrepreneurs to promote commercial spectator contests. The cities were where major technological breakthroughs were employed to facilitate the growing interest in sport, ranging from communication and transportation innovations to mass production of sporting equipment. Once a sound base was established for the rise of a modern sporting culture, people from different social classes and ethnic groups operating within the constraints of the industrial radial city shaped the emergence of sport as a popular mass institution.

CHAPTER TWO

Sport and Class

Americans like to believe that sport has always been a democratic institution that crossed class, racial, and ethnic boundaries. The sporting experience of Americans between 1850 and 1920 was anything but democratic, however; it was largely a product of social class. An individual's social class was determined primarily by his or her occupation and income, along with education, religion, race, ethnicity, and residency. The American social structure in this era was strongly influenced by the rise of industrial capitalism. At the apex was a tiny upper class of white native-born Americans. The urban middle class, also predominantly white and native born, comprised 30 to 40 percent of a city's population depending on the extent of local industrialization. The majority of urban residents were lower-class blue-collar workers, mainly immigrants and their children. Members of these three major social classes had dissimilar lifestyles, a result of differing amounts of discretionary income and leisure time, as well as distinctive social values, attitudes, and behavior.

The upper class were the richest 5 percent of the population, and at the apex of the upper class were the elite. The social elite comprised about 1 to 3 percent of Americans and were drawn from the most socially distinguished families. Their status depended on how their affluence was achieved, their access to power, and individual social characteristics. The antebellum elite of leading merchants and great planters had the wealth, time, and self-confidence to indulge themselves as they pleased, and they emulated the English gentry in their leisure activities. In the post–Civil War period, sport was particularly important to the new rich who had made their fortunes from commerce and industry. They used their participation in sports to gain recognition and social status.

On the other hand, northern, middle-class citizens largely frowned upon sports such as horse racing and boxing as immoral and wasteful. Evangelical Protestants were the leading critics of early American sport, and even in the late nineteenth century they remained opposed on moral grounds to gambling and blood sports. As reformers portrayed sports as health-promoting and character-building activities in the years before the Civil War, attitudes of middle-class men changed, and they became active sportsmen, participating in ball games and other forms of exercise. The growing bourgeois interest in fitness increased toward the end of the century as a new professional and bureaucratic middle class evolved for whom sport had important social and cultural functions.

Manual workers, especially artisans, were often very active members of the antebellum sporting culture. Their athletic options were generally curtailed, however, by the rise of industrial capitalism. As historians Benjamin G. Rader and Elliott Gorn point out, these options were particularly hindered by the decline of small artisan workshops in industries such as textiles and shoemaking where employees originally had considerable control over the pace of work and substantial free time. Such a working environment was supplanted by an increasingly proletarian, modern capitalist production system characterized by time and work discipline and weakened ties between workers and management. The rise of the factory system eliminated or devalued the skills of many artisans. By the late nineteenth century 85 percent of industrial workers were semiskilled or unskilled. These employees were increasingly working in larger and larger factories. For example, in 1919 Chicago, over 70 percent of manufacturing wage workers labored for companies with at least one hundred employees, and nearly one-third worked in firms with over a thousand workers. They had modest incomes, back-breaking jobs, and limited discretionary time (although free time was often involuntarily increased because of underemployment and unemployment) that hindered their recreational choices.

Sport and the American Elite

The American elite were prominent sportsmen ever since the colonial era, when they raised fighting birds, raced horses, and hunted foxes. The first voluntary associations established to encourage sports were upper-class organizations, including Philadelphia's Schuylkill Fishing Club (1732) and the Charles Town Jockey Club (1735). In the antebellum era, the elite sustained their historic interest in expensive sports such as horse racing, while certain rakish sons slummed among the demimonde, becoming members of the male bachelor subculture. For those "swells with money to burn," debaucheries like spending a night at a fashionable brothel or a cockfight provided a rite of passage into manhood.

The leading antebellum sportsman was financier John Cox Stevens, son of a rich Hoboken, New Jersey, inventor-merchant. He restored thoroughbred racing to New York in 1823 by arranging the Eclipse–Sir Henry race, the first great competition between northern and southern horses. Eight years later he established the Elysian Fields, which became the first major site of antebellum ball sports, in a corner of the family estate in Hoboken. In 1835, to win a wager that ten miles could be run in under an hour, Stevens promoted the first major pedestrian race. Then in 1844 he organized the New York Yacht Club (NYYC) among the elite Knickerbockers of the city. Its goals were to promote pleasure, sociability, good health, and American naval architecture. In 1851, Stevens's yacht *America* won the Royal Yacht Squadron Regatta held in conjunction with London's Crystal Palace Fair. This remarkable victory over eighteen squads representing the masters of the seas was a source of great national pride, and it symbolized the coming of age of American seamanship. The winning trophy became known as the America's Cup. The NYYC became one of New York City's leading men's clubs, and the nation's preeminent athletic organization. Membership tripled, and the makeup of members shifted away from the old elite to such nouveau riche as John J. Astor, Cornelius Vanderbilt, and James Gordon Bennett, Jr., all of whom believed that membership in such an elite club would certify their social status.

Bennett was the foremost post–Civil War elite sportsman. Son of a Scottish immigrant who had made a fortune publishing the plebeian *New York Herald*, Bennett used his inherited wealth and athletic proficiency to achieve recognition and social cachet. In 1857, at age sixteen, he joined the New York Yacht Club, and nine years later won the first trans-Atlantic yacht race. Bennett was also active in track and field, promoting the first intercollegiate track meet at Lake Saratoga in 1871 and financing professional pedestrians like Daniel O'Leary. He was an avid horseman who belonged to the American Jockey Club (AJC), rejuvenated fox hunting in Virginia, and, in 1876, organized the first polo club in the United States, the Westchester Polo Club in New York. Bennett also built the Newport Casino Club in Rhode Island, site of the first thirty-four U.S. men's tennis championships between 1881 and 1914.

The upper-class fascination with sport remained strong throughout the century. Social critic Thorstein Veblen argued that late-nineteenth-century elites enjoyed sport because it was fun, provided opportunities to be trendsetters or conspicuous consumers, and promised prestige based on prowess and the exclusivity of their games. Sport provided a means to separate themselves from lesser folk. Men of new wealth tried to gain acceptance from the established elite by marrying into old aristocratic families and emulating their lifestyles. They built costly mansions and estates, staged extravagant balls, financed cultural institutions, secured membership in high-status men's clubs, and participated in fashionable sports.

Upper-class young men looked to sport as a means to prove their manliness. Social commentators, as well as the elite young men themselves, felt upper-class men had lost power and influence; commentators questioned their courage and manliness in a society whose culture seemed to become increasingly feminized and excessively refined. These men had few opportunities to demonstrate the bravery their fathers had exhibited during the Civil War. Historian George Fredrickson argues that by the 1890s, one answer was to participate in tough sports, especially football, considered a moral equivalent of war, and even boxing, which enjoyed a brief fad in the 1890s. The elite eastern establishment worried that the Anglo-Saxon male had become effete and was losing his sexual potency. There was a lot of fear about declining family size, although that had less to do with virility than with planned parenting. For example, Congregationalist minister Josiah Strong in *Our Country: Its Possible Future and Present Crisis* (1885), argued than native-born white Americans and their small families would soon be overtaken by hordes of fertile new immigrants from eastern and southern Europe. The future of the Anglo-Saxon race and their control of the United States seemed in doubt because the sons of leading families were not measuring up.

Theodore Roosevelt, who promoted the concept of the strenuous life, exemplified the elite manly spirit. He had been a sickly child, but he had built himself up through physical activity. Young Teddy boxed, rowed, and wrestled on intramural teams at Harvard. He also enjoyed swimming, mountain climbing, and big-game hunting. Roosevelt was typical of elite Americans concerned about the future of their country and their class who saw sport as a means to facilitate social, sexual, and cultural regeneration. In 1898 he organized the Rough Riders, a volunteer company, to fight in the Spanish-American War, composed of former cowboys and college football players from elite eastern institutions.

A strenuous lifestyle was instilled at elite prep schools. Sociologist Christopher Armstrong credits Groton's headmaster Endicott Peabody with making athletics compulsory in emulation of English public schools and elite eastern colleges. Peabody's goal was to build his students up physically, morally, and spiritually. They would learn to play by rules, control their aggression, work as a disciplined unit, and do their best. Once-pampered boys would be ready for New Haven, Cambridge, and Princeton playing fields or the battlements of San Juan Hill.

The Elite Sports Club

Sports clubs were voluntary associations organized to facilitate athletic competition among people of similar backgrounds. Clubs obtained the necessary playing space, built facilities, purchased equipment, and arranged contests. Elite clubs provided a socially segregated, nonthreatening environment that fostered camaraderie. They guaranteed the integrity of competitors by establishing eligibility requirements, and they formulated playing rules in cooperation with local, regional, or national associations.

Elite athletic organizations had secondary functions that often became more important than their primary purposes. Membership was restricted by high initiation fees and annual dues and by requiring the unanimous approval of applicants by members. The sports club became a comfortable community of like-minded people who shared the same social origins, beliefs, values, customs, and lifestyles. It offered a safe haven from the problems of the industrial city. Members could close ranks against social inferiors and integrate their families into an elite subculture. The club also provided a place to strengthen bonds between the well-born and the new rich. By the late nineteenth century it was no longer possible to personally know everyone that counted, but members knew that fellow club members were the proper people with whom to socialize and do business. Membership also provided a stepping stone to higher status nonathletic men's clubs. The sports club was an integral part of the elite social world that encompassed patterns of speech and fashion, prep schools, Ivy League colleges, and Episcopalian parishes.

Late-nineteenth-century sports clubs catered to a wide range of interests. A small segment of the elite enjoyed field sports, particularly big-game hunting. The one-hundred-man Boone and Crockett Club, which included Theodore Roosevelt among its members, arranged expensive wilderness trips led by professional guides. Cricket became an exclusive upper-class sport in metropolitan Philadelphia, although it had nearly disappeared elsewhere in the United States. The city's five major clubs had up to thirteen hundred members whose elaborate clubhouses and pitches were located in the most prestigious neighborhoods.

Thoroughbred Racing and the Jockey Clubs

Thoroughbred racing was sponsored by rich men who craved public attention and social acceptance. The sport of kings was the leading elite colonial sport, but its gambling and aristocratic British connotations made racing inappropriate during the Revolution, and it was widely prohibited. This ban continued in northern states for several decades because of religious objections and the perceived need for citizens of a Republic to be especially virtuous. Northern racing was revitalized by the Eclipse–Sir Henry race and by four subsequent intersectional contests, culminating in the Fashion-Peytona match in 1845, which drew crowds estimated at well over fifty thousand. These races symbolized the relative achievements of the free North and the slaveholding South. Northern racing largely died following the 1845 match, however, because of rising costs, moral disapproval, and the impact of the depression of 1837. Southern racing, on the other hand, centered in cosmopolitan New Orleans, flourished with the support of great planters and wealthy merchants. But the coming of the Civil War killed the southern turf.

Thoroughbred racing made a comeback in 1863 when professional gambler and ex-boxing-champion John Morrissey, together with upper-class New York City sportsmen, organized a four-day meet at the elite Saratoga Springs resort to promote gambling at his casino. The event was a success and racing became a fixture at Saratoga. The results encouraged capitalist Leonard Jerome, financier August Belmont, chairman of the national Democratic party, and their friends to restore racing to New York City. They organized the American Jockey Club (AJC) in 1865 to make thoroughbred racing fashionable again, improve the breed, and promote social intercourse. The American Jockey Club established Jerome Park Race Track one year later. It attracted the carriage trade by building a luxurious clubhouse, banning liquor sales, and discouraging professional gamblers.

Membership in a prominent jockey club such as the AJC was less prestigious than belonging to the New York Yacht Club or the leading metropolitan men's clubs, yet it offered horsemen public recognition and status. Adelman found that the American Jockey Club's original 862 members were mainly New Yorkers of new wealth in finance or commerce who lived in the best parts of town, especially fashionable Fifth Avenue. The fifty life-members of the Board of Governors who ran Jerome Park were more than twice as rich and of significantly higher social status than the other members. Prestigious jockey clubs ran the new elite racetracks that included Pimlico (1870) in Baltimore, Churchill Downs (1875) in Louisville, Sheepshead Bay (1880) in Brooklyn, Washington Park (1884) in Chicago, and Belmont Park (1905) in Long Island. Opening day at these courses marked the start of the social season. By the turn of the century, major races at these tracks regularly drew over thirty thousand spectators. The thoroughbreds racing there cost as much as forty thousand dollars a piece, and they competed for stakes that could exceed fifty thousand dollars.

The elite operated the most prestigious tracks, owned the most valuable horses, and governed the sport. In 1891 major track owners established the Board of Control to regulate racing, primarily because of problems such as fixing bets and abusing animals at more plebeian, profit-oriented proprietary tracks. Widespread dissatisfaction with the board's performance, and fears that the New York State legislature would ban horse racing, compelled leading turfmen to create the Jockey Club in 1894 to establish national standards of conduct and behavior. The Jockey Club licensed racetrack workers, divided up racing dates, investigated dubious races, boycotted substandard tracks, and banned horsemen who raced at outlawed facilities. The Jockey Club received quasi-governmental status one year later when the state legislature established a racing commission to supervise the sport in New York in conjunction with the Jockey Club.

The Athletic Club

Well-to-do sportsmen organized athletic clubs that emphasized track and field, a sport previously dominated by professional pedestrians and Scottish Caledonian clubs that sponsored traditional Highland games. In 1866 three upper-middle-class New Yorkers established the first athletic club, the New York Athletic Club (modeled after the London Athletic Club), to arrange competition among men of similar backgrounds. By the mid-1880s nearly every major city had an athletic club.

The New York Athletic Club played a major role in track and field as an archetype for other athletic clubs. In 1876 it built the first cinder track and sponsored the first national track-and-field championships. The club also established the standard rules of amateurism, barring those who had competed for money, vied with professionals for a prize, or taught athletics to earn a living. This practice differed from the antebellum era or from contemporary English cricket where amateurs played for fun on the same teams as professionals who played for pay. Under the new system, professionals were barred because, since they devoted themselves completely to sport as a full-time job, they had an unfair advantage. These men *worked* at play, training more diligently and practicing against other full-time athletes. Rader further asserts that athletic clubs supported strict amateur rules out of fear that social inferiors would take over their games and their select communities.

Benjamin Rader, in his *American Sports: From the Age of Folk Games to the Age of Televised Sports* (1990), argues that in 1882 the New York Athletic Club's focus shifted from athletic competition to social rivalry. The club altered recruitment policies to seek members from among "the most prominent and successful men" without regard to athletic prowess. Membership shifted from young athletes to older, more socially oriented men in the Social Register. By 1885, the New York Athletic Club reached its limit of fifteen hundred members despite raising initiation fees to one hundred dollars and annual dues to fifty dollars.

Athletic organizations were on the low rung of metropolitan men's clubs, although membership could be a stepping stone into more prestigious sports clubs or male associations that emphasized wealth, ancestry, culture, or politics. Hierarchies existed among sports and between sports clubs. For example, the New York Athletic Club was less prestigious than the Manhattan Athletic Club or the University Athletic Club (which required a college degree), but more prestigious than athletic clubs in lesser cities such as Rochester or Buffalo.

Upper-class athletic clubs flourished in the 1880s, constructing superb facilities. The New York Athletic Club's $150,000 five-story downtown clubhouse built in 1885 included a gymnasium, swimming pool, bowling alley, billiard tables, dining rooms, a wine cellar, and sleeping quarters. Within three years, the club had secured a country site where a clubhouse, tennis courts, running track, and boathouse were built. A lavish new clubhouse was constructed in 1892, although even its fine facilities were surpassed by certain New York clubs and a few out-of-town clubs such as the Boston Athletic Association, with its three hundred thousand dollar clubhouse.

These clubs offered extensive social calendars with various activities for members and their wives. The social emphasis displeased many original members, who resigned in the mid-1880s. Nonetheless demands for victories did not slacken. The athletic clubs began heavily recruiting top white (primarily Protestant) athletes, regardless of social background, to assure victories and enhance the club's prestige. Inducements included free initiation, room and board, cash, and even jobs, a breach of the amateur spirit. In 1884 the prestigious Manhattan Athletic Club recruited the great Jewish athlete Lon Myers, a bookkeeper by profession, by hiring him as club secretary. Myers was invincible at races from three hundred to one thousand yards, and at different times held American records from fifty yards to the mile. He took advantage of his opportunities to compete to win medals, silverware, gold watches, and other prizes, which he could turn into cash.

In 1879 the National Association of Amateur Athletes of America (N4A) was established by the most elite athletic clubs to enforce amateur rules strictly. Myers's actions seemed to violate the association's ban on professional athletes, but a hearing in 1884 sustained his amateur standing. Dissatisfied with the association's position on the amateur question and jealous of the Manhattan Athletic Club's success, the New York Athletic Club dropped out of the N4A in 1886. The New York Athletic Club continued its fight against professionalism by helping to establish the Amateur Athletic Union (AAU) in 1888 to organize competition and to monitor strict amateurism better. The Amateur Athletic Union banned from its meets athletes who participated in N4A competitions and destroyed its rival after one year. The Amateur Athletic Union assisted athletic clubs to survive as status communities, but the over-building of expensive facilities and the depression of 1893 killed many prominent associations.

Women and the Elite Sports Clubs

Upper-class women constituted a leisure class whose ostentatious lifestyle reflected their fathers' or husbands' economic success. Contemporaries saw them as heavily dependent upon men for sustenance and physically debilitated "by modes of dress and enforced idleness." Yet elite young women were among the first sportswomen. Their social prestige protected them from ridicule or a challenge to their femininity, which made it easier to break social conventions. Lower status women, on the other hand, could not participate in a traditionally male sphere such as sports without having their femininity and place in society seriously questioned. Elite daughters may have been unwelcome at the workplace or the voting booth, but fathers and male friends supported their presence at country clubs and tennis courts. As historian Cindy Himes points out, the elite women "used sport to establish more casual and friendly relations between the sexes, to discredit myths about feminine weakness, to adopt more practical forms of dress and to reject physical idleness and disability as a lifestyle."

Women were admitted to male athletic clubs as spectators, social guests, and competitors. The Brooklyn Athletic Club, for instance, opened its billiard and bowling facilities to women on Mondays and Fridays, and they hired a female fencing instructor. In 1889 New York's Berkeley Athletic Club constructed a two hundred thousand dollar midtown clubhouse (library, gymnasium, pool, and dressing rooms) for women members, set aside tennis courts and a running track at the Berkeley Oval in the Bronx for them, and allotted time for female scullers at its boathouse.

Upper-class women also organized their own athletic clubs and in 1901 established the Federation of Women's Athletic Clubs. The Chicago Women's Athletic Club was the most outstanding. It was opened in 1903 at a cost of one hundred thousand dollars by the city's leading women, including club president Mrs. Philip Armour. Its 275 members paid one hundred dollars for initiation and forty dollars for annual dues. The club had a billiard room, bowling alley, gymnasium for fencing, basketball, and gymnastics, and pool for swimming, diving, and water polo.

The Country Club

The country club, modeled on the lifestyle of English country gentry, was a particular focal point for elite sportsmen and sportswomen. Country clubs were large suburban resorts used for a wide range of activities. Himes maintains that because women had more leisure time than men, they spent as much or more time at country clubs than did men. The first, simply called the Country Club, was established in Brookline, Massachusetts, in 1882 and became a model for subsequent facilities. Members were of the highest rank, with names like Cabot, Forbes, and Lowell—a genuine *Who's Who* of Boston Brahmins. As historian Stephen Hardy has pointed out, half of the founders were Harvard men; and 30.5 percent were in the Union and 69.7 percent in the Somerset, Boston's most prestigious men's clubs.

Hardy described the club as "part of an interlocking constellation of financial, cultural, medical and industrial institutions." The suburban country club provided an asylum or escape from the anxieties of work and the problems of urban life. As journalist Casper Whitney observed, it was a serene rustic oasis that encouraged a sense of identity, community, and stability. The club was a resort that preserved traditional values and insulated, protected, and taught upper-class youth essential social skills. Elite sons and daughters socialized with their peers at club dances and parties, sometimes finding romance and future spouses.

Tuxedo Park, built by tobacco magnate Pierre Lorillard in 1885 in a fashionable New York suburb, was America's most stylish country club. Members living in nearby mansions enjoyed the huge clubhouse's glass-enclosed verandas, ballroom, theater, and billiard room. Outdoor sports included fishing, hunting, pigeon shooting, golf, steeplechasing, ice skating, ice boating, sleigh riding, and tobaggoning on a mile-long electrically lit slide.

The country club set dominated the new sports of golf and tennis. Golf was an expensive sport enjoyed by the English elite, who served as role models for rich Americans. The first American course was St. Andrews, built by John Reid in Yonkers in 1887. Most courses, however, were modeled after the professionally designed Shinnecock Hills Golf Club, built in 1891 for William K. Vanderbilt and his friends in swank Southhampton, Long Island. Golf required eye-hand coordination, timing, and concentration, but the sport was not physically taxing. Consequently the game became popular with rich older men. It quickly became the principal country-club game, in part because foursomes offered a comfortable atmosphere for socializing and for consumating business deals. By the turn of the century about one thousand American golf clubs existed, mainly at the outskirts of cities.

Golf was considered an appropriate sport for well-to-do women because it did not require much physical exertion. Women were rarely barred from men's courses, although they were usually restricted to certain off-peak hours. In the 1890s women not only established their own golf organizations, but even their own golf course, New Jersey's Morris Country Club. The women's national championship began in 1895, just one year after the men's. Five years later golfer Margaret Abbott became the first American woman to win an Olympic gold medal.

Lawn tennis was an English game developed in 1873 by Major John Wingfield. One year later Mary Outerbridge brought lawn tennis to the United States from Bermuda. Her brother laid out a court at the Staten Island Cricket and Baseball Club, which he then managed. A ladies club was organized and given exclusive use of the courts on weekday mornings. The game quickly became popular at Philadelphia cricket clubs and fashionable summer resorts such as Newport, Rhode Island. Tennis was not considered a virile sport, and many courts were specifically built for country-club wives and daughters who enjoyed doubles matches that did not require strength or vigorous exertion. "The game is well enough for a lazy or *weak* man," noted the Harvard *Crimson* in 1878, "but men who have rowed or taken part in a nobler sport should blush to be seen playing Lawn Tennis." Male interest emerged mainly after the turn of the century because of international competitions such as the Davis Cup (1900).

Women preferred a sedate baseline game, positioning themselves as far from the net as possible, because they played in full-length skirts; running around was considered unladylike. May Sutton, America's first Wimbledon champion (1905), pioneered by playing more vigorously and shedding her high collar and long sleeves for more comfortable clothes. The women's national championship began in 1887, and it was an important venue for America's first outstanding sportswoman, Bostonian Eleanor Sears, four-times doubles champion. She was also the first national squash champion, a sport that was even more elite than tennis. Renowned for her fashion and her romances, Sears wore men's trousers, rode horses astride instead of sidesaddle, raced cars and airplanes, and challenged men in sports contests.

The elite sportswoman provided a model for the athletic Gibson girl of the 1890s who participated in coed cycling, golf, tennis, and horseback riding. She abandoned the corset in favor of a shirtwaist and long skirt that provided greater freedom than most contemporary apparel. This ideal American woman was attractive, tall and slim, physically fit, "aglow with the ruddy color of physical health and energy." She was well-to-do and independent, sexy, yet innocent. Historian Elliott Gorn, author of *The Manly Art: Bare Knuckles Prize Fighting in America* (1986), argues that the athleticism of the "new woman" symbolized the more active role that upper-class and upper-middle-class women were taking in American life.

Sport and the Middle Class

The middle class in 1850 comprised professionals, shopkeepers, clerks, prosperous farm owners, and future-oriented labor aristocrats, who were well-paid craftsmen. Middle-class skilled workers were "loyalist" artisans who worked in small shops. They supported capitalism, lived by Victorian norms, and had considerable control over the pace of work. Middle-class workers at midcentury were usually their own bosses, except for ambitious young clerks who were learning a business and had realistic expectations of advancement. These men believed in hard work, had little discretionary time, and found many contemporary sports to be time wasting, immoral, and debilitating, if not illegal. They did not seek to demonstrate manly traits through the vile pleasures of the sporting fraternity, but through hard work, providing for their families, and making the home the center of their lives.

The antebellum middle class abhorred the sporting fraternity with its culture and social ethic that emphasized immediate gratification and whose favorite sports, such as baiting contests, cock fighting, and boxing, attacked the moral fiber of society. As Gorn points out, boxing inverted the Victorian value system and posed a dangerous threat to capitalist values such as hard work and deferred contentment. Clergymen, journalists, physicians, and other social reformers ardently criticized such immoral and time-wasting pastimes that undermined self-control, promoted disorder, and often defiled the Sabbath. Such games stimulated gambling, debased humanity, and encouraged the assembling of potentially dangerous crowds. Hence middle-class reformers sought to civilize and restrict the male bachelor subculture. Henry Bergh's American Society for the Prevention of Cruelty to Animals (1866) opposed blood sports that harmed animals, while Anthony Comstock's Society for the Suppression of Vice (1874) sought the elimination of gambling sports.

Ironically, given their opposition to gambling, the antebellum sport first identified with the middling sorts was harness racing. Historian Melvin L. Adelman argues that harness racing was the first modern American sport. It gained popularity in the 1820s because standardbred horses were relatively cheap, cost little to maintain, and were useful for transporting people or freight, unlike thoroughbreds whose only function was to race. About seventy harness tracks existed in the 1850s, when it had become the most popular spectator sport. The trotter was seen as a democratic "American" horse in comparison to the aristocratic foreign thoroughbred. Trotting was an urban sport. New York City served as the locus of the breeding and training industry, and contests were originally staged on city roads. Trotting provided an exciting diversion that enabled owners to display their property, demonstrate their prowess, and make wagers. The sport first became organized in 1825 when the New York Trotting Association (NYTA) was formed by middle- and upper-middle-class horsemen. The association arranged semiannual meets instead of the spontaneous races, known as brushes, that had been customary.

Trotting's middle-class nature was reflected by the sport's modest origins and by the low cost of many top horses. For example, the great Lady Suffolk, winner of over thirty-five thousand dollars in purses, was discovered pulling a butcher's cart. By the 1850s, however, the sport began to attract the interest of the nouveau riche, such as Cornelius Vanderbilt of the New York Central Railroad and newspaper publisher Robert Bonner, who used the sport to gain publicity and promote their status. These rich owners bought up the best trotters, began to scientifically manage the breeding industry, and made it hard for less affluent horsemen to compete in the top events.

Negative middle-class attitudes toward sport changed once sport's public image as a depraved, immoral, time-wasting amusement was reversed into a positive, uplifting social force. The new sport creed claimed that physical exercise would provide sedentary individuals with a substitute for the lost rustic world of vigorous agricultural work and fresh air. The middle class became convinced of the salutary power of sport to remake the character and personality of Americans, enhance public health, and promote order in the cities. A modern middle-class leisure ethic arose that encouraged men to stop working themselves to death and to take time off for exercise and other recreational activities. The middle class became fascinated with sport. Team games furnished fun, camaraderie, excitement, and healthy outdoor competition. By the 1870s and 1880s nonmanual workers were employed about eight hours a day with a half-holiday on Saturday that left considerable discretionary time for sports or other uplifting recreations.

Finally, other factors that encouraged white-collar sports were changing middle-class conceptions of manly behavior and the identification of sport as a respectable activity. As with the upper-class, middle-class young men in the last third of the nineteenth century exhibited considerable uncertainty about their manliness. Oriard points out they faced conflicting calls for pugnacity and constraint. Social critics feared that these men were becoming "overcivilized" and losing their sexual identity through the feminization of culture at home, church, and school. New terms emerged, such as "sissy," "stuffed shirt," and "mollycoddle." Manliness, formerly perceived as the opposite of childishness, had become the antithesis of femininity. Middle-class men had previously relied upon their work as a means of demonstrating manliness. In the post–Civil War era, however, white-collar workers were less likely than in the past to be independent workers or entrepreneurs and more likely to be bureaucrats in the growing corporate world or the expanding government. Consequently they often lacked the sense of self-worth, creativity, and accomplishment that their predecessors enjoyed. This feeling was especially true among clerks, whose occupation in the late nineteenth century was becoming increasingly feminized, as women were hired as sales clerks and typists. Furthermore, the job of junior clerk, if measured by level of income and lessened opportunities for advancement, was becoming working class. Sport became a means for middleclass men to demonstrate physical prowess, strength, and other manly characteristics and to gain the kind of recognition that work had previously supplied. Vigorous physical activity became a solution to the loss or imagined loss of masculinity. The strenuous life of hunting or competitive sports would prove one's manliness as warfare or feeding the family had done in the past. The emerging cult of manliness was a popular middleclass response to feared inadequacies, and it fit in with the jingoistic spirit of the 1890s.

Middle-Class Sports Clubs

The popularization of athletics, particularly team sports, was a major boost to middle-class sport. Prior to the 1840s, team sports were for children and students playing various versions of football, cricket, and baseball. But thereafter they became a welcome source of recreation for young, middle-class men. Voluntary associations were established among people with similar backgrounds to socialize, arrange contests, and compete. These clubs provided the means to gain a sense of self-esteem and identity.

With the exception of Native American sports, such as lacrosse, that never became very popular among the Euro-Americans, the first organized team sport was crickct, an English sport played informally during the colonial era. Organized matches were rare until the 1840s, when cricket enjoyed a brief fad. Englishmen regarded cricket as a manly, complex, competitive sport that required considerable skill and mental exertion. Anglo-American sportswriter Henry Chadwick believed that cricket taught such virtues as sobriety, self-denial, fortitude, discipline, fair play and obedience. In the 1830s, English textile-mill workers in Philadelphia played on organized teams, and over the next two decades, English merchants and workingmen organized teams throughout the Northeast.

At midcentury, cricket was the preeminent American ball game, highlighted by intercity and even international competition. Games were played on Saturday afternoons, betting was commonplace, and some teams featured professionals. International test matches would last two innings in which all eleven players would have to be put out. Such matches could take two or three days, although teams playing less consequential games might agree to a score or time limit. By 1860 about four hundred clubs operated with ten thousand players. Cricket did not sustain its popularity with the middle class, however, for whom time was money. They preferred the simpler, more dramatic, fast-paced game of baseball, referred to by the late 1850s as the "national pastime."

Baseball evolved in the early nineteenth century from the English game of rounders, a ball game played on a square field with stones or posts at the corners, twelve to twenty yards apart. The batter hit the ball, and then ran clockwise around the stones. A number of American versions developed, most notably the Philadelphia game of town ball, first played regularly in 1831. The Massachusetts game, popular in the late 1850s, was played on a square field with bases or tall stakes at the corners. The batter was stationed halfway between first and home. An inning lasted until an out was made, and the game continued until one side scored one hundred runs. The New York version, known as baseball, was played as early as 1842 by respectable and prosperous upper-middle-class young men, who three years later became known as the Knickerbockers. Historian Melvin L. Adelman has described this team as the "first important and long-term club." The first known interclub game was played in October 1845 between a team known as the New York Club, already at least two years old, and their opponents, referred to as the Brooklyn Club. One year later the New York Club defeated the Knickerbockers 23-1 at the Elysian Fields in Hoboken.

The Knickerbockers' main contribution was to formalize the basic patterns and rules of baseball in writing and to provide an organizational model for future teams. The club played on a diamond field, with the batter stationed at home plate. The offensive team had three outs before they were retired. Outs were made by striking out the batter, catching the batted ball on a bounce or on the fly, forcing runners out, or tagging them when off base. The first team to score twenty-one runs, called aces, won.

Baseball, like cricket, fit in well with the new sports creed, promoting good health by providing exercise in the fresh air, encouraging cooperation through teamwork and morality by adhering to the rules. Yet baseball had several important advantages over cricket, and it became the most popular team sport in the 1850s. Baseball was based on widely enjoyed childhood games, was considered a sport of "American" origins, and did not demand as high a level of skill, important for a newly popularized sport. The new game was more exciting, with rapid changes from offense to defense, and took less time to play (in 1857 games were limited to nine innings and usually took under two hours), an important quality in a time-conscious society. In addition, baseball did not require as large and level a plot of ground as was needed for high-level cricket contests, which by midcentury were becoming hard to find. Urban expansion made such parcels of land too valuable for sporting purposes.

Most scholars discount historian Steven Gelber's argument that a major part of the game's early appeal was its congruence to ballplayers' work experience. He claimed that baseball was characterized by a strict division of labor and collective success or failure, similar to a job in a bureaucracy or factory. Most ballplayers at midcentury did not work at such occupations, however.

Adelman found that the first baseball teams were mainly voluntary associations of upper-middle-class and middle-class men. Three-fourths of the combined cohort of Brooklyn and New York players in the early 1850s were white-collar workers. They were principally located in metropolitan New York, although the game spread quickly along the Atlantic seaboard to Philadelphia, Baltimore, and other cities. As late as 1870, about 70 percent of all ballplayers were still nonmanual workers.

Clubs had a constitution, by-laws and officers, and they charged dues. They secured a playing field, organized practices, and arranged contests. Teams gave themselves patriotic names or referred to themselves by the occupation, neighborhood, or political affiliation of the members. They wore uniforms (like volunteer firemen, an important segment of the male bachelor subculture) that set them apart as a community of respectable athletes, whom contemporaries identified as "the baseball players' fraternity." The ballplayers largely stressed the serious nature of play, and practiced on a regular basis. They also emphasized sociability, however, inviting girlfriends and wives to games. Competition ranged from friendly intrasquad games to earnest matches against other clubs, highly ritualized proceedings that often included public advertising, the presentation of the game ball to the winning captain, and a dinner hosted by the home team.

In 1858 the top metropolitan New York teams organized the National Association of Base Ball Players (NABBP) to define the rules of play (they used the Knickerbockers' rules), resolve disputes, and control the sport's future. The game became increasingly democratized, and by the late 1850s three-fourths of the ballplayers were low-level white-collar workers or artisans. The lowest classes were largely unrepresented, even though one-third of New York's labor force was unskilled. They lacked the time, money, and access to playing fields, as well as the status necessary to gain acceptance into the early ball clubs.

Pre–Civil War employers criticized playing ball as a waste of time that led workers to neglect their duties. The new sport ideology, however, convinced bosses that baseball would make their employees healthier and more productive by teaching values congruent with the needs of the white-collar workplace. Chicago entrepreneurs John V. Farwell and Marshall Field were among the first businessmen to sponsor white-collar company teams. They believed baseball was a rational recreation that would keep young men away from saloons, gamblers, and loose women. It would teach such values as thrift, sobriety, virtue, and hard work, which in turn would produce reliable, cooperative, and self-sacrificing employees. Furthermore, sponsoring baseball would promote employee loyalty, advertise the company's name, publicize a positive image of the city, and help to maintain its social stability at a time of incredibly rapid change. By 1870 over fifty teams were supported by companies.

In addition to team sports clubs, the middle class organized cycling, target shooting, track, and other sports clubs to arrange athletic competition, and, in emulation of the elite, to promote sociability and gain social status. Target-shooting companies, the largest sports organizations in New York after the Civil War, were a substitute for traditional field sports that were becoming too expensive. Upper-middle-class athletes joined clubs such as the Boston Athletic Association, with its expensive costs as a stepping stone to a more prestigious club. These sportsmen also enjoyed less competitive and more social sports such as croquet, a popular fad in the 1860s, tennis, and golf. Tennis became popular with the middle class once public courts were constructed in municipal parks in the 1880s. The cost of golf made it less accessible, but in 1898 the first municipal golf course was opened in Boston, and other cities slowly followed.

Middle-Class Women

Victorian women were held up on a pedestal for their piety, morality, and self-sacrifice. These attitudes, known as the cult of domesticity, meant that wives occupied a separate sphere from men, with a focus on raising children and creating an upright and godly domicile. Men, on the other hand, lived a more public life outside the home, which included earning a living. Urban women were typically pale, physically unfit, and often ill. As we have noted, reformers during the 1830s and 1840s had asserted that physical fitness was important for women to alleviate Victorian frailty. Noted feminist Catherine Beecher championed such activities as walking, swimming, horseback riding, and exercise to prevent common female maladies. Physicians in the post–Civil War era agreed that moderate exercise served as a preventative and partial antidote. By the 1880s general-interest magazines gave serious attention to women's health and exercise. Women educators advocated physical training to prove that mental strain did not cause reproductive and nervous disorders and to improve their students' health, attractiveness, and strength, good preparation for motherhood. Anne O'Hagen's "The Athletic Girl," which appeared in 1901 in the popular *Munsey's* magazine, argued that sport would improve women's morality (an antidote to narcissism) and provide freedom, fun, vigor, and health. Journalist Christine Herreck asserted in *Outing* in 1902 that women athletes were not unfeminine. They were taught logic, patience, and discipline in place of selfishness, snobbery, and over-emotionalism. Athletics made them graceful and efficient, superior companions to men. Health crusader Bernarr McFadden, whose motto was "Health is Beauty, Ugliness a Sin," was among the most-noted advocates of women's fitness in the early 1900s. McFadden argued in books such as *Power and Beauty of Superb Womanhood* and in his *Journal of Women's Physical Development* that better nutrition and exercise would make healthier, more beautiful women.

Many critics, among them Dr. Arabella Kenealy of England, felt that women had no place in sport. Kenealy claimed in *Nineteenth Century* magazine that women could not be athletic and feminine since their bodies had limited constitutional capital that would be squandered by physical activity. James Cardinal Gibbons of Baltimore feared "the restless women" who moved into traditionally male spheres, such as business, politics, and sports, and gave inadequate attention to women's traditional domestic role. Critics of women athletes also asserted that sport taught qualities appropriate for business, not the home, citing as evidence that athletes tended to be single and, if married, had fewer children than the norm.

Early proponents of female fitness emphasized gymnastics systems ranging from calisthenics and precision drills, known as Swedish gymnastics, to Dr. Dio Lewis's system of light gymnastics that relied heavily on apparatus. Lewis became prominent in the late 1860s for a program that emphasized rhythmic exercises with rings, wands, and wooden dumbbells to promote flexibility, agility, and grace. Lewis's regimen was supplanted in the 1880s by Dr. Dudley Sargent's "corrective gymnastics" program, which stressed individual programs to ameliorate each student's weaknesses.

Women's fitness advocates stressed moderation in sport for fear it might induce women to become too boisterous, competitive, sexual, and exhibitionist. Physicians feared that highly competitive sport could seriously damage reproductive organs. Sargent claimed that women's preference for passive entertainment and sports such as bowling, tennis, and swimming was evolutionary because their narrow waists, wide hips, and sloping shoulders made them genetically less capable of vigorous physical activity. Doctors and educators believed that women's psyches were very vulnerable and prone to stress and nervous illness, making them less competitive than men. Overaggressiveness would badly damage women by allowing sexual passions to get out of control. Sport was perceived as situated at the border of civilized behavior and primitive aggression. Too much competition would erode women's self-control. Hence moderation in sport was necessary to protect modesty and prevent immorality.

The few fashionable middle-class women's sports at midcentury included horseback riding, sledding, ice skating, and croquet, often enjoyed in company with men. Evening skating in the park under gas-lit lamps was an extremely popular social sport. A skating fad emerged in the winter of 1858–59 after a frozen pond was opened in New York's Central Park. In the late 1860s the park reportedly averaged twenty thousand skaters a day (one hundred thousand for Christmas, 1860), including two thousand women. Good skates cost from thirteen to thirty dollars, but skates could be rented for a dime, plus a one-dollar deposit. Along with horseback riding, skating was about the only exertive sport appropriate for Victorian ladies in the Civil War era, and it gave middle-class women an opportunity to exhibit skill, exercise vigorously, and socialize with men. By the 1890s newly acceptable coed sports included cycling, tennis, and golf.

Women's participation in sports that were identified as physically demanding did not gain social acceptance. When college girls participated in team sports such as basketball, baseball, and crew, it was only acceptable if the sport was adapted for women, did not stress competitiveness, and limited spectators to other women. One of the rare middle-class women who dared participate in a male sport with men was Alta Weiss, of Ragersville, Ohio, daughter of the town physician. In 1907 when she was seventeen she pitched for a semipro men's team wearing a gym suit with a long skirt, shedding the skirt the following year. Her first season was highlighted by a victory against one of Cleveland's top semipro teams at League Park, home of the American League's Indians. Alta went on to pay her way through college and medical school by playing semipro baseball.

Working-Class Sport

As Adelman has pointed out in *A Sporting Time*, certain workers in the antebellum era, referred to as labor aristocrats, particularly well-paid printers, construction workers, and food tradesman, were prominent sportsmen. They had considerable control over the pace of work and hence, free time. The introduction of labor-saving machinery displaced many craftsmen, however, such as shoemakers.

Labor aristocrats could be categorized by their value systems: loyalist, radical, or traditionalist. Loyalists and radicals shared the same Victorian work and leisure ethic as white-collar workers, although they had greater esteem for physical prowess and strength. In the first half of the nineteenth century, loyalists were part of the middle class that identified with capitalism. They believed that Victorian virtues and self-discipline would result in personal advancement. In the second half of the nineteenth century, however, their incomes did not keep pace with that of most nonmanual workers, and their lifestyles were closer to other blue-collar workers. Labor radicals also championed self-restraint and Victorianism to prepare themselves to fight capitalism through unions and cooperation. They wanted to preserve their traditional control of the workplace against mechanization, the factory system, and the growing power of capitalists. Labor radicals believed that libertine values that rejected hard work, piety, sobriety, and sexual continence was destructive to the labor movement.

Traditionalist artisans wanted to maintain customary values, which included respect for physicality, honor, and toughness. These blue-collar sportsmen drank on the job, occasionally took off extra days from work to extend their weekend, and earned sufficient discretionary income to enjoy themselves as they chose. They enjoyed illegal blood and gambling sports, as well as the more respectable sport of baseball. Adelman argues that baseball enabled them to demonstrate their respectability; they were not just rowdy carousers. The traditionalists included shoemakers, handloom weavers, and workers in the food trades, especially butchers who were renowned for their strength.

Traditional artisans were an important segment of the male bachelor subculture. Members of this community did not believe in work before pleasure, deferred gratification, humanitarianism, self-control, accumulation of property, and devotion to domesticity. They preferred the company of other young men and encouraged such manly values as courage, honor, prowess, strength, virility, and violence. Most members of this subculture had little control over their work; instead they turned to their leisure for fulfillment, identity, a sense of manliness, and satisfaction. They enjoyed such vile pleasures as drinking, frequenting prostitutes, gambling, and watching such bloody sports as boxing and cock fighting. Adelman argues that participation in sport reflected a veneration of physical prowess and an effort to preserve traditional values.

Members of urban street gangs and volunteer fire companies were particularly prominent members of the antebellum sporting fraternity. Their overlapping memberships were composed of journeymen and apprentices. They were very involved in municipal politics and in sustaining the male bachelor subculture's traditional way of life in opposition to the core middle-class value system. Boxers often headed the gangs, which was useful, because one of their major activities was fighting with rival gangs. The sporting fraternity supported a preindustrial sporting world that centered around plebeian billiard halls, firehouses, gambling halls, and especially taverns.

Working-class volunteer firemen typically had boring jobs. But at the firehouse they could drink and play cards with their buddies and look forward to the excitement of the fire alarm ringing, when they would rush breathlessly to the scene of a fire. One historian described fire companies as "frat club-cum-athletic teams," who were particularly renowned for their fights with rival companies from different neighborhoods or ethnic groups at the scene of blazes. As historian Elliott Gorn points out, they recruited boxers such as Yankee Sullivan, the American boxing champion (1849–53), and street toughs such as Butcher Bill Poole, a nativist politician and gang leader, to bolster their fighting crews. Antebellum fire companies also organized sports competitions that encompassed various athletic contests related to fighting fires, such as hook-and-ladder races. These matches were attended by as many as twenty-five hundred spectators. One scholar has described these contests as an early equivalent of modern spectator sports, where firemen gained respect and pride by displaying their physical prowess.

After the Civil War, the male working-class sporting tradition was hindered by urbanization, immigration (most new immigrants had no sporting heritage), and the industrial revolution. The growth of cities and the loss of traditional playing sites limited blue-collar sports. In post–Civil War Pittsburgh, for instance, workers originally had easy access to sites for baseball, aquatics, and hunting, but increasing demands on open spaces for residential or industrial purposes in the 1880s and 1890s curtailed traditional sport. In addition, the large new suburban parks were largely inaccessible for inner-city youth. Consequently slum children were forced to compete with pedestrians and trucks to play in crowded streets where they ran the risk of getting run over.

Industrialization in the last third of the nineteenth century, beginning with its impact on the workplace, had a very negative impact on working-class recreation. The rise of the modern factory system weakened the relationship between master craftsmen and journeymen, reducing their personal relationships to questions of wages and productivity. Factory workers were given little latitude and were closely supervised. Workmen who came in late, took off an extra day, or were drunk, would be severely disciplined or fired. The change from small artisan shops to the factory system created a low-skilled, low-wage proletariat labor force who worked long hours and had few holidays. The least desirable and most dangerous factory jobs were shunned by native-born white Americans and more established immigrants, and were largely held by hard-working eastern and southern Europeans who had no alternatives. At the turn of the century, unionized skilled employees worked about fifty-four hours a week, with only Sunday off, while nonunion semiskilled and unskilled workers averaged sixty hours a week. The worst case was steelworkers, who worked twelve hours a day, with only every other Sunday off. In general, men engaged in physically exhausting work were often too tired for any after-hours activity more exerting than raising a beer mug to their mouths.

This is not say that industrial workers labored all the time. They often had unwanted free time when underemployed or laid off because of seasonal unemployment or widespread unemployment during recessions and depressions. During these periods of unplanned leisure, many employees could not afford to buy tickets to sporting events because of familial responsibilities. In 1910 about 40 percent of the work force was under the five hundred dollar poverty line, and entire families had to work just to survive. A visit to the neighborhood saloon for a nickel beer was about all the recreation low-income married men could afford.

Blue-collar sporting options were further curtailed by Sunday blue laws. An American Sabbath of restricted Sunday activities was especially commonplace in the pietistic South where it was maintained by custom and social pressure. The only exceptions were the cosmopolitan and heavily Catholic port cities of New Orleans, Mobile, and Memphis, as well as Texas cities with large Mexican and German populations. Sabbatarianism was weakest in the West and Midwest, where Sunday baseball was widely played in the late nineteenth century. Influential midwestern German communities used their clout to prevent enforcement of the blue laws, and both regions had a strong tradition of social democracy that discouraged any one group exercising social control over another.

In the Northeast, small-town WASPs who controlled state legislatures used their power to impose restrictive blue laws to regulate Sunday behavior in cities dominated by immigrants and their children. Local machine politicians who sympathized with their constituents' desire for Sunday recreation sought lax enforcement of Sabbatarian laws, pointing out that the rich could go golfing, but city boys were hassled for playing ball in the streets. Amateur or semiprofessional ballplayers were often allowed to circumvent the blue laws by selling programs rather than admission tickets. Professional games were usually halted, however. Major-league Sunday baseball was banned in New York City until 1919, when the legislature liberalized its Sabbath laws. The first Sunday games held there drew about thirty-five thousand fans. Blue laws prevented Sunday ball in Boston until 1929, and Philadelphia and Pittsburgh until 1934.

As a result of these circumstances, the typical working-class sports fans in the late nineteenth and early twentieth centuries were mainly native-born Americans, German artisans, and Irish municipal workers. These men had grown up familiar with sports and had a sufficiently high standard of living to enjoy athletic entertainments. Artisans earned about twice as much as laborers (skilled workers' wages rose by 74 percent between 1890 and 1914 compared to 31 percent for unskilled workers), toiled shorter hours than most blue-collar workers, and lived in neighborhoods where public parks and commercial sporting facilities were relatively accessible. Many, such as bakers or policemen, worked evening shifts so they could go to afternoon sporting events and not skip work.

The Working-Class Saloon

The tavern was the most accessible working-class sporting site, located on nearly every corner in the urban blue-collar neighborhoods and across the street from most factories. The "poor man's club" was the most important semipublic institution in working-class neighborhoods and the center of the male bachelor subculture. Historian Perry Duis, author of *The Saloon: Public Drinking in Chicago and Boston, 1880–1920* (1983), describes Chicago's saloons as quasi-gymnasiums. The largest had full-sized handball courts in the back room, while smaller rooms held billiard tables, bowling alleys, and dart boards. By 1909 half of the city's seventy-six hundred saloons had a billiard table, which, according to Duis, was "almost as much a necessity as the bar itself." Taverns had been important sites for sports since the colonial era, when they provided facilities for table sports, animal baiting and gambling, and rooms for clubs to meet. In the mid-nineteenth century, less respectable taverns were still the primary site for blood sports. The most famous animal-baiting arena was Kit Burns's Sportsman's Hall in New York, a barroom hangout for some of the city's roughest and toughest criminals. Despite the American Society for the Prevention of Cruelty to Animals' opposition to animal baiting in the late 1860s, cock fighting remained a popular sport, especially in southern backwater areas and bachelor communities such as mining camps, where it reportedly detracted from efforts to organize labor unions.

Taverns served as a major center for the boxing crowd. There they could pick up a copy of the *Police Gazette* and admire pictures of champions on the walls. These pugilists were among the leading working-class heroes. Early bouts were usually arranged at taverns with the saloonkeeper acting as promoter and stakeholder. In the 1870s, when Harry Hill's Dance Hall in New York was the sporting fraternity's leading hangout, Hill helped many prominent boxers get their start. Since prizefighting was illegal virtually everywhere in the late nineteenth century, many minor matches were secretly held in saloon backrooms for twenty-five cents a ticket. Gorn points out that combat sports epitomized a lower-class style of raucous play that affirmed lower-working-class values such as prowess, bravery, honor, and valor. Well-trained boxers were admired for their well-proportioned bodies and craftsmanship, exhibiting expertise at a moment when workingmen's skills were threatened.

The saloon was a popular site for sports gambling with book-makers who also worked barbershops and other male institutions. Offtrack bookmakers were accessible, paid track odds on any horse in a race, accepted bets as small as one dollar, and gave credit. The largest cities, like New York and Chicago, also had poolrooms, located mainly in midtown or the local vice district, where clerks were reportedly their principal clients. In the late nineteenth century, workingmen avoided elite tracks that had high entrance fees, were located an expensive ride away at the outskirts of town, and were inhospitable to the small bettor. They preferred business-minded proprietary tracks that catered to mass audiences, such as Brooklyn's Brighton Beach, or "outlaw" tracks such as New Jersey's Guttenberg, owned by bookmakers and machine politicians. Outlaw tracks were unsupervised by any racing regulatory agency, and they were frequently guilty of abusing horses, holding meets year-round, and fixing races.

Track and Field

Young blue-collar athletes competed successfully in those sports most appropriate to their socio-economic situation and their overcrowded neighborhoods, particularly sports that did not require expensive equipment and could provide an avenue for social mobility. Youth who grew up in working-class zones of emergence played baseball, inner-city lads boxed and played basketball, and all participated in track and field.

The top amateurs in track and field in the last decades of the nineteenth century were rarely blue-collar workers, hardly surprising considering their lack of regularly scheduled free time, long working hours, and low wages. Furthermore, they lacked suitable equipment, sound coaching, and sponsorship. Most amateur champions in the 1880s were either students or clerks, some of whom were subsidized by prestigious athletic clubs. Blue-collar athletes who participated on a high level were mainly labor aristocrats such as printers, who were well paid and worked relatively short hours, or municipal workers such as policemen who had job security, decent wages, and worked flexible hours so they could train. They had a job where physical fitness and strength were important, and New York policemen were especially successful in field events.

Late-nineteenth-century blue-collar track-and-field athletes competed mainly at annual picnics sponsored by their employer, union, benevolent society, ethnic organization, or political party. Just a handful of working-class track-and-field clubs existed in the late nineteenth century. By the early 1900s an increasing number of ethnic track clubs sprang up, such as New York's Irish-American Athletic Association (1903). Picnic games dated back to midcentury, when they were organized as fund-raisers for middle-class charities. Companies in the 1880s began sponsoring picnics to curry favor with their employees, primarily the office staff, and to gain publicity. Sporting events included bowling, marksmanship, and track-and-field contests, some of which were exclusively for employees and others open to all competitors. There would often be a couple of events for professionals for cash purses. The outings typically ended with a dinner dance.

Union picnic games in the late nineteenth century were staged by Knights of Labor locals, as well as unions of artisans such as typographers, plumbers, stonecutters, and bricklayers. They were typically on Decoration Day, July 4, or on Labor Day, in conjunction with marches and other demonstrations. These events were reported in the 1880s by the middle-class *Spirit of the Times*, but usually with a condescending tone. The *Spirit's* editor was a founder of the New York Athletic Club and regularly criticized the annual games of the Printers' Benevolent Association of New York for sloppy preparation and bad judging. By the early 1890s, however, the *New York Times* and the *Clipper* were both impressed by the quality of the "typestickers" athletic picnics.

The purpose of the union-sponsored picnics, historian John Cumbler reminds us, was to promote the recreational life of their members and keep alive a sense of community and class consciousness. Unions encouraged sociability and camaraderie at their halls, where they might have a poolroom.

Neighborhood political organizations sponsored picnics to improve relations with constituents. Machine politicians were leaders of the sporting fraternity and played a prominent role in promoting participatory as well as commercialized spectator sports. The most famous affair was New York City's East Side ward boss Tim Sullivan's annual outing, paid for by local businessmen to curry favor with the machine. The event drew up to six thousand participants, mainly Irish-American, who would enjoy the sports, a parade, and a political rally.

Professional opportunities in track-and-field sports dated back to pedestrianism in the 1830s, and the Scottish Caledonian Games of the 1850s. Professional long-distance runners in the late nineteenth century were mainly clerks and blue-collar workers who competed in highly organized events, most notably six-day-long marathon contests. The most prestigious was the 1878–79 International Astley Belt races for purses of up to twenty thousand dollars at arenas such as Madison Square Garden. The winners routinely exceeded five hundred miles. Marathon events remained popular throughout the 1880s. Other professional athletic contests were staged at Caledonian Games, working-class picnics, and at amusement parks. Short-distance sprint races for purses became popular in the 1870s. The runners were often sponsored by saloonkeepers or local politicians who bet on the matches and shared their winnings with the athletes. By the 1880s races were sponsored by amusement parks at Coney Island, Hoboken, Newark, Paterson, and Philadelphia for purses of one hundred to three hundred dollars. They drew up to twenty-five hundred spectators at twenty-five cents a ticket.

Blue-Collar Baseball

The first blue-collar ballplayers were artisans, primarily loyalists who supported capitalism, rather than traditionalists who wanted to maintain the old male bachelor subculture. Their teams were regimented and serious and gave players a chance to temporarily escape their problems, demonstrate prowess, make friends, gain a sense of belonging, and enjoy themselves without the boss looking over their shoulder. There is little evidence, however, contrary to the views of Marxist historian Bryan Palmer, that baseball established a collectivist subculture antagonistic to core American values.

The first artisan baseball players were from metropolitan New York. Historian Melvin Adelman found that nearly one-fourth (23.4 percent) of players active in Brooklyn or New York clubs in the first half of the 1850s were artisans, and virtually none were unskilled laborers. By the late 1850s, almost half (48.2 percent) of the most active players were skilled craftsmen. Furthermore, workers also played a prominent role in the sport's leadership. Roughly one-third of Brooklyn club officials were blue-collar workers, and one-fifth of Brooklyn and New York delegates to the National Association of Base Ball Players were artisans. The Brooklyn Eckfords, founded in 1855, was the first blue-collar club. The Eckfords were mainly prosperous shipwrights and mechanics (77.8 percent), economically middle class with bourgeois, modern values. Well-to-do dockbuilder-president Frank Pidgeon believed in "business first, pleasure afterwards." He advocated amateurism because he wanted to give all teams a fair chance. Pidgeon feared that with professionalization, wealthier clubs would hire the best players, and ballplayers would lose their independence, a common fear among midcentury artisans. However, sporting journals such as the *Clipper* and *Porter's Spirit of the Times* supported professionalism as a means to democratize baseball by making it easier for gifted working-class athletes to participate.

The best blue-collar team was the Brooklyn Atlantics, mainly composed of Irish Catholic food-industry employees with strong Democratic party ties. In 1860 they played a series with the middle-class WASP Excelsiors that drew enormous interest because the teams represented opposing ethnic, political, and class groups. The first two games were split, but the third and decisive game, attended by over fifteen thousand, was halted by rioting Atlantic fans.

Early working-class teams were organized along occupational lines, neighborhoods, and political divisions. They mainly played other workers because higher-status groups did not want to play beneath their station. These clubs had a strong fraternal and social aspect, and games were usually followed by a dinner; nonetheless, they played to win. Club officials expected players to be disciplined, trained, and well-drilled. By the 1880s, teams were sponsored by ethnic groups, unions, benevolent societies, political parties, and companies. Union teams publicized the labor movement, drew crowds to rallies and demonstrations, raised money to aid striking comrades, and publicized issues such as the eight-hour work day. Employers originally feared that baseball disrupted work habits, but they quickly learned that ballplayers were highly disciplined, moral, and healthy young men who made good workers.

Manual workers were well represented on early professional baseball teams. The *New York Times* in 1869 claimed that the first professionals were mainly young mechanics. That opinion has recently been corroborated by Adelman who found that three-fifths (61.8 percent) of early New Yorkers in the National Association of Professional Base Ball Players were blue-collar workers. Adelman argues that young artisans tried professional baseball more readily than older white-collar workers who had better job alternatives and less time for arrested adolescent behavior. Furthermore white-collar ballplayers were also put off by the low status of the new occupation, and they were less eager to leave home for a new and untried enterprise, especially if they had a family.

Industrial Sport

When the industrial revolution emerged in antebellum America, capitalists justified low wages, long working hours, and constant supervision as essential to keep workers in line and prevent dissipation from vile amusements. In the late nineteenth century, however, they learned from British capitalists the benefits of industrial relations in producing a happy, contented, loyal work force that would be punctual, efficient, hardworking, and non-union. American industrialists used sport as well as other features of welfare capitalism, such as bonuses and healthcare programs, to improve relations with their employees and kill unions by demonstrating to workers how much their company cared about their needs.

As early as 1872 railroad moguls relied on the YMCA to provide programs for their workers, and they greatly increased their support following the nationwide rail strikes of 1877. The company-sponsored YMCAs provided food and shelter, baths, libraries, work-related classes, religious instruction, and athletic facilities to discourage future labor disputes. During the 1880s, the YMCA reached out to such alienated workmen as Pennsylvania miners and Wisconsin lumbermen, although it remained a predominantly middle-class evangelical association. Workingmen found it too expensive, too Protestant, and too moralistic, and they resented having a middle-class value system imposed on them. In 1902 the YMCA tried to improve its working-class appeal by organizing an industrial department. Many memberships were paid by employers trying to ingratiate themselves with their workers. By 1903, ninety-eight thousand industrial workers belonged to the YMCA, but they made up just 20 percent of its membership.

In the 1880s, companies began sponsoring their own athletic programs, and within twenty years these programs became an integral element of welfare capitalism. Industrialists supported athletic programs for several reasons. They wanted to promote morale and bolster their firm's public image. Management believed sports programs would attract new workers, maintain control over the workplace, forestall unions, and encourage company loyalty. Sports would help instill workers with proper behavior and values such as punctuality, and enable the firm to oversee their discretionary time. Finally, management believed welfare capitalism would keep taxes down by averting any need for municipal recreational facilities.

Through welfare capitalism, bosses felt that they were doing something positive for their workers while simultaneously increasing profits. Welfare capitalists felt responsible for helping workers adjust to the dislocations caused by the industrial revolution at the workplace and off the job. Among native-born white Americans, these problems were particularly acute in southern textile-mill towns, where workers had been torn away from their traditional, independent, rural lifestyle.

The first outstanding industrial sports program was at the company town of Pullman, a model community on the outskirts of Chicago established in 1881 by George Pullman. He provided quality housing, good schools, and clean streets in order to exert social control over his skilled work force. He banned saloons and unions, and he spied on his workers. The town offered various amenities such as Sunday concerts, a public library, and sports programs. In 1882 the Pullman Athletic Association (PAA) was organized and was open to all employees. It helped attract workers, provided a moral alternative to vile amusements, and gained the company considerable positive recognition. The PAA stressed highly competitive sports, especially cricket and crew. The oarsmen, among the finest in the United States, were experienced athletes, many of whom had been recruited by a job offer. In 1883 Pullman hosted the national crew championships, which was attended by fifteen thousand spectators. Track contests were also very popular, so much so that they were not even disrupted by the 1894 Pullman strike.

Industrial sports programs were adopted in the early 1900s by companies such as the Pennsylvania Railroad, National Cash Register, and U.S. Steel, whose president, Andrew Carnegie, was a leading proponent of welfare capitalism. Carnegie believed that leisure-time activities influenced his workers' mental, physical, and moral development. Industrial sports programs proliferated among major firms, and by 1918, 152 of the 400 largest manufacturers provided indoor recreational facilities, and about half sponsored outdoor recreation or annual picnics. By 1920 Ford workers in Dearborn, Michigan, enjoyed a twenty-acre athletic park with facilities for football, baseball, and tennis, while in Pittsburgh, the Pennsylvania Railroad had thirty-two baseball fields, thirty-three tennis courts, seven athletic fields, and even a golf course. Certain firms even sponsored semiprofessional and professional teams to improve labor relations, exercise social control over the workers, and make a profit. In 1897 when a miners' strike hit eastern Pennsylvania, one prominent mine owner responded by organizing and funding an entire minor league. In Paterson, New Jersey, the local Atlantic League team was owned by Garret Hobart, soon to become William McKinley's vice president. His club was expected to deflect public interest from labor issues at a time when the local silk mills and locomotive works were on strike.

Historian Ted Vincent has argued that the first professional football teams, composed of mill hands or former collegians, were organized by western Pennsylvania and midwestern industrialists to alleviate labor tensions. In 1900 Carnegie executives organized professional teams in the mill towns of Homestead and Braddock. Braddock's club consisted mainly of steelworkers who received a bonus to play and were excused from mill work during the season. In 1902 the first professional football league was organized, purportedly to reduce the strains caused by an anthracite coal strike. Thereafter the center of professional football shifted to small industrial Ohio towns such as Canton and Massillon, where most spectators were rubber or steel workers. By the mid-1910s there were about eighty-six professional and semiprofessional teams sponsored by social clubs, ethnic fraternities, and especially the labor relations departments of industrial companies. As Harry A. March recounts in *Pro Football: Its Ups and Downs* (1934), boilermakers playing for the Columbus Panhandles, a division of the Pennsylvania Railroad, "worked in the shop until four Saturday afternoon, got their suppers at home, grabbed the rattlers to any point within twelve hours' ride of Columbus, played the Sunday game, took another train to Columbus, and punched the time clock at seven Monday morning." Several original National Football League teams were company-sponsored squads established to deflect labor unrest. They included the Dayton Triangles, financed by Delco and other local firms, the Packers of Green Bay's Indian-Acme Packing Company, the Hammond Pros, funded by a local steel magnate after the 1919 industrywide strike, and the Decatur Staleys (the future Chicago Bears), backed by a starch manufacturer, object of a 1919 strike and the brainchild of labor relations director George Halas.

Working-Class Women's Sport

Working-class sport was all but completely a male sphere because of restrictive social norms and lack of access. Lower-class sportswomen were looked down upon, and their femininity was questioned. A handful of professional sportswomen dated back to rowing contests in 1867, and, in the 1870s, boxing matches and pedestrianism. These sports were covered with relish by the *Police Gazette* because of their incongruity with the cult of domesticity. Lib Kelly, who fought in 1878 at Hill's Dance Hall, was the first outstanding female boxer. Two years later a woman covered 364 miles in a six-day marathon. Women also competed in feats of strength such as weight lifting, endurance contests such as walking a narrow plank (a popular saloon sport) for time, sports that required both strength and endurance such as wrestling, and exhibitions of bodybuilding. An 1898 charity exhibition of women wrestlers at the Polo Grounds drew twelve thousand spectators.

Baseball attracted working-class young women. There were numerous female teams of touring baseball players, such as Harry H. Freeman's "buxom beauties." These women's clubs had a bad public image and their members were occasionally presumed to be prostitutes. Probably the best female ballplayer of the nineteenth century was Lizzie Arlington, a coal miner's daughter from Pottsville, Pennsylvania. Arlington was considered such a good pitcher and gate attraction that she was paid a hundred dollars a week to play in exhibition games against professional teams. Arlington even appeared in a minor-league game in 1899 when she pitched one inning for the Reading, Pennsylvania, team of the Atlantic League.

Between 1850 and 1920 the sporting options of American men and women were heavily shaped by their status in society. The rich enjoyed the greatest options, and they used sport to escape from urban problems and withdraw into their own private world. Sport provided a means to certify one's social prestige and boundaries to identify people of similar status. Sport offered young men an opportunity to prove their manliness and women to display their independence. Middle-class people found in sports a new and socially approved form of recreation that fit in with their value system. They had the time, money, and access to public and semipublic sporting facilities, and they used them to have a good time while improving their health, teaching children morality, and making new friends and business contacts. On the other hand, working-class sport was hindered by urbanization, industrialization, and a civilizing process that tried to eliminate traditional sports that emphasized gambling and violence. The decline of the independent artisan and the rise of the factory with its time and work discipline curtailed leisure time and discretionary income, and the rapid growth of cities supplanted traditional playing sites. Sport remained a vital part of lower-class culture, but it was largely limited to the neighborhood tavern and billiard hall.

By the 1920s working-class sport participation would become commonplace among male old-stock Americans and second-generation immigrants. It had limited appeal to their sisters, who wanted to retain an image of femininity and respectability. Blue-collar workers enjoyed a significant boost in their standard of living after World War I, when industrial workers earned fourteen hundred dollars a year, approximately the same as clerical workers. Furthermore, working hours declined to forty-eight hours for skilled workers and fifty-four for unskilled, and Sunday blue laws outside the Bible Belt were becoming less restrictive. In addition the working class had greater access to participatory sports with the completion of small public parks and spectatorial sports with expanded cheap mass transit. By the 1920s the working class had become full-fledged members of the consumer society.

CHAPTER THREE

Sport, Ethnicity, and Race

The sporting culture of the industrial era was in large measure a product of ethnic and racial variables. Mid-nineteenth-century sport was significantly influenced by the athletic practices and values that western European immigrants brought with them to America in the period between 1840 and 1880. These newcomers established voluntary sports organizations to maintain their athletic heritage and ethnic identity. The immigrants from eastern and southern Europe who flocked to America primarily between 1882 and 1914 came with little if any sporting background, and they were uninterested in physical culture. Yet their sons became ardent sports fans, idolizing noted athletes, especially men from their own ethnic group. Second-generation Poles, Italians, and Jews used sport to prove they were real Americans and not greenhorns, becoming particularly prominent in sports that fit in with their socio-economic conditions. The African American experience was quite different from that of immigrants. They were American born and reared, and they had participated in American sports at a high level of accomplishment. They encountered enormous discrimination, however, when they competed in or attended sporting events and were even forced out of several professional sports, a reflection of America's pervasive racism.

Athletes from ethnic and racial minorities were prominent heroes who were idolized by fellow group members for their accomplishments. Ethnic folklore, particularly among the most downtrodden groups, recounted the accomplishments and legends of their champions to promote group pride and teach valuable lessons. Some of the earliest sports legends were Irish superstars such as boxer John L. Sullivan and the fabled baseball player Mike "King" Kelly, or African American icons such as heavyweight champion Jack Johnson.

The Old Immigrants

British-Americans

In addition to the many traditional rural sporting pastimes such as cricket, animal baiting, cock fighting, and field and equestrian sports that British colonists brought with them, they also transferred various indoor games such as billiards. Nineteenth-century English, Scottish and Welsh immigrants continued the most vigorous sporting tradition in the western world. Their interest in sports became a focal point for voluntary organizations that sustained these three ethnic heritages and promoted a sense of community. In addition, by the 1840s professional British athletes were coming to America to compete for money, particularly boxers (one-fifth of antebellum New York boxers were English immigrants) and long-distance runners. Pedestrian matches at Hoboken's Beacon Race Course reputedly drew up to thirty thousand spectators. Race publicists built up interest by emphasizing the ethnic factor: "It was the trial of the peculiar American *physique* against the long held supremacy of the English muscular endurance."

The first British sports organizations in the United States were rowing and cricket clubs. Early cricket elevens were "steak and ale" clubs, organized by textile workers or wealthy English merchants. They mainly played on Saturday afternoons, as in England, where a Saturday half-holiday was becoming customary. New York's St. George Cricket Club (SGCC), organized in 1840, was the most famous of many northeastern clubs, arranging high-level competition, including an international match against a Toronto St. George team. Members were virtually all high-status English-born businessmen, although as late as 1848 one-fifth were artisans. The St. George Cricket Club increasingly became more of a status than an ethnic association, however, and by 1865 merely 5.7 percent of its members were artisans. While New York cricketers were predominantly English, the sport became so popular that by midcentury it was considered the leading American ball sport. The numbers of American players grew, especially among the more prosperous folk in Brooklyn and Philadelphia. Even in heavily industrialized Newark, the number of American cricketers equaled the English representation.

Historian Rowland Berthoff found that Englishmen established sports societies wherever they went, recreating the atmosphere of a traditional country fair. After the Civil War Englishmen frequently organized Albion societies to promote familiar pastimes, particularly picnic games with running contests and dances. British settlers in rural southern Minnesota raced horses, organized a boat club, played rugby, and hunted foxes, while their urban counterparts formed curling and cricket clubs. British weavers in Fall River, Massachusetts, were so sports oriented that upon striking in 1889, they set aside space in the union hall to exercise with union-supplied athletic equipment.

Soccer was the most popular sport among late-nineteenth-century British immigrants. Soccer in the 1870s was mainly played by sandlot teams or loosely organized clubs of English and Scottish workers in industrial cities such as Paterson, New Jersey, Newark, Philadelphia, and New York. Elsewhere British and Irish miners, steelworkers, and stonecutters organized clubs and even leagues. In 1884 the forerunner of the American Football Association was organized by British soccer fans. Within two years

St. Louis and Fall River organized their own leagues. Fall River had twenty-five teams that averaged about two thousand fans per match. By the 1880s, when northeastern and midwestern companies began sponsoring teams, companies often recruited British soccer players. Chicago industrialist George Pullman hired several athletic British artisans to work at his sleeping-car factory and compete for the Pullman Athletic Association's renowned cricket and crew teams.

Scottish newcomers also used sport as a focal point for ethnic organizations that sought to renew their traditional culture. The most important were the Caledonians, a Scottish association initially founded in Boston in 1853 and described by historian Benjamin Rader as possibly "the single most significant ethnic community in encouraging the growth of nineteenth-century American sport." The association's goal was to provide Scotsmen with a sense of community by maintaining "the manners and customs, literature, the Highland costume and the athletic games of Scotland." Eventually over one hundred Caledonian clubs sponsored athletic meets and various Scottish social functions. Athletic contests emphasized such traditional Scottish events as throwing the caber and pitching the heavy stone. The Caledonians dominated American track-and-field until the rise of the track-and-field clubs and national amateur championships in the mid-1870s.

Caledonian competitions drew people from all ethnic backgrounds, and by 1870 admission-paying crowds surpassed twenty thousand. Besides the traditional Scottish games, there would be sprint races and field events such as the hammer throw, shot put, and pole vault. In 1886 New York Caledonians added a 220-yard women's race. Caledonian contests for cash prizes ranging from one hundred to two hundred dollars were opened up to all comers, but the stars remained Scotsmen such as Duncan Ross and Donald Dinnie. Dinnie used his stature as a major gate attraction to force meet sponsors to pay him appearance fees in addition to his purses. The Caledonians faltered in the late nineteenth century from the decline in Scottish immigration, the rapid assimilation of Scots immigrants into mainstream American culture, and the emergence of high-status athletic clubs that supplanted them as the leading track-and-field sponsors.

Irish Americans

The 1.7 million Irish who immigrated to the United States in the decade following the Great Famine of 1845–46 were mainly uneducated, impoverished, and unskilled Catholic peasants. They brought a traditional male bachelor subculture that included a lively sporting heritage. Single and married Irishmen spent their leisure time with their "mates" in pubs and other exclusively male surroundings where self-image and prestige were defined by their athletic, gambling, drinking, or sexual prowess. Once in America, the Irish readily moved into a similar subculture where they befriended men of comparable backgrounds, values, and behavior.

The Irish newcomers immediately distinguished themselves in boxing, a violent and bloody sport that required courage, strength, and skill. The sport offered tough Irish immigrants a possible escape from poverty. Boxing was most prominent in such cities as New York, Boston, Philadelphia, and New Orleans where there were a lot of Irish residents. As historian Melvin Adelman discovered, most New York prizefighters active between 1840 and 1860 were Irishmen (56.3 percent), many of whom had boxed in the Old Country, or Irish Americans (15.6 percent). Mid-century matches were mainly impromptu or secret events staged in neighborhood groggeries.

Second-generation Irish American boxers who grew up in New York were typically alumni of tough street gangs or fire companies closely tied to Tammany Hall. They fought for side bets and to protect personal honor, Irish pride, or the Democratic party. Irish pugilists preferred to fight Englishmen or native-born white Americans. The latter composed just 6.25 percent of the prizefighters. These were typically exapprentice mechanics or butchers who supported WASP gangs such as the Bowery Boys and nativist political parties such as the Whigs and the Know-Nothings.

Fighters in the 1850s could not earn a living from boxing because there were few formal matches. They generally depended on political sponsors for patronage jobs or work that required physical prowess, often becoming "shoulder hitters," or political intimidators. The most renowned antebellum Irish fighter was John Morrissey, who was born in Ireland but grew up in Troy, New York. Morrissey went to New York City as a young man seeking fame and fortune. He first gained recognition as a barroom brawler at Captain Isaiah Rynders's Empire Club and as an intimidator for the Democratic party. In 1853, in only his second formal bout, he defeated the American champion and fellow Irishman Yankee Sullivan, following the thirty-seventh round, for the title. Sullivan had been dominant until a free-for-all broke out, and he occupied himself punching Morrissey's second, or cornerman. When the timekeeper called the fighters for the thirty-eighth round, Sullivan did not join Morrissey in the center of the ring, and the referee awarded the fight to Morrissey. Morrissey won his only defense in 1858 against Irish American John C. Heenan in Long Point, Canada. Morrissey lacked technique, but he was courageous and determined. He retired a hero to most Irish Americans for his boxing prowess and impromptu brawls with nativists such as Butcher Bill Poole. Morrissey became New York City's most successful gambling-hall proprietor, and he played a prominent role in revitalizing northern racing at Saratoga Springs during the Civil War. Morrissey became a prominent Tammany Hall politician, serving two terms (1867–70) in the U.S. Congress. He broke with the crooked Tweed Ring, the machine that ran New York City politics, before its downfall in 1871, a move that salvaged his political career. Morrissey was elected to the state senate in 1876. He died two years later, having achieved a measure of respectability.

Considerable interest emerged in the Irish community after the Civil War in traditional Hibernian games such as hurling, a game similar to field hockey, but much wilder, in which players catch the ball on the side of a four-inch-wide stick and run with it down the playing field, and Gaelic football, similar to soccer, although the ball can be advanced with the hands, a game that had first been played in New York in 1858. Nationalists in Ireland advocated a rebirth of historic Irish sports at home and abroad to promote Irish freedom and ethnic consciousness. One of the first organizations to sponsor traditional sports was the Clan-na-Gael, also known as the United Brotherhood, a notorious, secretive revolutionary society established in 1867. In 1870 the Clan began sponsoring annual track-and-field games to promote Irish nationalism and to improve the Clan's public image. By the late 1870s, additional Irish sports clubs were created in Boston, Brooklyn, New York, and other heavily Irish locales. They provided members with a community of like-minded men, encouraged ethnic pride and Irish nationalism, and enhanced members' status and dignity. Boston's Irish Athletic Club's inaugural athletic meet in 1879 featured traditional contests such as goaling, trapping, and stone throwing. In 1884 the Gaelic Athletic Association (GAA) was founded in Ireland to promote historic Hibernian games. An American tour followed four years later, which helped to stimulate the movement in this country. Its American units became well known for organizing hurling, Gaelic football, and track-and-field contests on Sundays in Irish neighborhoods. A Hibernian spirit permeated New York's Irish football teams that played at Gaelic Park, and the teams named themselves for Irish heroes.

The Irish became widely recognized after the Civil War for their athletic prowess in American sports. Irishmen achieved success in track and field, a sport largely dominated by wealthier WASPS who could afford the cost of training, time lost from work, and admission into the more prestigious clubs. Some working-class Irishmen who were recruited by elite athletic clubs tried to parlay their physical dexterity into jobs or business opportunities. In 1886 nineteen-year-old Tommy Conneff, a promising distance runner and future mile record holder, came to America to better himself. He joined the prestigious Manhattan Athletic Club after the club's secretary hired him to work as a clerk in a company he owned. Irish track-and-field professionals had limited opportunities. The most notable were the six-day marathons that were popular in the late 1870s and early 1880s. Among the most successful Irish athletes was Irish-born Patrick Fitzgerald, a future Long Island city alderman, who won an 1884 Madison Square Garden marathon, completing 610 miles and earning over eighteen thousand dollars.

Beginning in 1903, New York's Irish American Athletic Club provided training facilities for world-class Irish (and selected non-Irish) athletes who were not welcomed at the more prestigious clubs because of their heritage. In 1908 it contributed nineteen of seventy-seven Olympic track-and-field competitors. Several working-class Irish athletes who belonged to the club, including five muscular policemen, won Olympic medals in field events between 1900 and 1912. They included Irish-born John Flanagan, who won three gold medals in the hammer throw (1900, 1904, and 1908) and Irish-born Martin Sheridan, who won five gold and one silver medal in the shot put and discus (1904, 1906, 1908). Johnny Hayes, winner of the marathon in 1908, was ostensibly a shipping clerk at Bloomingdale's, but the job was a sinecure, and he was able to train full-time for his race.

Sport was a major preoccupation for second- and third-generation Irish-Americans such as Danny O'Neill and Studs Lonigan, protagonists in James T. Farrell's novels about Chicago's Irish youth in the early twentieth century. They joined community baseball and football teams that played lads from different streets or neighborhoods. These teams were often based on turn-of-the-century formal gangs, known as social and athletic clubs. These clubs had about one hundred members, mainly in their late teens. They had streetfront clubhouses and were often sponsored by a local machine politician who expected the club to work on his behalf on election day. These clubs promoted camaraderie and sport, supplying uniforms and arranging contests. They could be either uplifting or destructive. Chicago's most famous club was the Ragen Colts, located in the Back of the Yards district adjacent to the stockyards. The Colts first gained renown for their athletic prowess, but by the late 1910s were mainly known as sluggers and political intimidators who terrorized the Southwest Side and the emerging Black Belt to the east. The Irish were frightened by the growing African American presence as stockyard workers and by African American support of the new Republican mayor, William H. Thompson, archenemy of Chicago Democrats. The Colts felt it was their duty to protect the Southwest Side Irish, just as they protected Washington Park, "their turf," from the infiltration of the black newcomers. When the Chicago Race Riot broke out in 1919, the Colts were second to none in their attacks against African Americans.

Club members and other Irish youth looked to professional sports, where they played a prominent role in the industrial era, as a way to get ahead. Irish immigrants and their families struggled to earn a living in America. As historian Stephan Thernstrom discovered, as late as the 1890s just 10 percent of Boston's first-generation Irish had white-collar jobs, compared to half of native-born white Americans. While the second generation fared much better—over one-third of Irish Bostonians born between 1860 and 1879 ended up in white-collar jobs—they did not do as well as second-generation western Europeans, who were 52 percent white-collar workers. Ambitious but poor, uneducated and unskilled Irish Americans sought success in such alternate areas as the church, politics, crime, and sports.

Irish continued to dominate prizefighting well into the twentieth century. In the 1890s, eight of fourteen American-born world prizefighting champions were of Irish descent, including John L. Sullivan, the last bare-knuckle heavyweight champion and the greatest sports hero of the nineteenth century. The Boston Strong Boy won his title in 1882 from Paddy Ryan, who admitted that "when Sullivan struck me, I thought that a telegraph pole had been shoved against me endways." Sullivan kept the crown for ten years until he was knocked out in 1892 by fellow Irishman James J. Corbett, a former bank clerk and boxing instructor. This was the first heavyweight championship under the Marquis of Queensberry rules, which had been adopted in the 1880s. The new rules required three-minute rounds and the use of gloves; wrestling was barred. A fighter who was floored by a punch and could not regain his feet in ten seconds was ruled knocked out.

Pugilism provided the Irish with heroes and promoted ethnic solidarity. Every Irish saloon proudly displayed a picture of Sullivan. He was the idol of all Irish Americans except the well-to-do "lace-curtain" Irish, who were embarrassed by his profession and racy lifestyle. He reputedly earned, and spent, over one million dollars during his career, mostly from national excursions known as "knocking-out tours" when he would offer one thousand dollars to anyone who could last four rounds with him.

Irish boxers were prominent members of the sporting fraternity and served as role models to indigent Irish Americans who grew up in rough neighborhoods such as New York's Hell's Kitchen on the Lower West Side. These communities were breeding grounds for future fighters, like heavyweight-champion Gene Tunney, who held the title from 1926 to 1930. These Irish learned to defend themselves in street brawls, usually against newer immigrants, to prove their manhood and gain their peers' respect. Youths learned the manly art at neighborhood athletic clubs, gymnasiums, and settlement houses. The best amateurs usually went on to the professional ranks. Irish preeminence in prizefighting declined between 1900 and 1919 to eleven out of thirty-one champions, which was still far superior to any other ethnic group. The decline resulted from improving job opportunities for Irish and the growing competition from impoverished second-generation southern and eastern European immigrants.

The Irish were also extremely visible in professional baseball, both as spectators and as players. Certain sections of ballparks in the early 1900s were popularly known by Irish names like "Burkeville," a part of the bleachers at New York's Polo Grounds that was frequented by Irish fans. In Chicago, Irishman Charles Comiskey purposely built his White Sox ballpark in 1900 a few blocks from heavily Irish Bridgeport. Comiskey expected to draw many fans from the neighborhood, especially with Sunday ball games and twenty-five-cent bleacher seats. Baseball appealed to Irish men; watching the game afforded enthusiasts a lot of time to drink beer with their buddies and provided boys with a rite of passage into young manhood and something to talk about with their fathers.

Irish Americans were disproportionately represented on the diamond. One expert in the late 1890s estimated that one-third of the major leaguers were Irishmen. This may have been an exaggeration, but at the turn of the century, only native-born white Americans exceeded them on the diamond. Their numbers were indicative of their sporting heritage and high degree of Americanization. In addition, the Irish could play baseball in fields near their homes, which were located in the zone of emergence. Irish boys hoped to follow in the footsteps of heroes such as catcher Mike "King" Kelly, the most famous nineteenth-century ballplayer, slugger Ed Delahanty, and Willie Keeler, who "hit it where they ain't." The Irish success was hardly limited to the playing field; in 1915, eleven of sixteen major league managers were Irish. They included John McGraw of the New York Giants (1902–32), the leading proponent of "inside" or "scientific" baseball, which emphasized intelligence, mastery of fundamentals, and scrappiness, and Philadelphia Athletics' owner Connie Mack, who managed his club from 1901 to 1950, longer than anyone in history.

Irishmen became very active in the business of sports as bookmakers, boxing promoters, and baseball-team owners, reflecting the close nexus that existed between urban politics, organized crime, and sports. Several major-league owners such as Mack, Comiskey, and James Gaffney of the Boston Braves were Irishmen. Gaffney was a member of New York's Tammany Hall, whose members were known as "Braves," hence the name of the ball club. Irishmen dominated the commercial side of boxing as promoters, operators of arenas, managers, and trainers. Even publisher Richard Fox of the *National Police Gazette*, the leading boxing periodical, was Irish. They also controlled sports betting, which was very popular among Irishmen. Bookmakers and poolroom operators in the late nineteenth century were overwhelmingly Irish, and they continued to dominate long into the next century as well. New York's poolrooms were dominated by the so-called Gambling Trust, which included Tammany's number-two man, state senator Tim Sullivan, and gamblers Frank Farrell and Jere Mahoney. Chicago's poolrooms were divided among Irish gambler James O'Leary (whose mother's cow supposedly started the Chicago Fire), Irish aldermen Jimmy Rogers, Bathhouse John Coughlin, and Hinky Dink Kenna, and the German gambler Mont Tennes.

German Americans

In the mid-1850s, Germans replaced the Irish as the leading immigrant group. The mid-nineteenth-century German migration was caused by potato blights, unprofitable small land holdings, political oppression, and the loss of skilled jobs resulting from the Industrial Revolution. They were skilled, literate immigrants with some money who were far better prepared for life in the United States than were the Irish. Germans were very proud of their culture, and they worked hard to maintain their ethnic identity in their rural communities and urban neighborhoods. They established German-language newspapers, theaters, choral societies, and other old-world cultural institutions, including the turnverein, which were gymnastic societies founded in 1811 in the German states by Friedrich Jahn. His goal was to promote German nationalism and physical fitness to prepare soldiers for future wars with France. As early as the 1820s a number of his students immigrated to the United States to teach gymnastics at prominent colleges. Members of the turnverein, known as turners, were typically students, artisans, and intellectuals. In 1848 the movement was brought to America by radical refugees escaping the defeated democratic revolutions. The first clubs were organized in Louisville, Cincinnati, and Newark, and in the next few years, other societies were organized in cities and even rural areas such as New Ulm, Minnesota.

In 1851 socialist turners established the North American Socialist Turner Association to promote their political, social, and athletic interests. Most turners, however, joined the progressive new Republican party, which was organized in 1854 in opposition to slavery, nativism, and laws curtailing personal freedom. The majority of turners were skilled workers, although the first societies in the booming midwestern cities of Chicago and Milwaukee were founded by conservative or apolitical businessmen, and the members were mainly white-collar workers.

Turner societies promoted gymnastics, liberal politics, German culture, and working-class interests. Turner halls, often the largest building in German neighborhoods, became important community centers. The finest ones had gymnasiums, billiard rooms, a library, dining room, club room, dance halls, and an auditorium. Turners frequently established militia units and sharpshooting companies for the purpose of returning home to Germany to fight for liberty. In the mid-1850s the militia had a more practical value because they defended the community against violent nativists who resented the German presence. When the Civil War broke out, turners enlisted en masse into the Union army. The Seventeenth Missouri was popularly known as the Western Turner Regiment because nearly all of its members were turners. German participation in the war significantly bolstered their public image.

The number of turners grew substantially in the late nineteenth century from about five thousand members in 1859 to nearly forty thousand by 1890. It was primarily a male institution, although women would join social auxiliary units. In 1865 the North American Turner Association (NATA) was established as a national organization for all turners. Membership in the post–Civil War era remained predominantly hard-working respectable blue-collar men (55.5 percent), chiefly craftsmen. Cities with large German communities, such as Chicago, had several turner units, some almost exclusively working class. These were the most politically radical.

Turners in the late nineteenth century continued to foster physical fitness, ethnic pride, and improved working-class conditions. They were a political pressure group that focused on such ethno-political issues as Sunday blue laws, prohibition, and foreign-language education. The turners were leading advocates of professionally supervised physical education and parks for vigorous exercise. As early as 1866, Chicago turners convinced the board of education to introduce exercise programs for elementary schools. In 1889 the program was expanded into the high schools, often with turner instructors. Athletic competition was not stressed, but in 1881 a group of Milwaukee turners competed in a gymnastic festival in Frankfurt, Germany, winning several medals. Annual national turnfests had limited appeal and became quadrennial events in 1885, though interest increased following the introduction of competitive gymnastics.

Turner membership in the late nineteenth century became increasingly bourgeois as Germans and their American-born children fared well economically. Nonetheless, many local units, as well as the national organization, still supported traditional socialist demands for worker control over the means of production, justice for all, factory inspection laws, restricted child labor, and the eight-hour day. Turner halls were used for union meetings and public debates on labor issues. Beginning in 1877, left-wing politics heated up following the violent nationwide railroad strikes. Nine years later, eight anarchists, including journalist August Spies, a Chicago turner, were sentenced to death for allegedly fomenting a conspiracy that led to the Haymarket Riot. Tensions erupted in Chicago between the bourgeois and socialist turners based on their positions on anarchism and the guilt of the anarchists. When radicals took over the national association, the middle-class societies temporarily dropped out.

Even after the middle-class turners returned to the association, the society remained active in left-wing politics. In the early 1900s members helped organize the Socialist party of America, assisted socialist turner Victor Berger in his election as mayor of Milwaukee, and repeatedly supported socialist Eugene V. Debs for president. All clubs, however, gave greater emphasis to nonpolitical social activities such as picnics, socials, balls, and theater. In the summer of 1906, for instance, Chicago's working-class Aurora turnverein sponsored a sports outing to Indiana that drew over five thousand people in five chartered trains.

Declining German immigration hurt the turners. In 1908 they began to use English as an official language at meetings. The society's main problem was its weak appeal to second-generation German Americans who preferred American sports to gymnastics. The viability of all German institutions in America was badly shaken after the United States entered World War I. Anti-German sentiment encouraged many Teutonic organizations to rename themselves to avoid public disapproval. German gymnastic societies became known as "Lincoln Turners." After the war, turnvereins became less prominent as membership sharply declined.

While the turners dominated German physical culture in America, Germans were also active in sports such as target shooting and bowling. Bowling in the second half of the nineteenth century was considered primarily a German sport. German immigrants brought a legacy of target-shooting companies, or *schutzencorps*, to America. These clubs comprised merchants and other "respectable" people, who held *schutzenfests* that became annual affairs after the Civil War. There were also plebeian target companies, such as the *Lehr und Wehrverein*, which were more politically oriented. German sharpshooting organizations were briefly banned in Chicago in 1877 for fear they would protect workers against the police or the National Guard.

The New Immigrants

Unlike the old immigrants who brought a sporting heritage to America, the new immigrants from eastern and southern Europe, who came in the late nineteenth and early twentieth centuries, had little if any sporting background. These impoverished newcomers were largely from premodern societies. They included about 4.5 million Italians, and over 2 million Poles and Russian Jews. The Italians and Poles were unskilled, uneducated, Catholic peasants. Over one-half of Italians and nearly 40 percent of Poles traveled back and forth between the United States and their homelands, not settling permanently in America. These newcomers ended up working at low-paying jobs and living in slums. They established their own ethnic villages, coping with culture shock by speaking their own languages and relying on old-world institutions, such as the parish church or synagogue, saloons, choral groups, and theatrical clubs, and starting new ones such as mutual aid societies and foreign-language newspapers. They were seldom interested in sport, which for most of them was a strange American institution.

The Bohemians (Czechs) were among the first of the new immigrants. They adjusted better to American life than most other groups because many were artisans and came from a relatively modern part of east central Europe. Unlike the other new immigrants, Bohemians brought an emerging sporting culture based on the *Sokol*, a voluntary society organized in 1862 by M. Tyrs and J. Fuegner to promote resistance to the Austrian Empire that controlled their homeland. The Sokol philosophy was modeled on the romantic nationalism of the turnverein. Its goal was to develop strong bodies and minds to lead the fight for liberation. The first American Sokol was established in St. Louis in 1865, and by 1900 there were 184 American Sokols. The organization promoted physical culture by establishing gymnasiums that emphasized calisthenics and championed Bohemian culture by supporting libraries, choral societies, and theatrical groups. Most members were freethinkers (religious skeptics) and got along poorly with devout Catholics, who established their own Sokols.

The Sokol hall, typically one of the tallest buildings in Bohemian neighborhoods, was a community center that housed the immigrants' major institutions. Sokols sponsored annual gymnastic shows and family outings involving gymnastic drills and folk dancing. Its physical culture program did not appeal to the second-generation Bohemians, however. Consequently, in the 1890s Sokols organized Sunday baseball leagues to attract the American-born and to sustain their ethnic identity. Chicago's Bohemian League performed at a very high level, and by 1910, several graduates had made the major leagues. Their achievements were a source of pride to the entire community, even to those who were not baseball fans.

Sport had a similar purpose among contemporary French-Canadian immigrants in New England. They also used sports programs to maintain ethnic identification and separation from other groups. Historian Richard Sorrell found that Francophone St. Ann's Church in Woonsocket, Rhode Island, built a gymnasium in the early 1890s "to keep the church as the center of social activities for youths and to prevent them from mixing with Irish Catholic and Protestant children at other recreational areas."

The new immigrants who came after the Bohemians had little if any athletic tradition. Sport was largely unknown among the Polish people whose homeland was divided between Russia, Prussia, and Austria. The main exception were the Falcons, organized in 1867 by Polish nationalists in Austrian-controlled Galicia on the model of the Sokols. They soon established hundreds of "nests" in Galicia and Poznan (German Poland). The first American nest was established in Chicago in 1887, followed by others in Polish mining communities in Pennsylvania and industrial cities of the Great Lakes. The Falcons encouraged ethnic pride, Polish independence, and strict morals, and they sought to promote a positive public image. The Falcons and Sokols both had paramilitaristic aspects. They wore uniforms, marched in parades, and organized military schools to train freedom fighters. When the United States entered World War I in 1917, about five thousand Falcons ineligible for the draft joined Polish military forces to fight for their homeland.

The impoverished two million Jewish newcomers pushed out of Russia were better prepared for America than other new immigrants. They were more likely to come from cities, were often skilled workers or had entrepreneurial experience, and had a keen respect for education. They had not been allowed to own farms in Russia, and they were stereotyped as weak, physically unfit, and unaccustomed to strenuous physical labor that Americans considered to be manly. These newcomers had no familiarity with sports. The rare Jewish immigrant who became a sports fan would be ridiculed by his peers as a fool.

Americanized German Jews whose families had migrated to the United States a generation or two earlier were embarrassed by the customs, odd clothing, and physical appearance of their devout eastern European brethren. Nonetheless, they accepted the responsibility of helping them adjust to modern American life. Philanthropic German Jews established settlement houses such as the Educational Alliance (1893) in New York's

Lower East Side and the Jewish People's Institute (1908) in Chicago's West Side. These institutions offered a wide variety of programs for children and adults to help the newcomers adjust. Settlements provided such useful services as civics classes, employment bureaus, and sports programs. Athletics provided bait to attract young people to settlements, where they could become acculturated. In addition, participation in sports could teach American values and behavior and destroy negative stereotypes about Jewish manliness and fitness.

Settlement houses were supplemented by the Young Men's Hebrew Association (YMHA), a German-Jewish organization dating back to 1854. Based on the model of the YMCA, the association promoted physical fitness, learning, sociability, spirituality, and "muscular Judaism." German-Jewish immigrants had originally participated in turner societies along with other Germans, but their sons preferred American sports. Furthermore, rising anti-Semitism in the late nineteenth century resulting from the new wave of immigration meant that German Jews were barred from top colleges, resorts, and sports clubs, such as the New York Athletic Club. Consequently, the YMHA gained prominence in the 1890s. The Young Men's Hebrew Association broadened its appeal in the 1910s to become a Jewish community center. It became more accessible to inner-city youth by constructing new facilities in slums such as Brooklyn's Brownsville.

Second-generation Jews became fanatical sports fans, as did Poles and Italians. Playing and talking about sports proved they were becoming real Americans. Success in sports gave them an opportunity to display prowess and gain status. Their sporting options were limited to neighborhood pastimes by parental attitudes, Sabbath restrictions, amount of leisure time, cost, and accessibility. Parents from southern and eastern Europe often saw sports such as baseball as a child's game and a waste of time. Their foreign-language newspapers rarely covered baseball, although the Yiddish *Forward* did publish an article in 1903 that sought to explain baseball.

The limited available public space often became ethnic battle-grounds. During the early 1900s, ethnic groups did not mix in the new small parks, but they divided them up to play with their own kind. Parks reinforced, rather than broke down, ethnic and racial barriers. The more established ethnic groups, such as the Irish, intimidated youngsters of the newest and least numerous groups who moved into their neighborhoods. Parks located between ethnic adversaries became focal points for Irish, Italian, Jewish, or Polish gangs. If no one group gained control, then the park became a no-man's land to be entered at great peril.

Second-generation youths were big baseball fans who followed their favorite players and teams in the daily press. However, they seldom attended games because ballparks were located far from their inner-city neighborhoods and tickets were expensive. Furthermore, it was difficult for them to become proficient ballplayers because they encountered parental opposition, had insufficient playing space near their homes, and missed out on secondary-school sports. Immigrant sons rarely attended high school; either they lacked interest or had to work to help support the family. Hence they had no chance to play interscholastic baseball under experienced coaches, and they had fewer opportunities to compete against highly skilled opponents.

Progressive reformers supported the second-generation interest in baseball because they considered the national pastime second only to public education as an agent of Americanization. However, playing the sport did not necessarily lead to acceptance by the core society, nor did it loosen the ties of ethnic identity. Ethnic teams and leagues existed to keep boys with their own kind. Furthermore, playing members of another ethnic group on a mixed team promoted ethnic pride and cultural pluralism as much as it did mutual respect and Americanization. French Canadians in Woonsocket became ardent baseball fans in the 1890s without losing their ethnic identity. They read baseball scores and followed the major league career of star second baseman Napoleon Lajoie in the French language press. The players became adept at signaling in French when they played Anglo teams.

The barriers that new immigrants faced in baseball resulted in underrepresentation on major-league rosters until the mid-1930s. In 1910, for instance, no major league rookie was of southern or eastern European stock. In 1920 there were just two Italians, two Bohemians, and no Jews or Poles out of 133 first-year men. New immigrants encountered a lot of discrimination in professional baseball. The first seven Cohens in the major leagues all played under an alias to hide their Jewish identity. Most Jews who made the majors were not from New York, where half of all American Jews lived, but from other communities and even small towns such as Hamburg, Arkansas, where Jews were much more assimilated.

While Jews were underrepresented on the diamond, they were overrepresented among major-league executives. German-Jewish entrepreneurs were involved with the Cincinnati American Association teams in the 1880s. Owners of German-Jewish origin in the early 1900s included Barney Dreyfuss of the Pittsburgh Pirates, Andrew Freedman of the New York Giants, and Julius Fleischmann of the Cincinnati Reds. At the time, Jewish owners outnumbered Jewish major-league players. The baseball business then was very similar to the fledgling movie industry, which was completely dominated by recent eastern European Jewish immigrants. These entertainment industries were new, and consequently were open to entrepreneurs willing to take risks, regardless of their social backgrounds. Neither venture encountered much competition from the more-established WASP businessmen, who preferred more conservative and higher-status investments.

Second-generation new immigrants were most successful at cheap indoor sports that did not require much space, namely track, boxing, basketball, billiards, and bowling. Although they were not welcomed at the most prestigious track clubs because of their religion or social class, Jewish youths had excellent role models to emulate, including Lon Myers, the greatest American middle-distance runner of the nineteenth century, and Meyer Prinstein, who won a total of three Olympic gold medals in the long jump (1904) and triple jump (1900, 1904). Prinstein also won the silver medal in long jumping at the 1900 Paris Olympics despite missing the finals, which were scheduled for the Christian Sabbath; officials at his school, Syracuse University, ordered him not to compete. After college, Prinstein competed for New York's Irish American Athletic Association because more prestigious clubs would not admit him.

Second-generation Russian-Jewish youths living in urban slums achieved considerable proficiency in track, a popular sport that did not require sophisticated equipment or highly experienced coaching. Jewish boys had lots of opportunities in the sport through the Young Men's Hebrew Association, intersettlement competition, and the Public Schools Athletic League, whose Manhattan meets were dominated by Lower East Side elementary schools. The Jewish American press applauded the public school athletic league for improving the health of inner-city children and giving Jewish youth a chance to gain the respect of the Gentile community.

Shortly after James Naismith invented basketball in 1891, it became very popular among inner-city youth because it was cheap and required little space. Second-generation Irish, Jews, and other ethnic groups played basketball in school yards, settlement houses, and church gymnasiums. By 1898 a professional league operated in Philadelphia. As one former New York University All-American remembered, "We played basketball in the streets with a rag ball and used ashcans for baskets. We stressed team play rather than shooting because rag balls didn't bounce." Top-level basketball was a bruising game that required a lot of padding. The playing floor was surrounded by wire mesh to prevent players from fighting over loose balls off the court and to protect them from spectators. Nonetheless, it was not considered a game of "brutality and brute strength," and the *American Hebrew* endorsed basketball for its "quick thinking, lightning-like rapidity of movement, and endurance."

Jewish and Italian youth were primarily identified in the public mind with prizefighting. Boxing was a very useful skill for inner-city schoolboys and young men to learn since they often got into fights with youth from other groups, particularly the Irish. Brawls occurred on the way to school, in the park, or when rivals encroached into one's neighborhood. As Benny Leonard, world lightweight champion from 1917 to 1925, remembered, "You had to fight or stay in the house when the Italian and Irish kids came through on their way to the [public] baths." Street fighters such as Chicago's Nails Morton became neighborhood heroes who protected youngsters and elderly Jews from rival ethnic toughs. Such experiences prepared rough inner-city youths, such as Chicago's Miller brothers, for future careers as boxers, hoodlums, or policemen. Rugged second-generation young men who learned to discipline their street fighting under the intense tutelage of experienced trainers at settlement houses or neighborhood gymnasiums often aspired to become professional boxers. They anticipated that success in the ring would lead to wealth and fame.

Professional fighters reared in the slums became ethnic heroes. Tough Jews, such as Joe Bernstein, "The Pride of the Ghetto," countered stereotypical images of physically weak Jews. Their parents, however, considered them an embarrassment to the family and to their ethnic group. Novices took pseudonyms to prevent parents from discovering what they were doing, to avoid discrimination, and to advance their careers. Benjamin Leiner fought as Benny Leonard to hide his career from his parents. He only gained paternal approval when he brought his winnings home. At first, ethnic fighters chose Irish aliases (Mushy Callahan was Jewish; Hugo Kelly was Italian) because the Irish were considered the toughest fighters. Once Jews had been recognized as outstanding fighters by the late 1910s, pugilists also took Jewish names (Italian Sammy Mandella fought as Sammy Mandell). Promoters tried to match men from different ethnic groups to heighten interest, such as the Leonard–"Irish" Eddie Finnegan match in a western coal-mining town. Finnegan took a bad beating, and in a clinch asked Leonard in Yiddish to take it easy on him because he was really Seymour Rosenbaum. Second-generation Russian Jews were the first new immigrants to gain success in the ring. For ambitious, uneducated, unskilled, and poorly connected second-generation newcomers who had little chance of succeeding through business or other traditional routes, alternate routes of success existed in fields such as entertainment, crime, and professional sports, particularly boxing. Historian Stephan Thernstrom found that in Boston one-fourth of second generation Russian Jews and three-fourths of other second-generation new immigrants ended up in blue-collar occupations. A substantial number of poor Jews, however, still resided in the inner city. A long tradition of Anglo-Jewish pugilists dated back to champion Daniel Mendoza in the 1790s, and a few, such as Barney Aaron, had fought in antebellum America. The first Jewish American champions were bantamweight Harry Harris, who won the crown in 1900, and featherweight Abe Attell, who held the title from 1904 to 1912. In the 1910s there were four Jewish champions, most notably Benny Leonard, probably the second-greatest lightweight in history. By World War I, there were more Jewish contenders than any other ethnic group. They were mainly in the lighter-weight classes, reflecting the slight stature of many new immigrants. The first Polish champion was middleweight Stanley Ketchell from 1908 to 1911, one of the all-time great fighters, while the first Italian was featherweight Pete Herman from 1917 to 1920. They gained their crowns about a generation before their groups produced a major-league batting champion.

The Native Americans

By the early 1900s, a little more than a decade after Wounded Knee, Native Americans had achieved a high degree of prominence in baseball and football. Among the first Native American major leaguers was Lou Sockalexis, who played for Cleveland from 1897 to 1899, and the team became known as the Indians in his honor. The novelty of having Native American players was part of the team's attraction, but that soon wore off. About thirty Native Americans played in the majors in the early 1900s, finding the baseball world less discriminatory than other segments of American society. A few had distinguished careers, particularly Hall of Fame pitcher Charles "Chief" Bender of the Philadelphia Athletics, who had a record of 210–128 and appeared in five World Series during his sixteen-year career.

National attention on Native American athletics focused on the Carlisle Indian School and its superstar, Jim Thorpe. Beginning in the late 1890s, Carlisle played all the top football powers, virtually always on the road. The public attitude toward Native American football players was originally racist and demeaning (in 1896 the *New York Journal* published nude photographs of Native American football players), but in time they were treated with more regard. Several Carlisle players earned All-American status, and their team became renowned for remarkable sportsmanship, which the school hoped would gain respect for Native Americans.

Jim Thorpe was a two-time All-American football player, who led Carlisle to an 11–1 record in 1911 that included a victory over Harvard. He set a national scoring record the following season with 198 points. Thorpe won gold medals at the 1912 Olympics in both the pentathlon and decathlon, and he was proclaimed "the greatest athlete in the world." In 1913, however, it was discovered that he had played professional baseball for Rocky Mount and Fayetteville, North Carolina (Eastern Carolina League), from 1909 to 1910, and he was stripped of his Olympic medals. Thorpe played in the majors from 1913 to 1915 and from 1917 to 1919. He also played professional football from 1915 through 1926, and he appeared as a placekicker as late as 1929, when he was forty-one years old. In 1920, he was the first president, albeit mainly a figurehead, of the American Professional Football Association, the forerunner of the National Football League. In 1950 Thorpe was named the outstanding American athlete of the first half of the twentieth century.

African Americans

The African American sporting experience differed from that of European immigrants because their ancestors had been slaves, they encountered discrimination because of skin color, and they were completely familiar with American sport. Slaves were employed as cock trainers, raced in crews at regattas, rode thoroughbreds at racetracks, and boxed in matches arranged by their owners. During the antebellum period, free people of color participated in working-class sports, particularly professional contests in boxing and pedestrianism, to gain recognition and make money. In antebellum New Orleans, which had the largest free black population in the United States, African American raquette clubs (a team sport similar to lacrosse) played on Sundays before racially mixed crowds of up to four thousand spectators.

During Reconstruction, southern sport outside of New Orleans was largely segregated well before the legalization of Jim Crow. African Americans participated in sports sponsored by their own fraternal, church, and political groups, which organized picnic games at black sections of municipal parks and "Colored Fairgrounds." Baseball games were organized by African American sports clubs. Such events promoted a sense of community, and, it was hoped, recognition by the white society. By 1876 African Americans had established YMCAs in Richmond and Nashville to promote sound morality and provide an uplifting substitute for "the sporting life." After Reconstruction, blacks had limited access to public parks, even in New Orleans, because of custom, inaccessibility, or police harassment. Following the enactment of segregation laws in the 1890s, a few separate and inferior parks were set aside for African Americans. The first black municipal park in Birmingham, Alabama, opened in 1908, only after seventeen white parks were constructed.

As historian Dale Somers has pointed out, interracial sporting competition existed in New Orleans, a uniquely continental city with relatively liberal racial traditions, until the mid-1880s. African Americans were permitted in general-admission sections of local racetracks until 1871, when the Metairie Course erected a separate seating area. Local African Americans responded with a boycott, and management was compelled to restore integrated seating in the public stand. New Orleans' lakefront facilities were segregated, however, and African Americans were barred from white athletic clubs. In the 1880s the color line was tightened. Game laws were passed to protect wildlife from black hunters, and white baseball clubs that had played African American teams were boycotted. In the early 1890s, local cyclists dropped out of the League of American Wheelmen (LAW) because northern clubs had African American members. By 1894 southern pressure compelled the league to ban African Americans.

The last sport in New Orleans to draw the color line was boxing because fighters were regarded as entertainers and lowlives, hardly the equal of spectators. On September 6, 1892, black featherweight champion George Dixon successfully defended his crown at Olympic Arena against Jack Skelly with an eighth-round knockout. It was the first time that African Americans had been admitted into the arena. The outcome so shocked local whites that no more mixed bouts were held in New Orleans.

Discrimination also existed in northern semipublic and public places ranging from restaurants and theaters to parks, beaches, playgrounds, and YMCAs. Separate black YMCAs were established in late-nineteenth-century Boston, Brooklyn, New York, and Philadelphia. Chicago's YMCA was integrated until the turn of the century, while in Detroit only the black elite could use the white YMCA. In 1913 an impressive $190,000 African American YMCA was constructed in Chicago's South Side ghetto by white philanthropists and meatpacking executives trying to gain the loyalty of their black workers.

Once the Great Migration of African Americans from the South began in 1916, white northerners perceived African Americans as a greater threat and discrimination increased. Recreational sites that bordered both white and black neighborhoods became disputed territory where African Americans were afraid to venture. Racial clashes in Chicago became more common at public facilities, particularly Washington Park and Lake Michigan's beaches. The Chicago Race Riot of 1919 was precipitated by the death of a black youth killed by rocks that were thrown by whites when he swam into "white" waters.

The extent of black participation in high-level northern sport was limited by social convention. African Americans living in the North occasionally played on high-school and college teams, but there were seldom more than one or two black players on any squad. Forty blacks played on white college football teams prior to 1915, including three All-Americans. Track-and-field athletes representing all-black clubs, such as New York's Smart Set Athletic Club, competed against whites. In 1904 George Poage became the first black Olympic medal winner with bronze medals in the two-hundred meter and four-hundred meter sprints. Despite Poage's accomplishments, racist attitudes and behavior were displayed at the 1904 St. Louis Olympics by the Anthropological Days exhibit. Aborigines who were employed at the city's world's fair were recruited to demonstrate their native games and then were called upon to compete in unfamiliar modern sports. They naturally had a difficult time with the strange games, and racists used their poor performances to justify prejudice.

African American sports clubs, like their white counterparts, sorted individuals by interest, class, or birthplace. Historian Stephen Hardy found that in turn-of-the-century Boston, long-term, upwardly mobile African American residents copied the city's white elite by forming tennis clubs, while natives of the West Indies organized cricket clubs, and newly arrived black southerners preferred boxing at neighborhood gymnasiums.

African Americans were particularly proficient in professional sports, where ability would presumably overcome prejudice, and where they could make money. Frank Hart starred in the grueling six-day marathon races of the 1880s and 1890s, with a best distance of over 550 miles. Cyclist Marshall Taylor, American and world sprint champion, had to overcome jealous white competitors who ganged up to defeat him by blocking his path or boxing him into a poor position. African Americans such as Willie Sims were among the finest jockeys of the late nineteenth century, and Isaac Murphy, who won three Kentucky Derbys and earned up to twenty thousand dollars a year, may have been the greatest of that era. The income and status of jockeys rose steadily in the end of the nineteenth century. Horsemen and bettors recognized that it was not just the quality of the horse but also the skill of the rider that determined success. Yet despite top performances, African American jockeys were quickly forced out of the sport by prejudice. At the same time they were forced out of cycling, organized baseball, and other relatively visible, well-paying occupations.

African Americans were not pushed out of prizefighting as they were in more respectable sports. Boxing's participants were desperate young men, recruited from the bottom layers of society. They were willing to chance having their brains bashed in to escape poverty. Fighters of color still encountered considerable racism and discrimination, which made it hard, if not impossible, to advance their careers by going against white fighters, especially contenders and champions. Black spectators preferred mixed bouts where their idols could win symbolic racial victories over white opponents, but local customs and laws restricted such contests, even in New York State as late as the mid-1910s. Thus a great fighter such as Sam Langford, who fought men from lightweights all the way to heavyweights in a twenty-one-year career, was rarely matched with white boxers. The top pugilists were afraid to fight him, so Langford never got a championship fight. The first black world champion was Canadian George Dixon who gained the bantamweight crown in 1890. He captured the featherweight title a year later and held it for nine years. There were four black champions in the early 1900s, including Joe Gans (1902–1908), the greatest lightweight of all time, who occasionally had to fix fights just to get a match, and heavyweight champion Jack Johnson (1908–15).

The heavyweight division was the most prestigious championship in the industrial era, and the one with which sports fans and nonfans were most familiar. A color line in the division was first drawn by John L. Sullivan in 1887 because he did not want to fight contender Peter Jackson, who was born in the West

Indies, and would have been a very difficult opponent. No African American got a title shot until 1908, when Jack Johnson gained a title bout against Canadian Jack Burns in Australia. Johnson's knockout victory jolted white feelings of superiority and raised fears that his championship would encourage black pride. Cartoonists drew demeaning racist caricatures of him, and journalists rationalized his victory as indicative of the lower evolution of the African American and his greater ability to absorb pain. Furthermore, white rage at Johnson was exacerbated by his flamboyant personality and his threatening behavior. Folklorist William Wiggins, Jr., recounted a tale told by his father about Johnson. Johnson was speeding through Georgia when he was stopped by a sheriff. "Where do you think you're going, boy, speeding like that? That'll cost you $50!" Johnson gave the officer a $100 bill and gunned his engine. The sheriff shouted, "Don't you want your change?" Jack replied, "Keep it, 'cause I'm coming back the same way. . . ." "Papa Jack" was a "bad nigger" who flaunted conventional norms and refused to accept an inferior status. He was a bold, lusty man who raced cars at record speeds, had white girlfriends and wives, and disregarded authority.

Promoters sought a "Great White Hope" who could defeat Johnson and regain the title for the white race. But Johnson dispatched them all with obvious ease. One of his most memorable fights was against the much-lighter champion middleweight Stanley Ketchell in 1909. Johnson promised to go easy so the fight would last long enough to produce a marketable film. In the twelfth round Ketchell surprised Johnson with a flurry and sent him down to the canvas. The stunned champion jumped up and knocked Ketchell out with one blow. Ketchell was unconscious for five minutes and short several teeth that were deposited in Johnson's glove.

The promoters brought the corpulent, formerly undefeated champion Jim Jeffries out of retirement for a July 4, 1910, match with Johnson that paid $101,000, what was until then the largest purse in history. Jeffries trained hard, but he was well past his prime and was knocked out in the fifteenth round. The outcome led directly to race riots across the United States. Considerable furor arose over exhibiting the fight film because it showed the white man's hero being humiliated. Fearing disorder, most major cities barred the film. In 1912, following Johnson's overwhelming defeat of "Fireman" Jim Flynn, a federal law was passed banning interstate commerce in boxing movies.

Unable to dislodge Johnson in the ring, white Americans went after the champion in court. The federal government hounded Johnson for his sexual escapades, and in 1913 convicted him of violating the Mann Act by transporting a woman across state lines for immoral purposes. He fled the country and spent the rest of his championship reign abroad. In 1915 when Johnson was thirty-eight, he lost his title in Havana to six-foot-six, 250-pound, Jess Willard in the twenty-sixth round. Johnson later claimed that he had thrown the fight in return for amnesty. He was an old fighter, however, untested in several years, and he probably lost fair and square. He returned to the United States in 1919 and served a year in jail. The color line in the heavyweight division was immediately redrawn, and no black got a title fight until Joe Louis in 1937.

The most popular sport in the African American community was baseball. The absence of African Americans from major-league rosters was purely a product of racism, not lack of experience. As early as 1862 African Americans were playing baseball in Brooklyn, and four years later there were middle-class black teams in Philadelphia. In 1872 Bud Fowler became the first African American professional when he played for New Castle, Pennsylvania. By 1898 fifty-five blacks had played professional baseball, including Moses Walker, a college-educated minister's son who was the first black major leaguer. Walker caught for Toledo (American Association) in 1884 and had a batting average of .251. The best African American ballplayers in the late nineteenth century were probably International Leaguers George Stovey, who won 33 games for Newark in 1887, an all-time league record, and Buffalo's second baseman Frank Grant, who hit .366 to lead the league that year and had forty stolen bases. Prejudice kept Stovey and Grant out of the major leagues, however.

Black players were insulted and threatened by fans, poorly coached, shunned by teammates, and spiked and thrown at by opponents. Second-baseman Grant reputedly invented shin guards for self-protection. Owners did not want to use black players because of prejudice and pressure from racist spectators and ballplayers, especially Cap Anson, the great player-manager of the Chicago White Stockings. Professional ballplayers were also afraid of job competition, diminished salaries, and lowered occupational prestige. Despite the excellent performances of men like Stovey and Grant, club owners in the high minor leagues agreed in 1888 to stop signing black players. By 1890 the International League was all white, and thereafter nearly all the remaining African Americans in organized baseball were on all-black teams. Following the 1898 season, there were no black players until Jackie Robinson played for Montreal in 1946.

African Americans responded to white prejudice by organizing their own touring professional teams beginning with the Philadelphia Orions in 1882. The first prominent African American pro team was the Cuban Giants, established in 1885 by Frank Thompson, a head waiter. He named them "Cubans" to lessen racial prejudice. The club was so good that within two years they were playing exhibition games against major-league teams. The press usually referred to these outfits as semiprofessional teams. Playing baseball, however, was a full-time job for the best independent clubs, who by the early 1900s were playing up to two hundred games a year. The Chicago Leland Giants, for instance, played at home on Sundays when African Americans had a day off work, toured the Midwest playing town teams during the week, and spent the winter playing in California. The Leland Giants were among the few black-owned clubs; the team even had its own ballpark. They played in Chicago's prestigious semipro City League from 1907 to 1909, and in 1909 they played a post-season series against the Chicago Cubs. They may have been the only black team then to play in an otherwise all-white association. In 1910 star pitcher Andrew "Rube" Foster gained control of the club. He renamed them the American Giants the following season and moved to the former White Sox field a few blocks from the growing Black Belt. In 1920 Foster organized the Negro National League to keep profits from black baseball in African American hands, to employ black athletes, coaches, and secretaries, and to symbolize racial pride. Every team but one was owned and operated by African Americans. Neither the players nor the community felt this was a substitute for the major leagues, however, and integration remained the ultimate goal.

The ethnic sporting experience was a product of cultural heritage, social class, and racism. European immigrants were largely influenced by their backgrounds. The old immigrants who brought a sporting tradition to America kept it alive, while many new immigrants had no such legacy. Virtually all second-generation sons were interested in sport, although their options were shaped by ethnic traditions, parental attitudes, and social class. Sport offered a means to disprove negative ethnic stereotypes, develop ethnic pride, bond with peers, become Americanized, and gain respect from the broader community. The most-gifted white ethnic athletes used sport as a potential route for social mobility. African Americans, on the other hand, regardless of generation, were familiar with the American sporting culture. Yet their participation was limited by *de jure* and *de facto* racism, as well as by poverty. Nonetheless, African Americans achieved a high level of proficiency in sports, which they employed to advance racial pride and to develop a sense of community. They sought, but did not always achieve, a begrudging respect from the broader society, and they were limited in their efforts to get ahead through athletic prowess.

CHAPTER FOUR

Sport and the Educational Process

The leading sponsors of sport for children, adolescents, and young adults were formal and informal educational institutions that sought to implement the positive sports creed, and thereby uplift, instruct, and socialize American youth. Intercollegiate male sport emerged in the mid-nineteenth century at elite eastern colleges. Athletic leaders at these schools were self-proclaimed defenders of amateurism where a win-at-all-costs attitude paradoxically led to professionalization. As historian Ronald Smith points out, by 1900 sport at institutions such as Yale had become rationalized, commercialized, and professionalized, and furnished a model for colleges across the nation. Collegiate sport also gave women the opportunity to contest conventional perceptions of femininity. The collegiate athletic experience served as an important role model for secondary school students, who in the late nineteenth century emulated their elders and organized their own sports programs. By the turn of the century, organized athletics were introduced by educators and youth workers into elementary schools, settlement houses, YMCAs, and playgrounds to acculturate and socialize immigrant children.

Sport and Higher Education

Men's Collegiate Athletics

In the antebellum era the principal collegiate sporting events were annual interclass contests. These matches promoted class loyalty, supplied a vehicle for hazing or initiation rites, and enabled students to work out excess energy. These amusements were not necessarily endorsed by parents, teachers, or administrators, but they were preferred to harassing the faculty or rioting in town. The main game was the football rush, a soccer-style game played on the first Monday of the fall term, which became known as "Bloody Monday," by fifty to one hundred freshmen and sophomores. The game gave the latter an opportunity to kick first-year students into submission. Other popular antebellum college sports included handball, fencing, boxing, running, quoits, horseback riding, and swimming.

College faculties in the second half of the nineteenth century originally tolerated, if they did not ardently support, emerging sports programs. Professors believed athletics kept students busy, taught proper social habits, developed manly traits and character, and advanced American civilization. Furthermore, sports promoted school spirit and publicized their institution.

The first intercollegiate sport was crew, a sport originally made popular by professional boatmen, upper-middle-class rowing clubs, and the Oxford-Cambridge races in England, which began in 1829. The earliest recorded college race in America took place fifteen years later when a four-man team of Yale seniors raced lowerclassmen. However, the initial intercollegiate athletic contest did not occur until 1852, when Harvard defeated Yale. Only a few races ensued over the next few years, but in 1858 students from four eastern schools established the College Union Regatta to arrange a championship race. The Regatta attracted considerable public attention, attested by the fifteen thousand spectators at its inaugural race in 1859. Within five years Yale's crew became dominant in the sport. Student supporters raised money for better sculls and a new boathouse, and they hired the first professional coach, John Ward. He followed rigorous training methods that included a strict diet of raw meat and little milk or water. Through sport, Yale sought to certify its parity with Harvard, the nation's most prestigious college. Winning was less crucial for Harvard, which had less to prove. Yet in 1869 Harvard participated in the most notable match of this era when its eight-man crew rowed against Oxford on the Thames. The match attracted enormous attention, and the results were reported almost instantly via the new Atlantic cable. The two-mile race provided an opportunity to display national pride and to compare the character, physical fitness, and technology of the competing nations. Harvard lost by six seconds, which was considered a marvelous showing. The results demonstrated how far the United States had come in just a few years of racing compared to the English, who had been racing longer. The outcome was perceived as a positive reflection on American culture, indomitability, and education. The well-publicized match increased interest in crew and led to the formation of the Rowing Association of American Colleges (1871). The organization included not only elite institutions, but also such upstarts as Massachusetts Agricultural College and Cornell. Their victories humiliated the elite schools and brought them national prominence.

Baseball was the second major intercollegiate sport; by the 1870s it had become the principal game on campus. The first contest was played in conjunction with a regatta in 1859, Amherst defeating Williams, 73-32 under Massachusetts rules, although subsequent college games were played by the New York rules. After the Civil War, northern and southern colleges organized baseball clubs. Established in 1865, the Harvard nine was the dominant college team for several years, and they traveled to New York to play top amateur teams. In 1870 Harvard's home games drew up to ten thousand spectators. The team made a forty-four-game western tour that season, playing professionals as well as amateurs, and winning two-thirds of its games against the pros. Other top colleges also played professionals; in the period from 1865 to 1875, Yale played twice as many professional clubs as it did college teams.

The College Baseball Association, established in 1879, was the first intercollegiate baseball league. It arranged a championship season and enforced the weak or nonexistent eligibility rules, which allowed students in experimental programs and postgraduate schools to play as well as junior faculty. Brown won the first league championship, led by Lee Richmond who a week before had pitched a shutout for the Worcester professional team in an exhibition against the Chicago White Stockings. The following year, just before graduation, Richmond pitched the first perfect game in major-league history for Worcester's. new National League team against Cleveland. Many top college teams used professionals on their rosters. In 1888 Harvard had four professionals, Yale five, and Princeton six. Few college men sought major league careers, however, because of its low social status and modest wages. During the 1880s, only about 2 percent of major-leaguer players had college experience, although the proportion quadrupled in the 1890s.

By 1900 it was common for top collegians to play for pay during the summer break and then return to school with their amateur standing intact. Summer ballplayers earned between thirty and forty dollars a week by playing in outlaw leagues (professional associations that operated outside of organized baseball), or on semipro, resort, and even professional teams, usually under a pseudonym or through some subterfuge. Players on hotel teams were on the payroll as waiters or cabana boys, so their amateur standing was protected. Semipro owners compensated players by betting they could not jump over a broom lying on the ground. Eddie Collins of Columbia, later a star major leaguer, played in 1906 for the Philadelphia Athletics of the American League under a false name to protect his college eligibility.

Summer ball became a major educational issue. Advocates such as President Nicholas Murray Butler of Columbia believed all students had the right to use their talents to pay for their education. Ballplayers had as much right to play summer ball as glee club members did to sing in church choirs. Leading critics such as Capt. Frank Pierce of West Point disagreed, however, castigating summer ball for encouraging cheating and lying and for giving violators an unfair advantage over their simon-pure collegiate competitors. Most college administrators frowned on summer ball, but they seldom initiated action against violators since they probably had many on their own teams. Jim Thorpe was the most famous athlete caught playing summer ball.

The third college sport was track and field, which like baseball started as an adjunct to intercollegiate regattas. The sport's main impetus came from the Caledonian Games, from Oxford-Cambridge athletic competitions in the late 1850s, and from track-and-field contests at Princeton, whose sport was heavily influenced by its strong Scottish heritage. The first intercollegiate track-and-field meet was held in 1873 in conjunction with the College Regatta in Springfield, Massachusetts, under the sponsorship of Scottish-American James G. Bennett, Jr., who donated a five-hundred-dollar silver cup to the winner of a two-mile race. Other events included the 100-yard dash, 120-yard hurdles, one-, two-, and three-mile runs, and a seven-mile walk.

In 1875 ten colleges established the Intercollegiate Association of Amateur Athletes of America (IC4A) to regulate track and field. Harvard and Yale completely dominated, winning all the team titles between 1880 and 1897. Competition was so serious that teams employed professional coaches or trainers, and they sought innovative training methods, new techniques (Yaleman Charles Sherrill created the crouch start), and superior equipment. By the mid-1890s collegians achieved international distinction by competing against Cambridge and Oxford and by setting world records. Bernie Wafers of Georgetown held world records in 1894 in the 100- and 220-yard dashes (9.8 and 22.6 seconds, respectively). Two years later, four Princeton juniors, a Harvard undergraduate, and five Harvard alumni represented the United States at the first modern Olympics in Athens; they won nine of twelve track-and-field events.

The fourth and ultimately the most popular college sport was football. The first intercollegiate game in the fall of 1869, won by host Rutgers, six goals to four over Princeton, used rules similar to soccer. Players were permitted to bat the ball, but not to carry or to throw it. Different versions of football were played at a small number of colleges over the next few years. In 1874 Harvard played two games against McGill University of Montreal in Cambridge with important consequences. One game was played under Harvard's soccer-style rules and the second under rugby rules. This was the first college rugby game in the United States. Players enjoyed the physical contact and the opportunities to carry the oval ball, so Harvard decided to adopt the new game. In 1876, Harvard, Princeton, Columbia, and Yale formalized common rules, and the first three established the Intercollegiate Football Association (IFA). They agreed to an annual Thanksgiving Day championship between the prior season's top two teams. Their rules included fifteen men to a team and two forty-minute halves. Scoring emphasized kicking (four touchdowns equaled one kicked goal). Controversies on the field were to be decided by a referee instead of by team captains, as in English rugby. Use of referees became necessary because Americans lacked a traditional football code to rely upon, were less deferential to a captain to decide disputes, and might have been less comfortable with the letter of a rule than in manipulating rules to gain an advantage.

Early football was dominated by Yale under the leadership of Walter Camp. During his varsity career from 1876 to 1882, during part of which time he was a medical student, the squad went 30-1-5. Camp became a watch manufacturer and served as volunteer advisor to the field coach (usually the prior year's captain) for nearly thirty years. He helped make all types of athletics popular, and he wrote twenty books on sports. But his special love was football, which he promoted as a member of the Rules Committee, from 1878 to 1925, and by his annual All-American selections, from 1889 to 1924. Camp was an innovative coach who stressed rational management. His practices consisted of warm-up exercises, repetitive drills to develop machine-like efficiency and precise play, and a rough, hour-long scrimmage. His innovations include using tackling dummies, filming practices, developing strategies, and coding signals to communicate plays.

Camp's methods were so successful that between 1883 and 1891 Yale outscored its opposition 4,660 to 92, losing just three games. At first, football was primarily a participatory game, but Camp recognized its potential profitability if games were moved off-campus to metropolitan New York. In 1876 the first Intercollegiate Football Association championship was played in Hoboken. The game was shifted to New York four years later and drew about five thousand spectators. Attendance thereafter steadily increased, reaching twenty-three thousand by 1887, an audience consisting largely of middle-class non-student fans. The game became recognized as the start of the winter social season, and rounds of parties would follow. The championship match became so popular that one-dollar and two-dollar tickets were soon being scalped for up to forty dollars. The three championship games between 1891 and 1893 drew thirty thousand to forty thousand fans each year. The competing schools in the 1891 match shared over twenty-eight thousand dollars in profits.

Football became a big moneymaker. As late as 1888, the student-run Yale Athletic Association made less money from football (twenty-eight hundred dollars) than either baseball or crew (five thousand dollars each). But during the 1890s Yale's annual football profits surpassed fifty thousand dollars. Given those returns it was surprising that in 1894 the faculties and trustees decided to move the big game back to campus. The Big Three colleges (Harvard, Yale, and Princeton) left the New York market because their leaders felt the games were getting too much attention and that post-game student riots in less respectable Tenderloin theaters were giving the schools a bad public image. As a result of the move, attendance dropped by one half.

Walter Camp was also responsible for most major rule and tactical innovations. They evolved by trial and error, according to football historian Michael Oriard, as much by accident as by design. In 1880 when Yale joined the Intercollegiate Football Association, Camp cut the number of players to eleven and decreased the size of the playing field to 110 by 53 yards. He developed logical standardized written rules to bring order to the sport and provide common understanding of play. Camp wanted to create an exciting spectator entertainment with greater drama and changes in the flow of play.

Camp addressed the problem of initiating play after a ball carrier was downed by having the team with the ball maintain possession. Teams would then line up across an imaginary scrimmage line, resuming play once the ball was heeled back to the quarterback. This innovation brought order to the game, but it also meant the offense did not have to surrender the ball. During the 1880 Thanksgiving Game, Princeton kept the ball the entire second half to preserve a scoreless tie and maintain its championship. These tactics were repeated at the championship one year later, and consequently in 1882 Camp introduced the "down system" to open up the game. The offense was required to advance the ball five yards in three plays to maintain possession. Camp also revised the scoring system to lessen the emphasis on the kicking game.

The new rules encouraged highly coordinated offensive units featuring wide-open attacks with prearranged plays signaled by a code. Blockers were assigned to run interference for the ball carrier, a technique that was illegal in rugby. In 1884 Pennsylvania introduced the V formation in which blockers wrapped their arms up around each other to form a convoy ahead of the runner. The wide-open offense was hindered in 1888 by a new rule that permitted tackling below the waist. This change made shifty, open-field running more difficult and encouraged the use of heavier players. (In 1883 the average Yale football player weighed 173.5 pounds.) Thereafter, coaches preferred dangerous momentum and mass plays employing closed formations, such as Harvard's fearsome flying wedge, developed in 1892, in which the biggest players grouped themselves twenty-five yards behind the line of scrimmage and then ran full-speed ahead of the runner. Rule changes after the 1894 season banned this hazardous tactic, but they did not end violent mass play.

The nineteenth-century intercollegiate sports programs were established and operated by student athletic associations that supported as many as twenty different sports. Membership cost fifty cents to one dollar, with additional capital coming from fund-raisers, private subscriptions, and gate receipts, which in the late nineteenth century became the primary source of athletic revenue. At first an elected captain arranged training programs and practices, selected line-ups, and supervised play during the game with the assistance of an athletic manager who scheduled games, oversaw finances, and checked player eligibility. By the 1880s captains were inviting alumni back to help prepare the team. As competition became fiercer, athletic associations began to recruit athletes and to hire professional coaches to mold winning teams. The employment of expert coaches fit in better with the growing professional orientation of American higher education than with the more elitist model of gentlemanly student control.

Students strongly backed the athletic association because they found sports more exciting than traditional extracurricular activities. Furthermore, the association promoted a feeling of community, provided publicity and prestige for their school, and operated independent of adult supervision. Students at large state universities had limited direct contact with their peers, but all could be sports fans who attended games and participated in the rituals of spectatorship. They cheered ("Eckie, Eckie, Eckie, Break his Little Neckie" roared Michigan fans when their team played against quarterback Walter Eckersall and the University of Chicago in 1905) and sang school songs, enjoying a moment when Victorian decorum could be temporarily forgotten. Furthermore, students found athletic participation more useful preparation for life in the modern, bureaucratic capitalist society they intended to enter upon graduation than was membership in literary societies or debate clubs. The suave, sophisticated behavior learned in fraternities, and the cooperation, leadership qualities, and hard work taught on the playing field were seen as valuable qualities for getting ahead. Walter Camp agreed. He felt that football developed a personality of leadership and brains that would help bring success after college in corporate America.

By the 1890s, midwestern and far western universities had growing intercollegiate sports programs, especially public universities that sought statewide, if not regional and national, recognition. Even predominantly female teachers' colleges began football programs to attract more male students. Sports programs were less developed at urban working-class commuter colleges and at impoverished southern institutions. Newer schools had a hard time gaining national recognition. Three-fourths (76.9 percent) of the All-Americans from 1889 to 1916 came from Yale, Harvard, Princeton, or Pennsylvania. Clarence Hergensheimer of the University of Chicago in 1898 was the first collegian not from an eastern school to make All-American.

Faculty members began to take leadership roles in regulating athletics in the late 1880s, following the model of Harvard's faculty committee, which was established in 1882 to protect amateurism. The board was restructured in 1888 as a nine-member athletic committee with equal representation from faculty, alumni, and students, and was granted full control over athletics. This mixed committee was widely emulated, but the system did not resolve intercollegiate sport's major problems. Yale students maintained free rein over the athletic association. Its faculty did not even seek control until 1905, when an investigation discovered the association had a slush fund in excess of one hundred thousand dollars for gifts, vacations, and tutors, and an income one-eighth that of the university's. Failure to control sports problems at individual schools led to interinstitutional cooperation. The Southern Inter-Collegiate Association, formed in 1894, was ineffective, but the Inter-Collegiate Conference of Faculty Representatives (or Western Conference, later known as the Big Ten) established one year later by their school's presidents, was somewhat successful. Freshmen were ruled ineligible, and bona fide students could participate for up to three years. However, while faculty in the Western Conference and in the Brown Conference, an association of Ivy League schools established in 1898, set policy, student organizations still managed the sports programs, and it took about twenty years for the conference model to become adopted widely.

Demands to win led to the practice of hiring a professional coach, who at first was usually hired just for the season. Hiring an experienced coach was in line with the growing trend toward professionalization in the United States. The days of the wealthy amateur such as Walter Camp, for whom coaching was an avocation, were rapidly disappearing. Amateurs were pushed aside, just as gentlemen-scholars were being displaced by highly trained specialists with Ph.D.'s. Paid coaches were under heavy pressure to win to keep their jobs, and they vigorously promoted the efficient management of college sport. The coach became one of the most visible people, if not the most important, on campus, and coaches were often paid more than top professors. Harvard's Bill Reid, the highest-paid football coach in the early 1900s, had a seven thousand dollar salary, 30 percent more than that of any instructor, and nearly equal to that of President Charles Eliot. Early football coaches were mainly Yale men (forty-five by the mid-1890s) recruited by schools across the country to elevate the quality of play, to win games, and to bring new status to their institution.

The most successful and respected football coach was Yale alumnus Amos Alonzo Stagg, a former ace Yale pitcher, who during the late 1880s had led Yale to five championships in six seasons. He also played right end as a graduate divinity student on the 1888 team that outscored the opposition 698-0, and he made the first All-American football team in 1889. Stagg's poor oratorical skills blocked his ministerial aspirations. Instead he studied and coached for two years at the Springfield YMCA Training School, preparing to promote muscular Christianity. In 1892 Stagg was hired by President William Rainey Harper of the new University of Chicago to coach football, basketball, baseball, and track. Although Harper sought a national reputation for his school as a research institution, he understood that success in sports would be a quicker route to recognition. Stagg was appointed chair of the physical culture department with a six thousand dollar salary, the first coach to receive an academic appointment and tenure. Stagg became the winningest football coach of the day. He set a record of 323 wins, unsurpassed until 1981 by Paul "Bear" Bryant. Stagg was a superb tactician who helped to invent many formations and plays such as the onside kick, and he trained twenty-four future coaches.

A collegiate coach's primary duties were recruiting, evaluating teams' strengths and weaknesses, determining tactics, supervising workouts and diets, and arranging schedules. Stagg so deftly arranged his team's schedule that between 1896 and 1905, 90 percent of its games were in Chicago, where the Maroons had a big home field edge and a large potential gate. Furthermore, he scheduled weak teams early in the season, a strategy that built up the team's record and bolstered its confidence and encouraged interest from fans.

Recruiting talented players was always a key to success. In the 1870s, certain athletic associations employed financial inducements to attract top baseball players. By the late 1890s colleges throughout the country offered scholarships or other inducements to attract top athletes. Teams often used players attending professional or graduate schools—two-thirds of Harvard's football team in the 1880s were in law school or another professional school—and it was not until 1905 that major colleges changed that policy to eliminate the "perpetual athlete." Top recruiters such as Michigan's Fielding Yost used players who never even enrolled in classes, "special students" who did not meet the normal admission standards, and transfers from other colleges. The most notorious of the transfers were known as tramp athletes who moved from school to school depending on the best offer. Yost's greatest player in the early 1900s was halfback Willie Heston, who had already played three years for San Jose.

Stagg originally opposed scholarships as contrary to amateurism, but he changed his mind after a couple of poor seasons. Stagg recruited top prospects by promises of scholarships, easy course loads, tutors, campus jobs, access to a Rockefeller trust for needy athletes, assignment to the best dormitories, their own dining facilities, and special parties and trips. Football junkets to the West Coast and baseball tours to Japan were excellent recruiting tools and superb advertising for the university. Stagg further enhanced the university's visibility by organizing in 1902 an annual interscholastic track meet on campus, and, fifteen years later, a national high-school basketball tournament. Such exposure gave Chicago first crack at many top athletes.

Competition for top recruits was fierce. They might sign up for classes at one school and be in uniform one week later at another. One of the most highly publicized recruits was James Hogan, who entered Yale in 1901 at age twenty-seven after a fabled career at Exeter. In 1904, when he captained the Yale football team, the athletic association paid for his one hundred dollar tuition, his board, a luxurious suite at the University Club, and a ten-day vacation to Cuba during the semester. In addition Hogan shared profits from the sale of programs at Yale's baseball games with two teammates, and the American Tobacco Company gave him a commission on all cigarette packs sold in New Haven. Despite his pampered treatment, Hogan was intellectually quite capable, and he went on to Columbia Law School, where he made the *Law Review*.

Once on campus, it was not difficult to keep players eligible. Lest Chicago fans worry, the *Inter-Ocean* reported, "It seems safe to say that no really valuable man will be lost to the team on account of any little educational deficiencies." Stagg selected easy classes for his players, often in his own department, enrolled them in courses taught by sympathetic instructors, hired tutors for them, and arranged for them to take special examinations, as late as the morning of a game. Chicago athletes were not required to take a full academic program until 1905. Two years earlier only three of twenty-three football players were fully registered. These practices seem to prove historian Ronald Smith's point that there never was a golden age of the intercollegiate student-athlete.

Playing major college football was a serious matter. The first football "game of the century" took place on Thanksgiving Day, 1905, between the undefeated University of Chicago ("Monsters of the Midway") and the University of Michigan, known as the "Point a Minute" team, who had averaged fifty points a game over the previous fifty-five contests. The contest for the mythical championship of the Midwest featured outstanding coaches and All-American players. Ticket requests were triple the twenty-seven-thousand seat capacity of Marshall Field, leading to a scalping frenzy. The game was a defensive struggle, and Coach Stagg, referring to William Rainy Harper, president of the University of Chicago, urged his squad to "win for the dying president's sake." The decisive play in the game occurred in the third quarter when a Chicago punt was carried out from behind the goal line by Dennison Clark. He was stopped after a few yards and dragged back into the end zone for a safety, the only score of the game. Clark was despondent after the game, and he talked about suicide. Twenty-seven years later Clark did commit suicide. He left a note hoping that his "final play" might atone for his error on the gridiron.

An important debate about the merits of football began in the late nineteenth century. America appeared ripe for a virile game that would verify courage and strength of character and foster such qualities as cooperation and obedience. Social Darwinists applauded football as a rough game, a test of the fittest, extolled by President Charles K. Adams of the University of Wisconsin for developing "those characteristics that have made the Anglo-Saxon race pre-eminent." As discussed in Chapter Two, elite and upper-middle-class young men were concerned about their physical fitness because of sedentary lifestyles, their ability to measure up to fathers who had been Civil War heroes, and their virility because of the feminization of culture. Football seemed a perfect test because it put young men under fire but spared them the carnage of warfare.

Criticisms of football focused on its violence—the sport caused more deaths than prizefighting—and its impact on the educational process. Journalists, such as editor E. L. Godkin of the *Nation*, chastised football for its violence and brutality, poor sportsmanship, and win-at-any-cost mentality. Godkin also admonished the sport's growing commercial nature and harmful influence on educational institutions. Religious periodicals compared football unfavorably to boxing because, unlike boxing, it lowered the morals of the respectable classes.

Some of football's most zealous critics were college professors. By the late 1880s, certain professors, among them Frederick Jackson Turner of Wisconsin, a former football advocate, became football's severest critics. These professors were concerned about the growing influence, upon their respective schools, of alumni and local residents who contributed to the athletic association and about the impact of intercollegiate sports on academic integrity and on their schools' reputation. The overemphasis on sport slighted their schools' mission of teaching and scholarship in favor of providing carnivals for the masses. Academics also complained that commercialization of sport fostered nonexistent or weak eligibility standards, the recruitment of tramp athletes, and unsportsmanlike conduct. Furthermore, it promoted bitter rivalries, raucous crowds, and betting.

The issues of football's brutality, professionalism, and commercialism came to a head in 1905. The game had become so violent that eighteen players died that year, although most were not collegians. As a result Columbia and several other colleges dropped football, while Stanford and California replaced it with rugby. In addition, devastating investigative reports appeared in newspapers and popular muckraking periodicals such as *McClure's*. Critical stories emphasized the commercialization, recruiting scandals, and win-at-all-costs ethic of the game that permitted unsportsmanlike tactics such as ganging up on an opponent's star player to put him out of the game. These stories were illustrated with frightening photographs of injured players, particularly the gruesome picture of Swarthmore star Bob Maxwell after he had been mauled by Pennsylvania players. President Theodore Roosevelt, a football fan, and the preeminent advocate of "the strenuous life," invited representatives of Yale, Harvard, and Princeton to the White House to discuss reform of the sport. Little concrete progress was achieved, although the meeting did publicize football's serious problems. At the end of the year Chancellor Henry MacCracken of New York University, which had just dropped football, organized a national conference attended by sixty-eight colleges to consider the game's future. Significantly, neither Harvard nor Yale chose to attend. The delegates decided by a narrow majority to reform the game, establishing the Intercollegiate Athletic Association (IAA) (renamed the National Collegiate Athletic Association [NCAA] in 1910). Only thirty-six schools joined at first. The traditional athletic powers such as Harvard and Yale, unwilling to share power with the less-prestigious colleges, did not. But by 1909 membership was up to sixty-seven, including Harvard and Chicago. The association guidelines banned freshman participation, required transfer-student athletes to sit out one year, and allowed students three years of eligibility. The association had little enforcement power over its rules, however.

Historian Ronald Smith argues that the democratization of the old boys' self-perpetuating rules committee in 1906 was just as important in reforming football as was pressure from the White House and the rise of the Intercollegiate Athletic Association. Harvard's Reid replaced Camp as secretary of the committee and secured significant rule changes to discourage mass play and open up the sport: ten yards for a first down; no tackling below the knees; and legalization of the forward pass, albeit under complicated restrictions that included a fifteen-yard penalty for an incompletion. Yet Smith points out that the so-called "revolution of 1906" barely changed the style of play since coaches were afraid to pass, and the sport remained very dangerous. More rule changes were added over the next three years, however: seven men on the line of scrimmage; no interlocking of arms for blocking; four tries for a first down; touchdowns were raised from five to six points; and the ball was streamlined to make it easier to throw in a faster and more accurate spiral. Coaches thereafter experimented more with the forward pass. In 1913 coach Jess Harper of Notre Dame, a former Stagg student, decided to use the forward pass as a tactic in its game against heavily favored Army. The small Catholic college won 35-13 by capitalizing on the passing of Gus Dorais to Knute Rockne. The results helped make the forward pass popular, for it did help to open up play and make contests more exciting to watch.

The popularity of college football in the 1910s encouraged the construction of new stadiums to house growing crowds. The first of the modern grounds was Harvard's Soldier's Field, built in 1903 for $250,000. The thirty-eight-thousand-seat, concrete-and-steel structure was the first major athletic field built on a college campus, and it had the largest seating capacity of any

American sports field. Named in honor of alumni who had fought in the Civil War, the field symbolized regeneration through sport. Ten years later the sixty-seven-thousand-seat Yale Bowl was constructed for four hundred thousand dollars, and similar edifices were completed at Syracuse, Princeton, and Chicago. Public institutions soon followed suit; Michigan constructed a forty-six-thousand-seat wooden structure, increased to eighty-seven-thousand capacity by 1928. Such large stadiums required top-flight teams, heated conference and intersectional rivalries, and the nationalization of the traditional Thanksgiving Day game to fill them up. Teams now had to reach out beyond student and alumni support to fill their stadiums. Colleges invited the local middle class to become vicarious alumni and demonstrate hometown (or home state) pride by attending games. The "Big Game"—a major rivalry or championship—became popular entertainment complete with pregame ceremonies such as rallies, parades, and bonfires, and game rituals such as organized rooting led by cheerleaders. Fan interest was enhanced in 1913 when Chicago began numbering players so they could be easily identified. Students purchased cheap season passes for end-zone tickets, while the higher priced choice seats were sold to the general public. Chicago charged three dollars for its best seats, the highest in the Western Conference. Football earned the university about $30,000 a year in the mid-1910s, with profits peaking at $212,000 in 1924.

Women's Collegiate Athletics

Scholars have recently suggested that as important as sport was for men on campus, women's physical culture may have been more consequential because physical education and sport shaped women's self-image, as well as public attitudes about femininity and women's relationship to men. Historian Cindy Himes, author of "The Female Athlete in American Society, 1860–1940" (Ph.D. diss., 1986), further argues that fitness programs protected women's access to higher education by assuring the public that women were healthy enough to stand up to academic rigors.

Physical culture was an important part of the curriculum at late-nineteenth-century women's colleges. Most instructors were trained by Amy Morris Homans, who established the Boston Normal School for Gymnastics in 1889. Homans directed the school for twenty-nine years. Another important mentor was Dr. Dudley Sargent of Harvard, who opened a gymnasium for women in 1881; a decade later it became the Sargent School for Physical Education. Sargent stressed individual programs of "corrective gymnastics" tailored to bolster each student's weaknesses. Sargent, an early anthropometrist, advocated increased muscularity. The professor kept detailed records of his students' weight lifting and calisthenics, activities that he preferred to games.

Homans's and Sargent's female students, predominantly young, unmarried, middle-class, and urban, developed the first woman-centered philosophy of sport that emphasized cooperation and friendship among sportswomen rather than competition. They stressed the feminine potential of sport that helped them gain credibility and advance their careers. They were very active in professional organizations such as the Association for the Advancement of Physical Education (later named the American Physical Education Association), founded in 1885. Historian Susan K. Cahn, author of *Coming on Strong: Gender and Sexuality in Twentieth Century Women's Sports* (1994) argues that these physical education pioneers forged an alliance with physicians by encouraging a middle-class model of sport designed to preserve gender differences, protect women's delicate sexual sensibilities, ensure the health of future mothers, and guard female athletes from male sports promoters.

Women physical educators exercised more control over students than their male colleagues. They supervised expansive athletic programs, required health exams for all students, set posture standards, and organized classes for "defective students." Educators' concerns that physical culture could "unsex" women and their opposition to competition that might harm female camaraderie led to modifications in women's sports to make them less like men's. Professional educators opposed the stress on winning, individual achievement, and professionalism identified with intercollegiate competition. They preferred mass participation, fair play, and health-improving activities. Instead of competitive sports, athletic festivals such as play days were established to celebrate traditional feminine qualities. Play days attracted athletes from several colleges who played on mixed teams so that individual schools would not compete against each other. The athletes played under women's rules for female audiences.

Efforts to improve college women's fitness dated back to at least 1866 when Vassar instituted a mandatory fifty-minute daily walk. Physical education at Bryn Mawr was originally voluntary, but compulsory gymnastics was introduced because students skipped the boring classes. Smith students were required to do calisthenics with dumbbells, Indian clubs, wands, and chest weights while listening to slow music. While exercising, students were compelled to wear blouses and ankle-length skirts, but they preferred more comfortable clothing. In the 1880s they began wearing sensibly divided skirts (bloomers), stockings, and tennis shoes; they swam in sailor dresses worn over tights.

Students preferred sports to calisthenics. As early as 1866 there were two women's baseball teams at Vassar. Despite parental opposition, Vassar women also participated in recreational archery, croquet, tennis, rowing, and horseback riding. In 1878 Smith College women organized a baseball game, but two players were injured and the game was halted. School officials then banned the sport because they feared violence and broken windows. Baseball was not resumed until an interclass match in 1892.

Organized women's collegiate sport developed in the 1890s, as female students demanded more control over their extracurricular activities. Bryn Mawr's Women's Athletic Association, formed in 1891, became a model for other campuses. Basketball, track and field, and field hockey were introduced between 1892 and 1901, primarily on an interclass basis. Although the athletic associations experimented with intercollegiate competition in basketball and tennis, faculties preferred intramurals, so intercollegiate matches were few and infrequent.

In 1892, Smith's new gymnasium director, twenty-four-year-old Senda Berenson, modified the newly invented rough game of basketball to make it more appropriate for feminine young ladies. Unlike the students, she did not come from a blue-blood background but was the daughter of Jewish-Lithuanian immigrants. She believed that "carefully supervised games" promoted self-reliance, self-control, and teamwork, which were "so necessary to the modern woman." Her rules prohibited physical play by banning anyone from snatching the ball and promoted teamwork by permitting no one to hold the ball for more than three seconds or dribble it more than three times. Berenson also redesigned the basketball court, placing three women in the offensive zone, three in the defensive, and two in midcourt to encourage team play, lessen reliance on a dominant player, and reduce fatigue (reflecting contemporary views of women's limited physical capacity). Excellence was recognized with varsity letters, and top ballplayers became campus leaders. Himes claims that sport at women's colleges was a culture-creating activity that promoted camaraderie, class spirit, and school pride. Women's sports also became enormously popular at coed western colleges. Although elite eastern women's colleges played a leading role in encouraging basketball, the first match between institutions occurred in 1892, when the University of California played Miss Head's School. Four years later, Stanford defeated California 2-1 in the first women's intercollegiate contest. Only women were allowed to attend.

Berenson justified college athletics as preparation for the physical strength women would need in their future professions, although these occupations were then just barely opening up to women. Respected middle-class-women's periodicals such as *Godey's Lady's Magazine* decried women's sports for developing muscles and tanned bodies. But the students sided with Berenson. The 1898 Wellesley yearbook applauded the faculty's acceptance of basketball, asserting, "The grimy and generally disheveled appearance of the players as they emerge from the fray, fills our athletic souls with pride."

The conflict between faculty and students over competitive sport was reflected by a change in preparations for Wellesley's Float Day in 1898. Class crews were originally chosen for beauty rather than ability, and victory was determined by form and grace rather than speed. The students preferred competition, however, and candidates trained ardently during the winter with rowing machines in hopes of being selected to row for their class. The regatta that year drew about seven thousand spectators, including women and men. The athletes were not worried about ridicule from men and wanted them present so the women could demonstrate their prowess.

Nonetheless, physical educators in the early 1900s succeeded in downplaying competition in favor of sport for sport's sake. They only supported athletic activities such as play days, which stressed traditional feminine qualities. Participants would enjoy themselves, gain health benefits, and learn teamwork without the taint of masculinity. Their sports would promote friendship and sociability rather than individual accomplishment.

Secondary School Sport

Secondary schools in antebellum America were originally private college preparatory institutions, but after the Civil War growing numbers of communities established public high schools to socialize middle-class youth and train them for college or clerical occupations. In 1890 there were two hundred thousand high-school students in the United States, mostly girls, whose graduation rate far surpassed boys. Thirty years later the number of high-school students had risen by 711 percent. Just one-third of elementary-school students attended high school, however, and one-third of those graduated. High-school student populations became more inclusive in the 1920s when the national standard of living rose and the prevailing educational philosophy shifted from emphasizing academics to promoting life adjustment.

Antebellum academies allotted perhaps fifteen minutes a day to physical education to alleviate health problems caused by a sedentary lifestyle. During the Civil War era health reformers such as Dr. Dio Lewis advocated programs for urban boys that stressed military drill and gymnastics to cultivate the body and develop traits such as courage, perseverance, and self-control.

Few schools had physical education programs until the late 1880s. At that time, New England schools adopted the Swedish system, which emphasized calisthenics, the Midwest favored turnerian gymnastics, based on the turnverein model, and a mixed system was implemented in Brooklyn, New York, and Washington, D.C. Girls were encouraged to participate in light gymnastics, dance, and exercises to break up the school day, prevent mental strain, improve their posture, and prepare them for their future. Physical culture would enhance their appearance, grace, and poise so they could better capture a mate, would train them to be cooperative for involvement in women's clubs, and would make them fit to become healthy, happy mothers.

School administrators preferred exercise programs over team sports because they were cheaper, less time-consuming, and therefore a better fit for the curriculum. Students, however, preferred sports. High-school students in the 1870s and 1880s established their own athletic organizations without formal school ties in emulation of collegiate associations, and, in the biggest cities, they established intracity leagues in imitation of intercollegiate leagues. Students financed Boston's Interscholastic Football Association, formed in 1888, secured playing sites, and arranged matches, sometimes traveling out of town to play. All students were expected to join the school's athletic association, attend games, and root for the team. Interest in school sports provided a common topic of conversation, a diversion from academics, and a means to encourage school spirit. Sports provided a focal point for developing a shared identity among students and alumni, extremely important for citywide institutions such as Boston Latin, as well as for new schools in neighborhoods that lacked a sense of community and local pride and needed something to rally around.

High-school sport suffered many of the same problems as their college counterparts, and by the mid-1890s administrators questioned student control. Headmasters wanted to protect their institution's reputation from such problems as unsportsmanlike-play, lack of attention to schoolwork, and unenforced eligibility requirements. Furthermore, administrators were under parental and student pressure to play star athletes regardless of their academic standing. Administrative control was generally welcomed by student leaders, however, who recognized their inability to deal with the win-at-all-costs mentality. Students did not regard adult supervision of interscholastic sport as an effort to subvert their independence, but rather to manage sport programs professionally, prevent difficulties from arising, and respond to pervasive problems. The secondary-school community agreed on the need for fair play and control of abuses: they wanted to see the realization of the positive sports creed. Administrative governance did not dampen the competitive spirit; instead, a wide variety of championship matches developed at the local, regional, and state levels. The New York Public Schools Athletic League, founded in 1903, had the most prominent and varied citywide championships, including basketball, baseball, track and field, riflery, soccer, cross-country, swimming, tennis, crew, and lacrosse.

Student interest in sport also worked its way into physical education programs and intramurals as instructors sought to promote sport for all male students. Physical educators taught sports to promote physical fitness and to help students adjust to an industrial capitalist society that demanded discipline, punctuality, and teamwork. Instructors contributed to the preparedness movement prior to America's entry into World War I by teaching riflery and military drill.

Adult-Directed Youth Sport

Children in the nineteenth century received little physical education, and their recreational activities were mainly self-designed. Boys played pick-up baseball games in vacant fields, played stick ball or stoop ball in crowded city streets, and swam off the docks or in local watering holes. They also gambled with dice, played with fire, got into fights, and joined gangs that taught destructive values and encouraged antisocial criminal behavior. Turn-of-the-century progressive reformers who were frightened by life in the slums and wanted to promote order in the cities advocated rational recreation as an alternative to deleterious street amusements. In particular, they recommended adult-supervised sport programs to provide city children with pleasurable, self-improving activities. Reformers believed sport would provide a replacement for the small-town lifestyle of earlier days. Reformers founded boy-workers organizations such as the Public School Athletic League and the Playground Association of America, and they supported established societies such as the YMCA to uplift inner-city youth by providing them with wholesome pastimes. Sport would help newcomers adapt to a new culture and strengthen ties to their new home.

The YMCA originally focused on young clerks, but so many youngsters drifted in to use the gym that leaders decided to enroll boys who could pay the five-dollar membership fee. Junior departments were established in the 1880s to keep ten- to sixteen-year-olds occupied in the afternoon. The YMCA sought to prolong childhood and delay the dangerous years of adolescence, when sexuality and emotions would weaken self-control. Rader contends that after the turn of the century the philosophic foundation for YMCA boy-workers shifted from muscular Christianity to G. Stanley Hall's theory of recapitulation. The Clark University psychologist argued in *Adolescence* (1904) that an individual's psychological development (ontogeny) occurred in fixed stages that recapitulated the cultural evolution of mankind (phylogeny). Hall asserted that adolescence was a time of optimism and uncertainty when youths, especially urban boys, were vulnerable to moral degeneration. They often lacked close familial and community ties, the experience of hard work, and the religious influences that had protected rural youth from dissipation.

In 1899 Dr. Luther Gulick, a son of missionaries who was an instructor at the YMCA Training College and editor of the *American Physical Education Review*, employed the recapitulation theory to justify adult-directed boys' sport. Gulick developed an evolutionary theory of play. He believed man had acquired an instinct to play during evolution. Children ages seven to twelve enjoyed games like tag and track-and-field sports, which had evolved from the hunting instinct acquired during the presavage stage of evolution, while teenagers preferred team sports, which combined the hunting instinct with a predisposition for cooperation, a trait that emerged in the savage stage of development. These instincts encouraged the modern child's proper physical, mental, and moral growth. Gulick looked to team sports to promote sound morality in youth, particularly inner-city male teenagers. These youths were attracted to gangs, where thievery, vandalism, and violence recapitulated a heritage of tribal hunting and warfare. Adult-supervised team sports would provide a substitute and, by appealing to the cooperation instinct, would teach teamwork, obedience, and self-control. Gulick's ideas influenced not only his attitudes toward sport, but they also prompted him to help establish the Boy Scouts and, with his wife in 1911, the Camp Fire Girls.

Rader explains that Gulick's biological theory of play provided a scientific rationale for boy-workers. First, the theory justified the creation of special institutions to organize adult-supervised team sports to encourage the development of socially desirable traits. Second, it encouraged boy-workers to deemphasize the promotion of piety, exemplified by the increasing secularization of the YMCA. Third, it encouraged reformers to downplay ethnocultural differences, focusing on boys' shared experience of maturation. And fourth, Gulick's theory justified single-sex play. Boys and girls were believed to prefer play activities based on sex-specific instincts acquired during evolution. Gulick believed girls should not play strenuous competitive sports, but they should participate in amusements such as folk dancing, cooking, and singing around the campfire, that would help prepare them for domesticity.

In 1903 Gulick became director of physical training for the New York City Board of Education, and he implemented his play theories. He sought to replace traditional fitness programs that emphasized gymnastics and calisthenics and only reached a small proportion of urban youth with a new approach. To do so, Gulick organized the Public Schools Athletic League (PSAL), a private corporation that received no public funding. He was backed by the school board, progressive educators, the Amateur Athletic Union, and prominent philanthropists such as Andrew Carnegie and Solomon Guggenheim.

The new league proposed the most comprehensive and sophisticated sports program ever initiated for schoolboys, offering interscholastic sport for the athletically gifted, sports for all students in New York's 630 public schools, and special events including field days, public exhibitions, and "Safe and Sane" July Fourth Games. The league received instant credibility when it organized the world's largest athletic meet at Madison Square Garden on December 26, 1903. The meet drew 1,040 competitors, primarily elementary-school boys.

Mass participation was encouraged through class competition in the fifth through eighth grades, with the winning team in each grade determined by the highest average performance. Individual eligibility required good behavior and a B average. Each school held championships in events such as the broad jump, pull-up, and sprint, and the top teams advanced to compete for borough-wide titles. Students could also compete for athletic badges; elementary-school students needed a B average to participate; high-school students needed to show "satisfactory progress" toward graduation. Age-group standards were established, and competitors who achieved these scores in running, jumping, and chinning received a bronze or silver certificate. The program had a very beneficial impact on student fitness, reflected by the rise in medals awarded from 1,162 in 1904 to nearly 25,000 eleven years later.

In 1905 a Public Schools Athletic League Girls' Branch was established by wealthy women to provide exercise and activities for girls. Director Elizabeth Burchenal agreed with Gulick's theory of play, and she developed a program that stressed group participation ("Athletics for All Girls"). It comprised fifteen different sports and folk dancing to foster better agility, fun, and good health. Competition in athletics was restricted to interclass contests, and games were modified to prevent rough, unladylike play. For example, basketball fouls were more heavily penalized (a point for the offended team and a foul shot) than in boys' games.

The league organized athletics on the largest scale anywhere in the world, with programs that reached about one hundred thousand children. It provided a model for other major cities, including Baltimore and Chicago. By 1910 seventeen cities had organized similar programs to promote social control, good health, and traditional American values among the children of new immigrants. These programs were no panacea, however, as young athletes did not stop smoking or other bad habits, and they did not reach youth who were out of school.

Settlement workers who lived and worked in inner-city slums were ardent advocates of adult-directed sports for youth, and they tried to reach those youngsters that schools did not. Settlement houses were first established in the 1880s to improve living conditions in the worst urban slums. By the 1910s sixty-eight settlement houses operated in Chicago alone. The volunteers were mainly middle-class women; their goals were to identify a community's problems and then try to resolve them. Settlement houses used athletic programs to attract neighborhood youth and draw them away from gangs, poolrooms, and saloons. The settlement workers believed in the power of team sports to acculturate and improve the morals, character, and health of inner-city youth. Participation in sports would boost self-confidence, teach athletes to get along with different kinds of people, and prepare them to be team members in their future occupations. Soon after Jane Addams opened Hull House in 1889 on Chicago's West Side, volunteers organized gymnastic and calisthenics classes, recreational clubs for young boys, bowling and billiard tournaments, boxing classes for older boys, and competitions in boxing, wrestling, and basketball for its best athletes. Settlement sports programs were less attractive to second-generation immigrant daughters because of parental opposition and the unfeminine image of athletics among the foreign-born working class. Nonetheless, Hull House's women's basketball team achieved considerable renown.

In New York, sports programs at local settlements were so popular that by 1902 intersettlement competition began, and one year later established the Inter-Settlement Athletic Association.

The association claimed in 1911 that it reached more working boys than any other sports program. Their contests were held in the evenings to maximize the number of participants and spectators. Saturday night athletic programs followed by a dance were especially popular.

Settlement workers led the Progressive movement's efforts to develop public recreational facilities in the inner city. These neighborhoods desperately needed bathhouses, playgrounds, and gymnasiums, as well as professionally trained youth workers to organize and supervise sports programs. The Progressives helped quadruple to forty-three the number of cities with supervised recreation programs in the period between 1900 and 1906. In 1906 settlement workers and other Progressives established the Playground Association of America with Gulick as president and Addams as vice president. The association's philosophy was based on Gulick's biological theory of play; members sought to bring street-tough city children under control and to promote community pride. The Playground Association focused its efforts on publicizing the needs for supervised municipal recreation facilities, particularly in the inner city. While the precise impact of the association is difficult to measure, the concept of publicly organized leisure for urban youth certainly took hold. By 1917, 504 cities sponsored recreational programs, mostly in emulation of Chicago's small parks. They included such innovative features as New York's evening centers for working people and the use of piers to create additional recreational space.

Advocates of the sports creed overestimated its ability to remake society, in part because most physical educators, coaches, administrators, high-school and college players, and spectators were native-born white Americans who already shared the same basic values. In addition, the ability of adult-directed sport to ameliorate inner-city youth was exaggerated. Most inner-city youth were outside of the umbrella of sports reform, and participation would not necessarily transform a bad character into a model citizen. Fewer than one out of ten urban children regularly used playgrounds, which were mainly enjoyed by middle-class WASP children. Many older youths never participated in adult-directed sports because they worked, had no access to a YMCA or settlement house, or simply preferred the spontaneity, disorder, and defiance of authority that characterized life on the street. Although reformers were often able to overcome the negative features of highly competitive athletics that stressed victory at all costs, they did not anticipate that the toughest youths would take over playgrounds and small parks for their own uses, or that such public space located between rival gangs would become contested turf. At the same time, reformers overlooked the potential of sport for self-directed growth. Boys left alone to play had to create their own field in a street or a narrow alley, make up their own rules ("anything to right field is out"), and respond to unique situations that established conventions could not cover ("do-overs").

CHAPTER FIVE

Baseball and the Rise of Professional Sport

The rise of commercialized professional spectator sport was the most significant development in post–Civil War athletics. Prize-fighting, although commonly illegal, had an enormous appeal among the sporting fraternity, who respected the ability of men to defend themselves and to knock opponents senseless. Horse racing, which had its own legal problems, was very popular with the elite and the lower class, who were thrilled by the sight of one-thousand-pound thoroughbreds ridden by one-hundred-pound jockeys spinning around the turn to the finish line. And everyone was excited by the drama of baseball. Unlike today, professional ball games did not take a long time to complete. Something thrilling was always happening or anticipated: a hit and run, a Walter Johnson fast ball, or the steal of third base by Ty Cobb. What could top the intensity of a game on the line: two out in the bottom of the ninth, tieing and winning runs on base, and a full count on the batter?

Before the 1860s, few sporting events were staged in enclosed semipublic facilities where spectators were charged admission fees, and only a few athletes made their living as oarsmen, jockeys, pedestrians, or cricket players. In the late nineteenth century, the spectator sports business boomed. External factors such as urbanization and the commercialization of leisure, which had acclimated people to paying for their entertainment contributed. Internal factors were critical as well: the modernization of particular sports, the emergence of sports entrepreneurs who were not affiliated with taverns, the interest of fee-paying spectators in watching highly skilled athletes perform, and the professionalization of sportsmen. There were a number of minor professional sports, including cycling, rowing, wrestling, track and field, and football, but public interest was dominated by baseball, boxing, and horse racing. The three major professional sports were all controlled by politicians and their closest business associates, often streetcar owners or professional gamblers. These entrepreneurs recruited top athletes, coaches, and trainers, and they promoted championship contests, organized baseball leagues, and established racing circuits. They also constructed or rented boxing gymnasiums, arenas, ballparks, and racetracks to stage their contests in front of paying audiences.

Prizefighting

Prizefighting was universally banned until the 1890s and thereafter permitted in only a few locations until the 1920s. Professional boxing was forbidden because of its brutality and corruption. The people who arranged bouts, participated in matches, and attended contests were viewed as lowlives. Throughout this period, urban machine politicians were especially prominent in the sport. Many of the leading managers and promoters were professional politicians who used their power to gain influence in the sport. Furthermore, political bosses used their clout to protect illegal bouts and ultimately to make prizefighting legal.

The earliest bouts were arranged personally by fighters or their managers in sporting taverns. After the Civil War notable fights were also arranged through the sporting press, particularly Richard Fox's *National Police Gazette*. Boxing historian

Elliott Gorn credits Fox, whom he considers the leading promoter of the 1880s, with cleaning up much of the sport's iniquity,
such as fixed bouts. Purses, if any, were usually small; most of
the fighter's earnings came from side bets. Illegal bouts occurred
in barns, river barges, or saloon backrooms, with spectators
charged as little as twenty-five cents. As late as 1889, even national championships, such as the John L. Sullivan–Jake Kilrain
heavyweight bout had to be held on the sly.

In the early 1880s the sport became increasingly popular in
New York City, where politically connected promoters arranged
boxing matches. Prizefights were against the law, so these bouts
were described as "exhibitions." They offered fans a demonstra-
tion of the art of self-defense or, more likely, a chance to see
someone's body pummeled into a mass of jelly. Several contests
were staged in spacious downtown opera houses, theaters, public armories, and multipurpose arenas such as Madison Square
Garden. Owner William Vanderbilt brought in other popular
events, including the prestigious Horse Show and long-distance
running races, but he emphasized boxing exhibitions. A few programs featuring champion John L. Sullivan were especially successful. The police would at times stop matches, however, for
"outraging decency and tending to corrupt public morals." In
1885 constables halted the Sullivan–Paddy Ryan bout, and
Vanderbilt discontinued his boxing shows.

The adoption of the Marquis of Queensberry rules in the
1880s, requiring gloves and timed rounds, had a big impact on
boxing, contributing to the legitimization of the sport by making
it more humane. Yet Gorn points out that these rules sped up
fights and actually made the sport more dangerous, because fighters could hit harder and throw more punches since their hands
were protected.

In 1890 New Orleans became the first major city to permit
prizefights staged by athletic clubs. The city's prestigious athletic clubs secured sites, provided purses, and negotiated with
managers to arrange bouts. New Orleans's boxing boom peaked
in September 1892 with three consecutive days of world champi-

onship fights. The boxing extravaganza climaxed with Gentleman Jim Corbett's defeat of the great John L. Sullivan for a twenty-five thousand dollar purse plus a ten-thousand dollar side bet. Two years later, however, following the death in the ring of a local boxing hero, the sport's popularity declined rapidly in New Orleans.

The center of boxing shifted back to metropolitan New York. In 1892, boxing was revived at Coney Island, under the protection of Brooklyn's Democratic bosses, who owned the most notable arenas. Four years later, state senator Tim Sullivan, who controlled New York City's most important boxing arenas, secured passage of the Horton Act, permitting sparring matches in buildings owned by athletic clubs. Over the next few years hundreds of prizefights, including several championships, were fought in Greater New York (Brooklyn and New York merged in 1898). In 1900, however, conservative upstate Republicans, who controlled the state government, opposed prizefighting on moral and political grounds and repealed the Horton Act. Championship bouts in New York were halted, although the sport survived under the guise of politically connected "membership clubs," private organizations that were permitted to stage weekly three-round matches between members for the entertainment of other members. This was simply a ploy to evade the law, because anyone who paid a one dollar fee could join the club and watch the fight. After 1900, the national center of boxing shifted west to San Francisco, where machine boss Abe Reuf protected the city's twenty-round championship bouts. He went to jail in 1907, however, for corruption stemming from local boxing promotions.

In 1911 New York regained its preeminence in prizefighting following a Democratic sweep in the state elections. The legislature passed the Frawley Act, legalizing ten-round, no-decision contests supervised by a state athletic commission. Lesser matches were staged in small gyms located in lower-class residential neighborhoods, but the big fights were held in large midtown arenas, such as Madison Square Garden, in the heart of New York City's entertainment district. The second Madison

Square Garden was built in 1890 on the site of the old Garden by renowned architect Stanford White at a cost of three million dollars.

Boxing crowds were exclusively male, and often rowdy, particularly in small neighborhood gyms. Spectators there sat close to the action and bet heavily, often on local ethnic heroes with whom the crowd identified. Promoters recognized the value of matching a Jewish fighter against an Irishman or an Italian against either of them. Riots occurred periodically because excited fans brought with them traditional animosities and longstanding rivalries that heated up during interethnic bouts. Fans would throw chairs into the ring, seconds would jump into the ring, and fistfights would break out among spectators. Riots occurred for other reasons as well, even at big arenas, because of unadvertised price increases, inadequate security, and overcrowding, not to mention unpopular decisions by the referee or an obvious fix.

The boxing revival was short lived. In 1917 the sport was again banned by antiurban, upstate Republicans who sought to regulate the behavior of New York's foreign-stock population. They also hoped to limit the power of those Tammany Hall politicians (and their hoodlum friends) who promoted the sport and controlled prizefighters.

In 1917 prizefighting was legal in twenty-three states, but the sport was severely restricted in its major markets. Even San Francisco, a city tolerant of boxing in the early 1900s, only permitted four-round bouts. During World War I boxing's image improved considerably because it was used for training soldiers. Consequently much of the press after the war, including the reform-minded *New York Times*, supported Democratic state senator James J. Walker's campaign to restore prizefighting as well as lift other restrictions on the personal freedom of returning veterans. In 1920, Governor Al Smith, part of the Tammany machine, signed the Walker Act, which reestablished a boxing commission and permitted twelve-round fights to a decision for the first time. New York immediately regained its position as the national center of boxing. Madison Square Garden, a financial white elephant for years, became the mecca for prizefighting under its new boxing impresario Tex Rickard. Championship matches at the Garden in the 1920s drew record crowds and were glamorous social events, attracting the rich and famous men and women of the day.

Thoroughbred Racing

If prizefighting was the sport of pugs, horse racing was the sport of kings. Nonetheless, its revival after the Civil War also required extensive political connections to protect it from critics who wanted to ban the sport. Moral reformers castigated racing because its primary appeal was betting. Furthermore, animals were abused, races were fixed, and the sport had close connections to machine politicians and syndicate crime. The political connections of the racing world were epitomized by the situation in New York, the national center of racing in the late nineteenth century. The sport there was dominated by politically active elites and their machine associates in the Democratic party.

The first major thoroughbred racecourse to open after the war was New York's Jerome Park in 1866, operated by the elite American Jockey Club. The club's original members included financier and national Democratic party chairman August Belmont as well as the notorious William Tweed, the crooked boss of Tammany Hall. Four years later, robber-baron Jay Gould, who virtually owned the New Jersey legislature, helped found the prestigious Monmouth Park in Long Branch. The success of these and other elite tracks encouraged entrepreneurs to establish proprietary tracks such as Brooklyn's Brighton Beach in 1879 and Gravesend in 1885. Brighton Beach was very successful, generating a two hundred thousand dollar profit by its third year. The success of New York racing over the next twenty-five years was a product of the political clout of leading elite Democratic horsemen such as transit magnates William C. Whitney and August Belmont II and such prominent Democratic Irish American sportsmen as Tammany boss Richard Croker and his colleague Tim Sullivan. These men all raced horses and used that common interest to form a coalition that worked together to protect horse racing and on-track betting in New York State.

A few proprietary racecourses operated by politically connected bookmakers and machine politicians were blatantly crooked outlaw tracks. In the early 1890s the most notorious were New Jersey's two outlaw tracks, Guttenberg, located just across the Hudson River from New York City, and Gloucester, outside of Philadelphia. These tracks ran year-round, rain or shine, and they were renowned for fixed races. Their Democrat owners controlled the state legislature in 1893, and they were presumed to be omnipotent. Political reformers made racing a major campaign issue that year, however, and in a surprising upset the Republicans gained control of the state government and closed the tracks. Racing in New Jersey did not resume until 1940.

Despite the political clout of racecourse operators, nearly all major tracks were forced to close for varying periods of time. Antigambling leagues in the late nineteenth century and Progressives in the early 1900s secured laws in most states against racetrack gambling. Without gambling, tracks could not survive. In Chicago, for example, the racing center of the West, reformers in 1892 forced the closing of the outlaw Garfield Park. Two years later, the prestigious Washington Park racetrack was also closed, followed by the rest of the tracks in 1895. Chicago had no racing until 1898, when Washington Park and certain proprietary tracks reopened. The city's tracks were closed again in 1904, and thereafter Chicago had virtually no thoroughbred racing until the 1920s. By 1908, 289 of 314 American tracks had been closed for varying periods of time. New York's courses managed to remain open through 1910 because of political influence, but even they were then closed for two years because of Progressive governor Charles Evans Hughes's successful campaign to halt racetrack gambling.

Racetracks required an enormous amount of space—racing ovals alone ranged from one-half to one-and-a-half miles—yet, except for the outlaw tracks, courses seldom operated more than a few months a year. Racecourses were the least accessible semipublic sporting facilities, located on the urban periphery or in suburbs where land costs were relatively cheap. The rich might ride elegant carriages to the course, but most fans traveled by mass transit or commuter railroads. For most of the nineteenth century, New York's elite tracks were a one-hour train ride from midtown Manhattan, although they were usually closer to midtown in other cities. Profit-oriented tracks that sought lower-class crowds were usually located nearer to the heart of population than were the high-prestige courses. For example, New Jersey's Guttenberg was a short ferry ride from the West Side of Manhattan, and Chicago's Garfield Park was a five-cent, thirty-minute ride from the Loop. A few facilities such as Monmouth and Saratoga were located in distant resort areas that were reached by a long railroad ride.

Racetrack ambience varied substantially from lavishly appointed, elegant clubhouses of elite tracks to spartan facilities at the plebeian tracks. Jerome Park set a high standard with its clubhouse that was comparable to a luxury hotel. It had an elegant ballroom and dining room, and bedrooms for overnight stays. The most prestigious tracks, such as Brooklyn's Sheepshead Bay, Chicago's $150,000 Washington Park, and New York's $2.4 million Belmont Park, had large grandstands with separate sections for jockey club members, women, and the masses. A grandstand seat was priced at two to three dollars, which discouraged class intermingling. The masses were confined to the seventy-five-cent standing room in the infield. Races with major stakes at elite tracks, such as the Futurity and the Belmont in New York, and the American Derby in Chicago, were great attractions, drawing as many as seventy thousand spectators in the 1890s and 1900s. The American Derby of 1893 was the single richest race, with a fifty-thousand-dollar purse to the winner. By comparison, plebeian tracks charged as little as fifty cents for admission, and outlaw tracks often opened the infield for free to encourage wagering. Crowd control was rarely a problem at the finest tracks, which were patrolled by Pinkerton detectives. Lesser tracks drew rougher crowds, which included petty criminals and prostitutes.

On-track wagering was originally conducted by auction pools. Pool makers organized betting pools in which they "auctioned" off the choice of horses in a particular race to the highest bidder. They might arrange several pools for each event. Pool makers took 5 to 10 percent off the top, and they distributed the balance to the winning bettor. With this gambling format, the small wagerer could not afford to bet on favorites, which won about 40 percent of the time. In 1871 Jerome Park introduced the French pari-mutuel system in which the track organized the betting. Bettors could wager on any horse in a given race, and the odds were determined by the amount of money wagered on each steed. This system seemed more democratic than the auction, because everyone could bet on the more popular horses. The system did not catch on, however. Heavy bettors disliked it because their big bets would drive odds down, while poorer participants deplored it because major tracks required a minimum bet of five dollars and offered no credit. In 1877 New York State banned auction pools following the heavy betting on the scandal-ridden Tilden-Hayes presidential election. The pools were replaced by bookmaking, which by the early 1880s became the dominant form of betting at American racecourses. Bookmakers rented space at the tracks where they posted their own odds on all horses in a given race, charging 5 percent for their services. They usually took bets as low as two dollars, which helped make the sport more accessible.

Racetrack wagering was widely criticized as immoral, but at least bettors attended the races and thereby supported the sport. Virtually no one had a good word for the illegal offtrack betting. It was aimed largely at a working-class clientele, although certain gamblers did cater to Society bettors. Offtrack betting was conducted through bookmakers and poolrooms that took wagers on races all over the country, saving clients the time and expense of going to the tracks. Poolrooms were found mainly in lower-class residential neighborhoods, vice districts, and even the central business district of major cities. The conventional wisdom was that their clients were mainly clerks and artisans. Bookmakers and poolrooms were protected by political bosses who worked with crime syndicates that provided fast results from the tracks via the racing wire. Organized crime made more money from horse-race gambling than from any other source. Gangsters provided the muscle to collect debts, payoffs to prevent police interference, and attorneys to fight indictments. Their political allies provided protection and advance warning about raids. New York senator Tim Sullivan's "Gambling Trust" reputedly monopolized the city's multimillion-dollar poolroom business.

Thoroughbred racing struggled during the 1910s, but the sport revived dramatically after World War I when peace and prosperity returned, and an increasing number of states legalized on-track gambling. Between 1918 and 1920 purses doubled, and they redoubled by 1926, which led to a 60 percent increase in the number of thoroughbreds during the 1920s. The widespread legalization of racing resulted from several factors, most notably the continued clout of Irish machine politicians and the growing political influence of their ethnic constituents, who enjoyed gambling and opposed traditional moral values being imposed upon them. In addition, state legislatures were under greater pressure from jockey clubs, breeders, and organized crime to legitimize the sport. Further, each state needed new revenues that could be generated by taxing racetrack admissions and gambling proceeds.

Professional Baseball

The commercialization of baseball began in 1862 when Brooklynite William Cammeyer enclosed his skating rink, which became the Union Grounds. He allowed local teams to play for free, charging ten cents admission to spectators. The public was already accustomed to paying for other forms of entertainment, and spectators had paid to attend the 1858 all-star series between New York and Brooklyn players to defray expenses. Cammeyer and other early promoters expected ticket sales would cover the cost of operating the field, provide a profit, and discourage the presence of rowdy fans. Teams were increasingly concerned about winning, and a championship system began in metropolitan New York. Teams competed for top players such as pitcher James Creighton, who in 1860 was recruited by the Brooklyn Excelsiors with financial incentives, making him the first professional baseball player. In the past, cricket clubs had previously hired bowlers, but the National Association of Base Ball Players (NABBP) opposed professionalism because it was considered unfair to amateurs who did not devote their complete attention to sport.

An enormous postwar boom occurred in baseball, partly a consequence of its increased national exposure in Civil War camps. By the late 1860s, more than two thousand organized clubs existed, mostly in the Northeast, of which thirteen were professional. Crowds approaching fifteen thousand were soon reported at major contests. The professional teams played over fifty games a year, including out-of-town contests. Players were paid in cash, given a political sinecure, or received some other form of compensation. Top teams, such as the Brooklyn Atlantics, raised ticket prices to twenty-five cents in 1867 and fifty cents three years later.

The first openly all-salaried team was the Cincinnati Red Stockings of 1869, which was organized by local boosters to bring fame and prestige to the city. The club became enormously successful under the leadership of manager Harry Wright, a former cricket player. The "father of professional baseball," Wright was a shrewd judge of talent who recruited players, mainly metropolitan New Yorkers, for annual salaries ranging from six hundred to two thousand dollars, and molded them into a powerful machine. The club toured the East in 1869, finishing with a remarkable record of 57–0–1, drawing about two hundred thousand spectators. The tie game came against John Morrissey's Troy (New York) Haymakers in a game on which he and his friends had reportedly bet sixty thousand dollars. With the score at 17-17, an argument occurred over a foul tip. Morrissey ordered the Troy team off the field, which ended the game and voided the wager.

Cincinnati's success encouraged urban boosters elsewhere, most notably in Chicago, to recruit professionals. In 1870 the Reds won their first twenty-seven games before losing to the

Brooklyn Atlantics 8-7 in an extra-inning contest marred by fan interference. But the Red Stockings were not making money, and following a loss to the Chicago White Stockings, the team cut expenses, going amateur the following season.

By the end of 1870 the National Association of Base Ball Players was in disarray. The amateurs split off because of commercialization, professionalization, and fears of gambling and fixed contests. In 1871 a nine-team National Association of Professional Base Ball Players (NA) began play under NABBP rules, charging only ten dollars for a franchise. Most of the teams were joint-stock companies that paid regular salaries. The weaker teams were generally cooperatives whose players got a share of the gate instead of a salary. Each team arranged its own schedule. The stock clubs charged fifty cents admission, and the co-ops twenty-five cents. The National Association lasted only five years because it could not resolve several serious weaknesses. Problems included players jumping to another team, weak competition, rumors of fixes, inept leadership, and minimal admission requirements that permitted too many small cities, such as Keokuk, Iowa, and Troy into the league.

Most association teams were weak, unstable, and rarely broke even. In 1872, for instance, five of eleven teams did not even complete the season. The only real pennant race occurred in 1871 when the Philadelphia Athletics (22–7) edged the Boston Red Stockings (22–10). Thereafter Boston completely dominated, taking the next four pennants, including a remarkable 71–8 season in 1875. The team was managed by Harry Wright, who brought with him most of his old Cincinnati club. Wright emphasized a spartan training regimen, discipline, fundamentals, pregame batting and fielding practice, teamwork, and strategy. He handled players as individuals and used salary as a motivator. Wright also controlled the club's thirty-five thousand dollar budget, arranged the schedule and transportation, and supervised groundskeeping and advertising.

Association players made about thirteen hundred to sixteen hundred dollars, about four times the typical nonagricultural worker, with stars getting up to twenty-five hundred dollars. Their social origins were similar to the leading amateur players from whose ranks they were drawn. Virtually all (over 90 percent) were American-born, and predominantly of native-born white American ancestry. Over four-fifths (83 percent) came from cities at a time when only one-fourth of the national population was urban. Players were drawn especially from Baltimore, Brooklyn, New York, and Philadelphia, all leading centers of amateur and professional baseball. Three-fifths of New York and Brooklyn professionals were previously artisans, and the rest were lower-level white-collar workers.

The Rise of the National League

In 1876 the National Association of Professional Base Ball Players was supplanted by the more profit-oriented National League of Professional Base Ball Clubs (NL). The National League sought to operate on sounder business principles. As reflected by its title, it was a league of "clubs" rather than of "players." Led by William Hulbert, a member of the Chicago Board of Trade and owner of the Chicago White Stockings, the eight-team National League sought to avoid its predecessor's weaknesses. A franchise cost one hundred dollars, instead of ten dollars, and member cities were required to have a minimum of seventy-five thousand inhabitants. The league office arranged schedules so that all teams played each other the same number of games, made rule changes, dealt with disputes, and supervised paid umpires. Each franchise was guaranteed exclusive rights in their hometowns. The National League sought to bolster its image by installing a United States senator as president; waging a moral crusade to ban gambling, Sunday ball, drunkenness, and rowdy behavior; and encouraging decorum and respectability by attracting women to attend games with Ladies' Day promotions.

The new circuit was not an instant success. Only Chicago made money in 1876, and New York and Philadelphia were expelled for not completing late-season western road trips. A number of teams came and went in the first few years, including Troy, which was added in 1879 even though the city's population was below the minimum. One year later Cincinnati was ousted for refusing to ban Sunday games or liquor sales. There were fifteen different clubs in the first four years of the new league, and by 1881 Boston and Chicago were the only surviving original franchises. The National League was also beset by corruption and by competition from professionals outside the league, including the loosely knit International Association. Front-running Louisville lost the pennant in 1877 because four prominent players fixed games. The players were immediately expelled for life.

National League owners devoted considerable attention to labor relations because salaries comprised over 60 percent of team budgets. They increased control over employees by introducing the reserve clause in 1879, which gave teams an option to renew, trade, or release a player, without any reciprocity on the team's part. The league argued that this policy encouraged fairer competition by preventing richer clubs from hiring all the best players. As a result, ballplayers lost any leverage they might have had negotiating contracts. The new policy helped increase profitability in the 1880s.

Management was also concerned about controlling players' behavior so that they would perform their best and not harm the sport's shaky public image. Ballplayers were young men, often bachelors, who liked to chase women, drink, and gamble. Some had undisciplined work habits. Consequently, management tried to impose a strict regimen through the uniform players' contract, which stipulated heavy fines and suspensions for poor play, lost equipment, and disorderly behavior on or off the field. In 1881, management began to blacklist players for dissipation or insubordination. Fines levied on players also helped management recoup some expenses. During the mid-1880s, White Stockings president Albert G. Spalding fostered respectability by fighting his players' gambling and drinking. He offered bonuses to certain players to stop drinking and hired detectives to spy on them. In 1886 when superstar catcher Mike "King" Kelly was accused of drinking lemonade in a saloon after midnight, he did not deny being there, but he took umbrage to the unmanly accusation that he had been imbibing lemonade. Spalding sold him the next season to Boston for the unheard-of sum of ten thousand dollars.

In 1882 the National League's major-league monopoly was challenged by the American Association (AA), organized mainly by entrepreneurs in the beer business who recognized the growing profit potential of baseball and the opportunities it would present them to sell their beverage. The American Association started with six clubs in major markets (Baltimore, Cincinnati, Louisville, Philadelphia, Pittsburgh, and St. Louis) of which only St. Louis had a National League franchise. The combined population of the six cities was five hundred thousand more than the combined population of the eight National League cities. The league sought a massive plebeian audience by setting the basic ticket price at twenty-five cents, permitting Sunday ball, and selling liquor at games.

The two leagues fought for control of ballplayers and markets, and a baseball war ensued as the American Association hired contract jumpers and blacklisted National League players. The association became very popular, and five of its six teams outdrew the Chicago White Stockings, whose gate receipts tripled any other National League team. In 1883 the American Association added New York and Columbus, and the National League responded by dropping Troy and Worcester in favor of Philadelphia and New York. This change put the National League head-to-head with the American Association in the nation's two largest cities. Nearly all association teams made money that year, led by Philadelphia's seventy-five thousand dollars, while the National League clubs averaged twenty thousand dollars in profits. The leagues made peace after the season by signing a national agreement, and they merged in February 1884. They recognized each other's contracts, initiated a post-season championship, or World Series, and together with the minor Northwestern League, set up an arbitration committee to settle disputes.

The White Stockings, who captured three straight National League pennants between 1880 and 1882 and three more between 1884 and 1886, and the St. Louis Browns (AA), who won four straight pennants between 1885 and 1888, dominated the 1880s. The Browns were owned by "Der Boss President," Chris Van der Ahe, who went into baseball to sell beer, while Chicago's

Spalding, the National League's most influential owner, was becoming a renowned sporting-goods manufacturer. The White Stockings continued to draw the largest crowd in its league with such stars as catcher Mike "King" Kelly, the most exciting, if not the best, player of the nineteenth century; manager and first baseman Adrian "Cap" Anson, selected for the Hall of Fame; and Ed Williamson, whose twenty-seven home runs in 1884 was a record until 1919. They were the most profitable team, with net returns often surpassing 20 percent. By 1887 the White Stockings had accumulated a one hundred thousand dollar surplus, and along with Boston and New York, were grossing nearly one hundred thousand dollars a year. Overall, the National League made seven hundred and fifty thousand dollars in the period between 1885 and 1889, a 300 percent increase over the early 1880s. By contrast, players' salaries rose by just 30 percent.

By the 1880s, the modern character of baseball had been largely established. Important improvements in equipment were introduced, including the catcher's mask and chest protector, shin guards, and small, lightly padded, pocketless gloves. Tactics stressed "inside baseball" (sacrifices, place hitting, stealing, hit and run, fielders backing up their teammates, and infielders playing off the base) and physically rough play. Most modern regulations were already in place, although rule makers struggled to maintain a balance between offense and defense to keep the sport exciting and entertaining. In prior years the offense had the upper hand; batters could request an area in which pitches were to be thrown, and fielding was difficult with poor gloves. In the 1880s new regulations gave the advantage to pitchers, who stood only fifty feet from the batter. Pitchers were allowed to throw overhand and to use deceptive deliveries to confuse the batter. The modern strike zone was introduced in 1887, a year when walks counted as hits, greatly inflating batting averages. Two years later the modern three-strike, four-ball rule was established. In 1894 the balance shifted back to the offense when the pitcher's mound was pushed back to the present sixty feet six inches, resulting in a thirty-five point increase in batting averages to .309.

Hall of Famer Mike Kelly, the most colorful, popular, and resourceful ballplayer of his day, would try anything to win. If Kelly caught the lone umpire following a base hit to the outfield, he would run from first base to third across the pitcher's mound, bypassing second, or even from second straight to home. According to legend, Kelly often dropped his catcher's mask along the third-base line to hamper runners coming home. In one game he took advantage of substitution rules that required the replacement to notify the umpire; he leapt off the bench, announced "Kelly now catching," and caught a foul ball for an out. Folklorist Tristram Coffin claimed Kelly's greatest stunt occurred while playing right field in the twelfth inning of a late-afternoon game when it was getting dark. There were two out, the bases were loaded, and a shot was hit over Kelly's head. He raced back, far beyond the vision of the umpire, leaped up, shook his glove in satisfaction, and jogged in to the bench. The batter was called out, and the game was suspended because of darkness. His teammates slapped his back and said "Nice catch, Kell." "Not at all," responded their hero, "'Twent a mile above my head."

In 1885 player dissatisfaction with the reserve clause and a new twenty-five hundred dollar salary limit (often broken for stars such as Kelly, who in 1887 signed a contract with Boston for two thousand dollars, plus an additional three thousand dollars as team captain for a photograph he sold the owners) resulted in the formation of the Brotherhood of Professional Base Ball Players. Led by law student John Montgomery Ward, a star Giants pitcher, it was the first sports union. Following the profitable 1889 season when most teams set attendance records, the underpaid players struck back. The 107-member Brotherhood established a separate league, the Players' League (PL), which was governed by a committee of players and capitalists. The new league had no reserve clause or salary classification. Ballplayers were guaranteed salaries based on 1888 wages and a share in any profits that exceeded ten thousand dollars per team. The new league was supported by trade unions and by the preeminent baseball weeklies, *Sporting Life* and *The Sporting News*.

Ironically the Players' League did not seek working-class fans, preferring spectators who could afford fifty-cent tickets.

The Players' League was a serious threat to organized baseball. Two hundred major leaguers, including nearly all the best players, jumped to the new league. The National League held on to only thirty-eight veterans. The National League and American Association established a war committee under Spalding, whose *Baseball Guide* chastised the newcomers as socialists and anarchists. Spalding pressured newspapers by threatening to pull his company's advertisements from papers that supported the interlopers. Organized baseball compiled a $250,000 war chest to bribe Players' League stars to return, to sue contract jumpers, and to hire thugs to intimidate Brotherhood fans. Members of the Brotherhood stood fast, however, including Mike Kelly who turned down a ten thousand dollar offer out of loyalty to "the boys."

The Players' League outdrew the National League, averaging 1,850 per game to 1,500. Attendance figures were inflated in 1890 by frequent Ladies' Days and lots of free passes, not to mention false reports. But it was a Pyrrhic victory; fans were turned off by the bickering in baseball. The Players' League ran a $385,000 deficit, mostly to pay for new ballparks, while estimated National League losses ranged from $231,000 to $500,000. The Brotherhood players and their backers were dismayed by the balance sheet, and after the season the National League coopted the Players' League financiers. Except for Buffalo, where there was no competing major-league team, all Players' League stockholders either sold out to, merged with, or bought out the local National League team. Spalding had outsmarted and outmaneuvered the Brotherhood. The Players' League failed to overcome the disadvantages of starting from scratch, and players put too much trust in the capitalists, who had their own agendas.

The baseball peace was short lived, because in 1891 American Association and National League relations collapsed when the latter reneged on an agreement to return players to their original clubs. After a financially difficult year, the leagues negotiated a dramatic settlement. The National League absorbed four of the American Association teams and bought out the other four clubs for $130,000. The enlarged, reinvigorated National League maintained its fifty-cent ticket price (with certain exceptions), and the league adopted Sunday ball in cities where it was legal. Players were badly hurt by the consolidation, which eliminated 25 percent of major-league jobs. Furthermore, a new twenty-four-hundred-dollar salary cap was introduced, and it was strictly maintained. By 1893 salaries had dropped between 30 and 40 percent as owners tried to recoup losses from the previous years. Cincinnati's popular pitcher Tony Mullane balked at the cuts and held out for half a season before signing for twenty-one hundred dollars, one-half his 1891 salary. As a result, the National League made money from 1893 to 1895.

The National League struggled on for the next few years, hurt by the effects of the 1893 depression and by a lack of competition among its twelve teams. Attendance in the 1890s probably averaged slightly more than two thousand per game, significantly below the National League average for the nineteenth century of about twenty-six hundred per game. Only three teams, Boston, Baltimore, and Brooklyn, all renowned for inside baseball, won pennants between 1891 and 1900. On the other side, Louisville and St. Louis always finished in the bottom third, and Washington escaped the low ranks but once.

Another problem at the end of the 1890s was syndicate baseball, when the same owners controlled two different teams. A classic case occurred in 1898 when the Baltimore Orioles owner secured a major share of the Brooklyn Dodgers. The Orioles manager, Ed Hanlon, moved over to the Brooklyn franchise and brought along his star players, who helped the Dodgers win pennants in 1899 and 1900. Another product of syndicate baseball was the Cleveland Spiders, who set an all-time record for futility in 1899 with a dismal 20–134 season. The team had collapsed after owner Stanley Robison shipped all his best players to brother Frank's newly purchased St. Louis Browns. Alienated Cleveland fans boycotted the team (attendance through June averaged less than two hundred), and the Spiders played their late-season games out of town.

The National League tried to cope with its problems after the 1899 season by further consolidation, lopping off its four weakest teams. The eight-team league (Boston, Brooklyn, Chicago, Cincinnati, New York, Philadelphia, Pittsburgh, and St. Louis) became extremely stable, and the National League had no more franchise shifts until 1953.

Baseball in the Early Twentieth Century

The small number of franchises, an excess of experienced major leaguers, a lack of cohesion among bickering National League owners, and poor leadership from league headquarters opened the door for a rival major league to emerge. In 1901 the American League (known until 1900 as the minor Western League) proclaimed itself a major league with eight teams, including franchises in three of the recently dropped National League cities (Washington, Cleveland, and Baltimore). Under the strong and aggressive direction of President Ban Johnson, the American League successfully filled its rosters with seasoned ballplayers. Eighty-two veterans jumped from the National League in the first two years; over 60 percent of American League players had major-league experience. The American League immediately went head-to-head in competition with the National League in Boston, Chicago, and Philadelphia. One year later it vied with the National League in St. Louis (replacing Milwaukee), and two years later New York (replacing Baltimore). Securing a New York franchise was considered crucial for certifying the American League's major-league status and its financial success. It was a difficult task, however, because Giants owner Andrew Freedman, a prominent Tammany realtor, used his substantial clout to keep out competition even after he sold his club in 1902 to John Brush. No suitable site for a ball field could be found until President Johnson awarded a franchise to local Tammanyites William Devery, a former police chief, and Frank Farrell, the city's leading gambler, who had their own political influence.

Competition for players raised salaries, forced profits down, and brought the National League to the bargaining table. The leagues signed a new National Agreement in 1903 that recognized the American League and its contracts. The National Commission (the league presidents plus a third party they selected) was established to control organized baseball, and the minor leagues were classified for the purpose of drafting players. The commission's main achievements included restoring a postseason championship (the World Series) in 1903, resolving conflicts over players' contracts, disciplining players, and supporting umpires.

The rise of the American League symbolized baseball's booming popularity, which surpassed all other sports at the turn of the century. America's fascination with the game was reflected and promoted by extensive coverage in the daily press, popular magazines, sporting weeklies, and specialized monthlies such as *Baseball Magazine* (1908). The press provided extensive game reports, in-season and postseason gossip, and feature stories analyzing everything from the business of baseball to the physics of the curve ball. Baseball became a staple of fiction, ranging from Burt Standish's juvenile Frank Merriwell series to Ring Lardner's humorous short stories such as "You Know Me, Al." The doubling of major-league attendance between 1901 and 1909 and the national expansion of professional baseball also indicated the popularity of baseball. The minor leagues grew from thirteen leagues in 1900 to forty-six in 1912, leaving few cities without professional baseball. Even Saugerties, New York, population seven thousand, had a team in the Class D Hudson River League.

Professional baseball's unsurpassed popularity was a result of several factors. The game itself was fun and was widely played. Spectators who had grown up playing baseball could watch high drama in well-played competitive contests that only took about two hours. Fans at the ballpark participated in the rituals of spectatorship, which included rooting for the home team, yelling at the umpire and the opposition, and eating hot dogs and drinking beer. Even fans who seldom or never attended ball games could follow the day-by-day achievements of their heroes and favorite teams through the daily press coverage.

Baseball's popularity was also a consequence of how well it fit in with prevailing American values and beliefs. Native-born white Americans in the Progressive Era worried that the growth of industries, cities, bureaucracies, and the immigrant population was creating a distended society whose future was in doubt. The popular press, baseball guides, and juvenile literature conveyed a new baseball ideology, which characterized baseball as a game of pastoral American origins that improved health, character, and morality. Furthermore, baseball fostered the American myths of agrarianism, social democracy, and social integration.

The baseball creed coincided with the prevailing broad-based progressive ethos that promoted order, traditional values, efficiency, and Americanization by looking back to an idealized past. The game's history and folklore expressed some of society's main values and goals. Baseball fostered social integration by promoting acculturation and hometown pride, by teaching respect for authority, and by giving factory workers much-needed exercise and diversion.

The game was said to exemplify democracy because people from different social backgrounds sat together at the ballpark, which would reduce class tensions, promote democratic feelings, and provide plebeians a model of proper behavior to emulate. Baseball was also believed to epitomize democracy since player recruitment and retention was based solely on merit. Because only talent, not social origins, counted, observers assumed that professional baseball was a route of social mobility.

Identified as a rural game, baseball supposedly built character and developed such traditional qualities as fair play, discipline, and rugged individualism. It extended small-town life into cities, where playing and watching the game helped indoctrinate newcomers. Yet at the same time baseball was also perceived as a means to teach boys modern values such as teamwork and self-sacrifice, as exemplified by a crisp double play or a sacrifice bunt. Such traits were considered essential for future bureaucrats and factory workers. Youngsters supposedly learned such behavior by playing and watching baseball and emulating heroes such as Christy Mathewson, a college-educated muscular Christian who abstained from playing Sunday games. He had 373 wins, the most in National League history, and he pitched three shutouts in the 1905 World Series. After retirement he managed the Cincinnati Reds for two-and-a-half years, resigning during World War I to become an army captain. Mathewson was severely injured after the Armistice when he breathed poison gas while inspecting German trenches. He subsequently contracted tuberculosis and died in 1925. Matty was eulogized across the country: "Clean power in the hands of a clean and vigorous personality."

The arcadian, integrative, and democratic attributes of professional baseball were largely myths. In reality, baseball was not a democratic game of rural American origins, a promoter of social integration, or a builder of character. Baseball was actually an urban sport that had evolved over time from the English game of rounders, and its finest players were raised in the city. Professional baseball was more democratic than most sports, but all social classes and ethnic groups were not equally represented in the audiences or on the playing field. Until the 1920s, ticket and transportation costs, inconvenient starting times, and the absence of Sunday ball prevented many people from attending games. Fans from different social backgrounds did not sit together in the ballpark; different-priced sections effectively separated the classes. Players in organized baseball did not represent a cross-section of the national population; virtually all were white and the overwhelming majority were from native-born American, Irish, or German stock.

Baseball's capacity to integrate as exemplified by hometown pride and hero worship, was substantially exaggerated. To begin with, not all Americans participated in the rituals of spectatorship, since they did not all attend games. In addition, baseball idols such as Ty Cobb were often poor role models. Cobb was respected for his work ethic, aggressive style of play, and statistical accomplishments, yet at the same time he was hated by his peers and was a notorious racist misanthrope. Furthermore, social psychologists Thomas Tutko and Bruce Ogilvie demonstrated that sport does not build character, and social psychologist such as Leonard Berkowitz discounted its cathartic potential.

Although the realities of baseball had little in common with its myths, the public accepted the ideology as truth, and their mistaken assumptions influenced the way people behaved and thought. Middle-class WASPs believed that traditional values still counted in a fast-paced, urban society. Social workers in the early 1900s considered playing baseball second only to the public schools as a means to acculturate immigrant children into the American way of life, and they stressed baseball and other team games in their recreational programs.

Another popular myth was that team owners were selfless, civic-minded men who sponsored teams as a public service or to promote hometown pride. In reality they were middle-class businessmen trying to make money in an untapped field that well-to-do WASPS disdained. Owners were typically professional politicians, business allies of politicians, or streetcar executives deeply involved in urban politics. Ted Vincent found that nearly one-half of the 1,263 nineteenth-century baseball stockholders and officials he studied were politicians, including fifty-six mayors and 102 state legislators. Their ball clubs, especially in the minors, were shaky small businesses. Vincent reported that only three-fourths of the nineteenth-century teams lasted more than two years. For example, from its formation in 1885 to 1899, the Southern League completed only four seasons and did not play at all during three.

In the early 1900s all major-league clubs had political connections. Political ties were especially strong in cities with powerful citywide machines, such as New York, where Tammanyites owned all the teams, but such connections also existed in most other cities. Politically connected owners used clout to benefit their baseball business just as they did for any other investment. Political influence assured lower-tax assessments and minimal license fees, cheap or free police protection, and security against interlopers. Friends at city hall also supplied inside information about property values, anticipated land uses, and mass-transit plans, invaluable knowledge for teams selecting a playing field. On the other hand, owners without protection were vulnerable to political pressure for passes or payoffs. Such owners might encounter repeated inspections by fire marshals or even the construction of city streets through the field. In 1902 John Brush sold the Cincinnati Reds to a coalition of local Republican politicians that included boss George B. Cox after it was rumored that streets would otherwise be cut through his ballpark.

Major-league teams in the early 1900s were very profitable. They achieved substantial annual earnings, while the value of their franchises, worth fifty to one hundred thousand dollars early in the decade, increased by about five times in little more than ten years. The teams in Chicago and New York had the greatest profit potential because of the size of their cities. The Chicago Cubs (the former White Stockings) were sold by Spalding for $105,000 in 1905; the team earned $1.2 million between 1906 and 1915. In 1916 the Cubs were sold for five hundred thousand dollars. The Giants were even more valuable. In 1902 Andrew Freedman sold the club to John Brush for $200,000, which was about four times more than he had paid in 1895 for his majority share. Brush made a good investment because the team earned about one hundred thousand dollars a year from 1906 to 1910. In 1919 Brush's heirs sold the franchise for one million dollars to Charles Stoneham, a Tammany curb-market broker. A profitable investment, the Giants earned $296,803 in 1920, a National League record. The Giants were surpassed by the Yankees, their tenants at the Polo Grounds, who made a record $373,862. That season, the Yankees featured a new star, Babe Ruth, arguably the greatest player of all time.

The early baseball parks were cheap wooden structures, which reflected the sport's financial weakness, the state of building technology, the frequent mobility of teams, and the high failure rate of teams. Nineteenth-century clubs moved frequently, exemplified by the Chicago White Stockings, who played at six different sites between 1870 and 1894. Teams shifted locations because of high rents, burned-down ballparks, declining neighborhoods, streetcar subsidies, or political pressure. In 1889, for example, the Giants had to move from the original Polo Grounds (just north of Central Park) to a new site two miles further north because prominent aldermen, disgruntled at the number of passes they received, opened a street through the site.

The best sites were accessible by inexpensive rapid transit, were cheap to rent or purchase, and were located in safe middle-class neighborhoods near their fans. They were rarely located in working-class neighborhoods and almost never downtown, where real estate was prohibitively expensive. The exception was Chicago's beautiful ten-thousand seat Lake Front Park, a model ballpark built in 1883 for just ten thousand dollars. The team had to relocate two years later, however, because it was occupying public land illegally. In the late nineteenth century, construction costs of a ballpark escalated to between thirty thousand and sixty thousand dollars. New York's Hilltop Park, built in 1903 for seventy-five thousand dollars, was the last wooden major-league park to be constructed. These fields had serious disadvantages. Their seating capacities had become inadequate, the ambience was plain, and they were dangerous buildings. Often built cheaply by politically connected contractors who sometimes used substandard materials, the wooden parks were also highly inflammable. Five fires occurred in major-league parks in 1894; St. Louis alone had six in a ten-year period. Five major conflagrations in ballparks occurred between 1900 and 1911, and in 1903 an overcrowded railing broke at Philadelphia's Baker Bowl, killing twelve.

The era of the dangerous wooden ballparks ended in 1909 with the construction of the first fully modern, fire-resistant stadiums. This major innovation occurred because of baseball's increased popularity and profitability, its growing stability as a business, and the dangers posed by wooden structures. Municipalities in the Progressive Era were extremely concerned about the threat of fires in public places, such as the 1902 Iroquois Theater blaze in Chicago that killed 603 people, and they compiled strict new building codes. Chicago's revised regulations of 1909 specifically barred future construction of large wooden ballparks. The construction of new playing fields was also stimulated by the existence of the necessary technology, decreasing labor and material costs, and growing competition from other popular entertainments, such as vaudeville, movies, and amusement parks.

The new modern ballparks, designed in a classical style with greatly increased seating capacities, charged higher ticket prices that largely killed the custom of twenty-five-cent bleacher seats. Philadelphia's twenty-thousand-seat Shibe Park, opened in 1909 at a cost of five hundred thousand dollars, was the first fully fire-resistant ballpark, soon followed by Pittsburgh's triple-decked Forbes Field, with elevators, inclined ramps, electric lights, and telephones. Between 1909 and 1916 ten new major-league parks were built at an average cost of five hundred thousand dollars, and nearly all the rest were modernized using fire-resistant materials. Navin Field (Tiger Stadium), built in 1912, Fenway Park (1912) and Wrigley Field (1914) are still in use.

These privately constructed civic monuments were located on the urban periphery in middle-class or underdeveloped areas; the relatively cheap sites had been either purchased or leased on a long-term basis. Their field dimensions were unique, being closely tied to the shape and size of the lot. At the Polo Grounds, for instance, right field was only 259 feet from home plate, compared to 480 feet in center field. Although the fields made a strong impact on the neighborhoods in the immediate vicinity of their entrances, where parking lots, restaurants, and taverns sprang up, they did not significantly harm peaceful residential locales. Named for an owner (Ebbets Field), team (Braves Field) or location (Fenway Park), these rustic, green oases were referred to as a "park," "field," or "grounds," rural metaphors that reinforced the pastoral imagery of the national pastime. An important change in nomenclature occurred with the opening of Yankee Stadium (1923), a more modern and urbane name. Constructed at a cost of $2.5 million (plus $675,000 for the land), the sixty thousand seat "House that Sunday Baseball Built" was by far the most expensive and biggest ballpark of this era.

Most historians believe that spectators were mainly lower-middle to upper-lower class, and of WASP or old-immigrant stock. Historian James Sullivan's study of Cincinnati (AA) crowds in the 1880s suggests that blue-collar fans were even under-represented at American Association games, despite its work-ing-class orientation. He found that except on Sunday, fans in the more expensive sections surpassed those in the cheap twenty-five-cent seats. The National League originally sought a middle-class audience by setting high prices for admission, dividing seating areas by price, using security guards, and banning Sun-day baseball and liquor sales. Games began at convenient times for white-collar workers (Chicago games began at 2:30 because the Board of Trade closed at 2:00 P.M.; Washington games at 4:30, reflecting the closing time of government offices). Blue-collar spectators were mainly artisans with half-holidays on Saturday; workers with unusual shifts like bakers, butchers, and police-men; men taking an unpaid holiday; or the occasional unem-ployed fan. High ticket prices, the absence of Sunday ball in eastern and southern cities, and the cost of transportation cur-tailed working-class attendance. A round-trip on mass transit cost at least ten cents, which was more than low-income work-ers, who rarely rode streetcars at the turn of the century, could afford.

The behavior of nineteenth-century fans was occasionally unruly. Disorder was usually caused by overcrowding, drunken-ness, and the misconduct of rowdy players who carried on vitri-olic exchanges with umpires and fans. If the umpire's ruling "robbed" the home team, cries of "kill the umpire" would come from fans and team members. Fans might throw food or bottles at or physically attack the umpire. In the early 1900s Ban Johnson's strong support of umpires helped discourage egregious umpire baiting, and the dimensions of modern ballparks elimi-nated overcrowding and placed fans farther away from umpires and ballplayers. Furthermore, spectators were not primarily from the sporting fraternity, whose members had a greater proclivity for the kind of antisocial behavior witnessed at boxing matches. Rather the audiences were more "civilized" and acted in a more acceptable manner at the ballpark. Middle-class women com-prised a small but visible segment of audiences since the earliest days of baseball; clubs encouraged their attendance with Ladies' Days, on which women were admitted free or for a nominal fee. Their interest was reflected in the popular song of 1908, "Take Me Out to the Ball Game," in which the refrain is sung by a girl who tells her date she prefers an afternoon at the ballpark eating peanuts and Cracker Jacks and rooting for the home team to the theater or any other alternative he would fancy.

Baseball crowds were less disorderly than contemporary British soccer fans, whose identity and world view was wrapped up in the success of the home or national team. Baseball spectators had an easier time than soccer fans accepting unfavorable decisions and defeats, partly due to baseball's long season, which meant that most single contests were not crucial. Furthermore, there was no intracity competition in baseball (except for exhibitions and the World Series), as there was in Glasgow between the Celtic Football Club (Irish) and Rangers (Scottish), which raised the level of fan excitement to dangerous levels.

The social origins of major leaguers changed substantially around the turn of the century. A slight majority of nineteenth-century ballplayers were from blue-collar backgrounds, about three in ten were white collar, and the rest were sons of farmers. Players were not well educated, saved little money, and often lacked marketable skills. These social characteristics combined with the low status of their occupation resulted in over one-third of players who were active between 1871 and 1882 sliding down into blue-collar occupations after retirement. Their short-lived fame had little impact on their future careers. It did help them in the liquor business, since one out of ten retirees ended up owning or working in a saloon.

By comparison, major-league players in the period from 1900 to 1919 were drawn from higher socio-economic backgrounds, attracted by professional baseball's enhanced status and higher wages, which averaged about two thousand dollars in 1901, three thousand dollars in 1910, and five thousand dollars in 1923. They were mostly white collar sons, 44.6 percent, a figure more than double the proportion of nonmanual workers in the American labor force in 1910. One-fifth of ballplayers were sons of farmers, and one-third were blue-collar sons. One-fourth had attended college, five times the rate of other men their age. Their social backgrounds, education, and the increased number of baseball-related jobs resulted in a much smaller number (14.1 percent) moving into blue-collar work upon retirement compared to earlier ballplayers. The less-successful retirees were typically poorly educated blue-collar sons who had lived for instant gratification and ended up unprepared for life after baseball.

Early-twentieth-century baseball was known as the "dead-ball era." Pitching dominated, and runs were hard to come by, averaging fewer than seven a game for both teams. Teams played for runs one at a time, stressing "inside baseball." The entire National League had only 101 homers in 1907, and in the following season major-league batting averages were the lowest ever until 1968. Pitchers had several advantages, beginning with the modern home plate, introduced in 1900, which was five inches larger than its predecessor. One year later foul balls were counted as strikes for the first time. Games were played with just one or two balls that would become softened and discolored and thus harder to hit. Hurlers used foreign substances like spit, sandpaper (emery ball), or talcum powder (shine ball) to roughen a ball's cover, which made it move unnaturally and befuddle batters. However, Rader argues that even more important than trick pitchers (whose earned run averages were similar to other hurlers) was the use of bigger and stronger pitchers, the introduction of relief pitching, and improved fielding. The introduction in 1910 of a livelier cork-centered ball increased home runs by 30 percent, but they were still rare. Frank "Home Run" Baker of the Philadelphia Athletics hit the most home runs in the American league for four years (1911–14), yet his yearly total never topped twelve homers.

Intraleague competition remained unbalanced since four National League teams won seventeen pennants, and four American League teams won nineteen from 1901 to 1920. The Pirates, led by eight-time batting champion, shortstop Honus Wagner, won the first three National League titles, while the McGraw-managed Giants took the next two, plus four more in the 1910s.

The Cubs took pennants in 1906, 1907, 1908, and 1910. They won 116 games in 1906, an all-time record, yet lost the "El World Series" to the Chicago White Sox, the "Hitless Wonders."

The American League's biggest winners were Philadelphia and Boston with six pennants each. Between 1910 and 1914 the Athletics won four pennants and three World Series, led by a brilliant pitching staff and the "$100,000 infield." In 1915, however, owner-manager Connie Mack dismantled the team rather than meet spiraling salary demands, and the team ended the decade mired in last place. The A's were supplanted by the Red Sox who won in 1912, 1915, 1916, and 1918. The Sox had an extraordinary outfield and a stellar pitching staff, which included Babe Ruth. As a twenty-one-year-old in 1916, Ruth went 23–12, with nine shutouts (all-time American League record for a left-hander) and a league-leading 1.75 earned run average. Ruth went 65–33 with a 2.02 earned run average in his first three complete years in the majors, and he was spectacular in the World Series, going 3–0 and establishing a record of twenty-nine and two-thirds consecutive scoreless innings. Then in 1919 he set a major-league record with twenty-nine homers. Ruth was sold to the Yankees one year later for one hundred twenty-five thousand dollars plus a three hundred thousand dollar loan because Sox owner Harry Frazee needed to raise money for his Broadway theatrical productions. Ruth became the Yankees right fielder, and he smashed his own home-run record with an astounding fifty-four in 1920, marking the end of the dead-ball era. Ruth eventually played twenty-one years in the major leagues with a lifetime .342 batting average and a record 714 home runs. He was a self-made man who demonstrated that America was still the land of opportunity. Idolized for his natural prowess, with his large income and insatiable appetite for women, food, and fame, Ruth symbolized the consumer ethic of the 1920s.

Organized baseball's monopoly was severely tested in 1914 when the year-old Federal League proclaimed itself a major league. Its owners included several extremely wealthy men who wanted to own a big-time sports franchise, and it seemed to them that baseball was popular enough to support a new major league.

The Federal League did not recognize the reserve clause, and owners openly vied for top players, such as Ty Cobb and Walter Johnson, who used the opportunity for leverage to negotiate lucrative new contracts with their old clubs. Cobb re-signed with the Tigers for twenty thousand dollars. Twenty stars who remained with their clubs secured an average 92 percent increase in pay. Only a few luminaries past their prime, such as "Three Finger" Brown and Joe Tinker, did change leagues. Consequently, the Federal League rosters were composed of players past their prime, journeymen, and minor-league players.

The Federal League challenged organized baseball when the major leagues were strong and well organized, and it lacked the outstanding leadership that Ban Johnson provided the American League when it took on the National League in the early 1900s. The Federal League, unlike the American League in 1901, was starting virtually from scratch, and its Brooklyn and Chicago franchises were weighted down by the need to build expensive fireproof ballparks (which would include the future Wrigley Field) to comply with their cities' strict new building codes. Following two years of competition during which the new league lost $2.5 million and the major leagues encountered skyrocketing salaries, costly legal action, and rumors that the interlopers were moving into New York, a settlement was negotiated. The intruders received six hundred thousand dollars to dissolve, and the Chicago and St. Louis Federal League franchises were allowed to buy the Cubs and Browns in their respective cities. The Federal League team in Baltimore balked at the settlement and sued organized baseball under the Sherman Antitrust Act. The case eventually went to the Supreme Court. In 1922 Justice Oliver Wendell Holmes, Jr., wrote the majority opinion, stating that baseball was not trade or commerce because "personal effort . . . is not a subject of commerce," nor was baseball an interstate activity because crossing state lines to play was merely incidental. This crucial ruling exempted organized baseball from antitrust legislation.

Baseball's darkest moment came in September 1920 when journalists revealed that the 1919 World Series between the Cincinnati Reds and the Chicago White Sox had been fixed. The White Sox were considered the best team in baseball, but they lost the Series five games to three. Baseball, unlike horse racing and boxing, was not identified in the public mind as a gambling sport, but as a pastime enjoyed for its own sake. But in reality baseball gambling was very popular, not withstanding ballpark signs forbidding it. Fans bet confidently because baseball was considered honest. They wagered on the outcome of games, statistics such as hits and runs, and even the call of a pitch. Statistics not only helped management and fans evaluate players, but they also helped gamblers make informed judgments when betting on baseball. Club owners were often avid bettors; many had connections to horse racing or gambling. The presumed fixer of the 1919 World Series was the notorious gambler Arnold Rothstein, a partner in a Havana racetrack with Giants owner Charles Stoneham. Several rumored fixes had occurred in the early 1900s, but they had been dismissed or kept quiet "for the good of the game." The news of what became known as the "Black Sox" scandal shook public confidence in the integrity of the national pastime and nearly ruined it.

Historians Eliot Asinof and Harold Seymour have argued that first baseman Chick Gandil convinced seven underpaid, uneducated, and unsophisticated teammates to fix the series for a one hundred thousand dollar bribe from gamblers. Third baseman Buck Weaver changed his mind and played to win, but he did not report the incident. The players were indicted on the basis of confessions given by pitchers Eddie Cicotte and Cy Williams, and the illiterate star outfielder "Shoeless Joe" Jackson, who batted a robust .375 during the Series. When the case went to trial, however, the prosecutor reported that the confessions had been lost. They had been stolen by the outgoing state's attorney and ended up in the office of Sox owner Charles Comiskey's attorney. The absence of this key evidence severely weakened the state's case, and the team members were acquitted. Nonetheless, all were banned from the sport in 1921 by baseball's first commissioner, Judge Kenesaw Mountain Landis. Landis became the arbiter of last resort in all baseball disputes, and he employed broad investigative and punitive powers to protect the owners' interests.

The Black Sox scandal was an important symbolic event at a time when many old-stock Americans were worried about the future of their country. People were disillusioned by the nature of the peace that followed World War I. The Treaty of Versailles, which featured a League of Nations, was rejected by the Senate. Economic discontent resulted in major strikes in the steel and railroad industries, a general strike in Seattle, and a police strike in Boston. Growing fears of Bolshevism and radicalism at home led to the Red Scare, and racial antagonisms erupted in the Chicago Race Riot of 1919. The country seemed to be coming apart at the seams. If baseball—the finest American institution that epitomized and taught our traditional values was corrupt—what hope was there for the future? The acquittal fortuitously redeemed baseball (the jurors carried the players out of the courtroom on their shoulders), restored national self-confidence, and paved the way for the golden age of sports of the 1920s. During the twenties, the stern leadership of Judge Landis and the slugging of Babe Ruth helped the country forget the Black Sox and restored baseball to its pedestal.

The rise of commercialized professional spectator sport in the industrial era strongly reflected the spirit of industrial capitalism. Entrepreneurs sold consumers entertainment that was provided by highly trained and skilled athletes. Businessmen in horse racing and especially baseball, like their contemporary oligopolists and monopolists, tried to limit entry into their business by creating organizations such as racing boards and leagues to control access to their sport and thereby assure greater revenues for themselves.

Sport in the industrial era was mainly controlled by urban politicians and their close associates. These men had the power and influence to aid their sports businesses. Sports promotion offered a means to make money, gain prestige and fame, create more patronage opportunities, and provide a service for sports-minded constituents. A strong nexus between ethnic machine bosses and organized crime developed in the gambling sports of horse racing and boxing. While the elite remained a vital force on the racecourse, offtrack betting provided a major source of underworld revenue. During the 1920s horse racing experienced a dramatic resurgence, and the sport became widely legalized. During the next fifteen years bookmakers and organized-crime figures gained control of several racetracks.

In the case of prizefighting during the 1920s, the underworld supplanted their political allies and became the dominant force controlling the ring. Boxing became widely legalized during the Golden Age of Sports, and suddenly became a glamorous and profitable sport. In 1927 the Dempsey-Tunney heavyweight championship fight in Chicago's new Soldier Field attracted over one hundred thousand fans and brought in $2.7 million in gate receipts, until recently the largest in the sport's history.

During the 1920s, other professional sports vied for public attention. The National Football League was founded in 1920, the National Hockey League in 1922, and the American Basketball League in 1926. Automobile racing, six-day bicycle races, and professional golf also competed. These sports, however, as well as boxing and horse racing, were dwarfed by professional baseball, even if major-league attendance increases did not keep pace with population growth. Baseball overcame the Black Sox scandal, and its image as the clean, all-American game that stood for all that was good in our country endured. It had the preeminent sports hero in Babe Ruth and the most-famous sports facility in Yankee Stadium, and while movie-going may have supplanted it as the real national pastime, baseball was still the sport of choice for Americans. Organized baseball had achieved near-monopoly status; it was a national sport (although the major leagues were just in the North and Midwest) that appealed to all social classes. Baseball was the only major professional sport whose allure was primarily the game rather than the potential gambling gain. It was considered a game that epitomized the finest qualities of American society and reminded us of our youth. Few saw it as the crass business that it was, owned by politically connected entrepreneurs.

BIBLIOGRAPHICAL ESSAY

General Surveys

A valuable introduction to the study of sport history is Allen Guttmann's *From Ritual To Record: The Nature of Modern Sports* (New York, 1978), which examines the nature of modern sport from a Weberian perspective by analyzing the characteristics of sport in premodern, ancient, medieval, and modern times. He argued that the development of sport has been a product of modernization, and that modern sport is characterized by secularism, equality, bureaucratization, specialization, rationalization (logical formation and adaptation of universal rules; application of scientific methods to athletic training), quantification, and an obsession with records.

The principal interpretations for the rise of American sport have emphasized the role of cities and industrialization in that process. Scholars originally focused on the negative character of city life in comparison to rural society and subsequently accentuated the influence of industrialization upon urban life. The first scholarly analysis of American sport history was Frederick L. Paxson's presidential address to the Mississippi Valley Historical Society (now the Organization of American Historians), "The Rise of Sport," *Mississippi Valley Historical Review* 4 (1917): 143–68. A student of Frederick Jackson Turner, Paxson argued that the late-nineteenth-century rise of sport was a reaction to the deprivation of urban life in comparison to that of the country-side or frontier. Following the disappearance of the frontier, Americans needed a new release, which they found in sport, as a means to manage urban tensions and sustain harmony in congested heterogeneous cities. Paxson's deprivation thesis was slightly modified by Arthur M. Schlesinger, Sr. [*The Rise of the City, 1878–1898* (New York, 1938)], who attributed the athletic boom to a reaction against the restrictions of urban life. Urbanites were deprived of traditional fresh-air recreations, and they turned to spectator sports to vicariously experience rural life. Foster Rhea Dulles reinforced the deprivation paradigm in *America Learns to Play: A History of Popular Recreation* (Englewood Cliffs, NJ, 1965), which pointed out that crowded urban conditions and the pace of industrial work "did not permit the familiar games and athletic contests of village life." Consequently city dwellers relied on spectator entertainments, particularly sports, as an "outlet for surplus energy and suppressed emotions." Dale Somers argued in *The Rise of Sports in New Orleans, 1850–1900* (Baton Rouge, 1972), a study of a wide-open southern city where all sports flourished, that the rise of sport reflected urbanization and industrialization's transformation of the social structure. He argued along the lines of Schlesinger that the nature of urban life (weak community identities, six-day work weeks, and remoteness from the countryside) "rendered the simpler, unorganized and often spontaneous diversions of rural America unsatisfactory or inaccessible." The void was filled by organized and commercial sport, which provided a safety valve in the stifling urban environment.

A new paradigm was established by John R. Betts in his seminal "The Rise of Organized Sport in America" (Ph.D. diss., Columbia University, 1951), largely summarized in his *America's Sporting Heritage, 1850–1950* (Reading, MA, 1974). Betts argued that sport was neither a "reaction against mechanization, the division of labor, and the standardization of life in a machine civilization" nor a romantic return to a lost pristine age. Rather the rise of sport was "as much a product of industrialization as it was an antidote to it." Betts argued that industrialization and the urban movement were the principal factors for the rise of organized sport. Betts recognized that while American sports were originally primarily rural, simple, individualistic, and mainly for youths, sport existed as an urban institution since the early colonial era. Among Betts's major contributions was his analysis of how a positive antebellum sport ideology helped sell sport to the middle class. He dated the boom in organized sport to the post–Civil War era, a product of industrialization that provided enormous fortunes, and a higher standard of living for the middle class. Technological innovations, improved access to sports sites, lowered equipment costs and new apparatus, and the emergence of entrepreneurs who recognized potential profits in catering to urban sporting interests facilitated the rise of a national sports market.

The most sophisticated and elegant explanation of the American sporting experience is Benjamin G. Rader's indispensable *American Sports: From the Age of Folk Games to the Age of Television*, 2d ed. (Englewood Cliffs, NJ, 1990). Rader seeks to explain how and why informal games evolved into modern spectator sport and to identify and explain developments in the internal history of sport (rules, ethos, management, and finance). Rader examines the emergence of an antebellum sporting counterculture that sought to maintain traditional athletic pleasures; he mainly focuses on how nineteenth-century industrial capitalism, the evolution of American society and culture in an urban setting, and the particular requirements of major American sports led to the rise of organized sports. Rader emphasizes the importance of spectator sports in the period from 1890 to 1950, stressing the role of entrepreneurs, heroes, and professional athletes; voluntarism; the emergence of a consumer society; and the impact of the progressive sports creed on public behavior. His excellent analysis of postwar sport examines the continued growth of commercial amateur and professional sports, the impact of television, and the growing roles of African Americans and women in major sports.

Other overviews of American sport history include John A. Lucas and Ronald A. Smith, *The Saga of American Sport* (Philadelphia, 1978); Douglas A. Noveer and Lawrence E. Ziewacz,

The Games They Played: Sport in American History, 1865–1980 (Chicago, 1983); and Allen Guttmann, *A Whole New Ball Game: An Interpretation of American Sports* (Chapel Hill, NC, 1988), a collection of essays on such topics as Puritans, southerners, women, and children, in which he seeks to demonstrate his modernization paradigm. The most recent interpretive analysis is Elliott Gorn and Warren Goldstein, *A Brief History of American Sports* (New York, 1993), which examines the connections between sport and American culture and society, how developments in culture and society influenced sport, and how sport influenced class and gender identities.

Recent scholars, especially Melvin L. Adelman in *A Sporting Time: New York City and the Rise of Modern Athletics, 1820–70* (Urbana, IL, 1986), have gone beyond examining the city as a principal site of American sport to analyze sport as both the product of urbanization and as an independent variable impacting upon city building. Adelman argues that the emergence of sport in the nation's leading city was a joint product of the modernization of society and of the modernization of sporting institutions. Stephen Hardy's *How Boston Played: Sport, Recreation and Community, 1865–1915* (Boston, 1982) examines such topics as interscholastic sports, elite sports clubs, boxing heroes, and park use in post–Civil War Boston. Steven A. Riess, *City Games: The Evolution of American Urban Society and the Rise of Sports* (Urbana, IL, 1989) shows how demographic growth, evolving spatial arrangements, social reform, the formation of class and ethnic subcultures, the expansion of urban government, and the rise of political machines and crime syndicates all interacted to influence the development of American sport. Sport, in turn, also influenced these social variables. For a similar analysis of British sport, see Richard Holt's *Sport and the British: A Modern History* (New York, 1989), which examines how class structures and urban experiences molded British sport.

A number of recent review essays on sport history provide valuable critiques of the booming literature and help make that scholarship accessible. See Melvin L. Adelman, "Academicians and American Athletics: A Decade of Progress," *Journal of Sport*

History 10 (1983): 80–106; Stephen Hardy, "The City and the Rise of American Sport, 1820–1920," *Exercise and Sports Sciences Reviews* 9 (1981): 183–229; Steven A. Riess, "The New Sport History," *Reviews in American History* 18 (1990): 313–25; and Robert M. Lewis, "American Sport History: A Bibliographical Guide," *American Studies International* 29 (1991): 35–59. Readers seeking accessible primary sources should consult Steven A. Riess, ed., *The American Sporting Experience: An Historical Anthology* (West Point, 1984), which combines secondary articles and primary documents; Peter Levine, *American Sport: A Documentary History* (Englewood Cliffs, NJ, 1989); and George Kirsch, *Sports in North America: A Documentary History, 1840–1860* (Gulf Breeze, FL, 1992), the first of a ten-volume series to be published by Academic International. Selections include rules and regulations, club and association bylaws and constitutions, contemporary articles, and press accounts of major contests.

Industrialization, Urbanization, and the Rise of Sport

The best introduction to antebellum sport is Adelman, *A Sporting Time*, which analyzes the modernization of sport in New York between 1820 and 1870. The author's superb research into baseball, cricket, harness racing, and thoroughbred racing indicates that the rise of sport predated the Civil War era. The book also contains considerable information about boxing, pedestrianism, and water, animal, and leisure sports. John Dizikes, *Sportsmen and Gamesmen* (New York, 1981) argues that the ideas and behavior of antebellum sportsmen changed from the values of sportsmen to gamesmen. While elite sportsmen accepted the written rules and unwritten conventions of a game, bourgeois gamesmen were manipulative and tried to bend rules whenever they could in order to win. Dizikes's analysis is based on just a few biographical studies, and he unfairly stereotypes middle-class Victorians, who had more integrity than he suggests.

The dynamics of urban growth and its impact on sport has received considerable scholarly attention, particularly the development of the municipal park movement. On sport and urban space, see Riess, *City Games*. Galen Cranz, *The Politics of Park Design: A History of Urban Parks in America* (Cambridge, MA, 1982) is an overview of park history that offers a very idiosyncratic periodization. On sport and the parks, see Riess, *City Games*, and Hardy, *How Boston Played*. On the origins and evolution of the naturalistic vision, see David Schuyler, *The New Urban Landscape: The Redefinition of City Form in Nineteenth-Century America* (Baltimore, 1986). Considerable attention has been given to Central Park. See especially Roy Rosenzweig and Elizabeth Blackmar, *The Park and the People: A History of Central Park* (Ithaca, NY, 1992), which is concerned with the role of the masses in the construction and use of public space. See also Ian Stewart, "Central Park, 1851–1871: Urban and Environmental Planning in New York City" (Ph.D. diss., Cornell University, 1973); and "Politics and the Park: The Fight for Central Park," *New-York Historical Society Quarterly* 61 (1972): 126–47. On the early park movement in Brooklyn, see Donald E. Simons, "The Public Park Movement in Brooklyn, 1824–1873" (Ph.D. diss., New York University, 1972).

For a positivist interpretation of the park movement, see Gerald Marsden, "Philanthropy and the Boston Playground Movement, 1885–1907," *Social Science Review* 35 (1961): 48–58, and Betts, *America's Sporting Heritage*. For a social control perspective, see Michael P. McCarthy, "Politics and the Parks: Chicago Businessmen and the Recreation Movement," *Journal of the Illinois State Historical Society* 65 (1972): 158–72; Joel Spring, "Mass Culture and School Sports," *History of Education Quarterly* 14 (1974): 483–95; Cary Goodman, *Choosing Sides: Playground and Street Life on the Lower East Side* (New York, 1979); and Cranz, *Politics of Park Design*. For a more moderate view that recognizes the selflessness of the reformers, see Paul Boyer, *Urban Masses and Moral Order in America, 1820–1920* (Cambridge, MA, 1978). While these studies largely examine the park movement from the top down, recent scholarship recognizes that motivation for reformers is quite complex and that many countervailing factors are involved, including the agency of working-class urbanites. See Hardy, *How Boston Played*; Roy Rosen-zweig, *Eight Hours for What We Will: Workers and Leisure in an Industrial City, 1870–1920* (Cambridge, MA, 1983); and Stephen Hardy and Alan G. Ingham, "Games, Structures and Agency: Historians on the American Play Movement," *Journal of Social History* 17 (1983): 285–302. On the origins of Chicago's park system see Glen Holt, "Private Plans for Public Spaces: The Origins of Chicago's Park System, 1850–1875," *Chicago History* 8 (1979): 173–84, which demonstrates how private citizens played a crucial role in initiating municipal change. See also Elizabeth Halsey, *The Development of Public Recreation in Metropolitan Chicago* (Chicago, 1940); and Gerald R. Gems, "Sport and Culture Formation in Chicago, 1890–1940" (Ph.D. diss., University of Maryland, 1989). On Frederick Law Olmsted, the leading park architect, see Cynthia Zaitzevsky, *Frederick Law Olmsted and the Boston Park System* (Cambridge, MA, 1982); Laura Wood Roper, *FLO: A Biography of Frederick Law Olmsted* (Baltimore, 1973); Elizabeth Stevenson, *Park Maker: A Life of Frederick Law Olmsted* (New York, 1977); and Thomas Bender, *Towards an Urban Vision: Ideas and Institutions in Nineteenth-Century America* (Lexington, KY, 1975). See also Frederick Law Olmsted, Jr., and Theodora Kimball, eds., *Frederick Law Olmsted: Landscape Architect, 1822–1903* (1922–28; reprint, New York, 1970); along with Charles E. Beveridge and David Schuyler, eds., *The Papers of Frederick Law Olmsted*, vol. 3, *Creating Central Park, 1857–1861*, and vol. 6, *The Years of Olmsted, Vaux, & Company, 1865–1874* (Baltimore, 1984–92). For a critical review of some of this literature, see Daniel M. Bluestone, "Olmsted's Boston and Other Park Places," *Reviews in American History* 11 (1983): 531–36. Rosenzweig and Blackmar in *Park and the People* argue that Olmsted has been given too much credit at the expense of his colleague Calvert Vaux, and they are critical of the elitism in early park planning.

Scholars have given little attention to rural sports, emphasizing competitive urban sports. See Ted Ownby, *Subduing Satan: Religion, Recreation and Manhood in the Rural South, 1865–1920* (Chapel Hill, NC, 1990) for a discussion of field sports and cock fighting in the evangelical South. On fishing, see, Colleen J. Sheehy, "The Rise of Urbanism and the Romance of the Rod and Reel," in *Hard at Play: Leisure in America, 1840–1940*, ed. Kathryn Grover (Amherst, MA, 1992), 77–92.

Nearly thirty years ago John Higham's innovative essay, "The Reorientation of American Culture in the 1890s," in *The Origins of Modern Consciousness*, ed. John Weiss (Detroit, MI, 1965), 29–48, pointed out how the elite worried about moral and physical decline. More recently considerable attention has been given to the history of sport, fitness, and health, undoubtedly a product of the 1980s fitness fad. James C. Whorton, *Crusaders for Fitness: The History of American Health Reformers* (Princeton, NJ, 1982); Harvey Green, *Fit For America: Health, Fitness, Sport and American Society* (New York, 1986); and Martha Verbrugge, *Able-Bodied Womanhood: Personal Health and Social Change in Nineteenth-Century Boston* (New York, 1988), date the rise of the health movement to the Jacksonian era when it was a product of urbanization, the rise of evangelical Christianity, the search for perfection, and the general thrust for social reform. These works all examine middle-class attitudes about health from then through the Progressive Era. They further consider the health movement of the Progressive Era, produced by fears of city life, the new germ theory, social efficiency, and concerns about individual character. See also Donald Mrozek, *Sport and American Mentality: 1880–1910* (Knoxville, 1983); Kathryn Grover, ed., *Fitness in American Culture: Images of Health, Sport, and the Body, 1830–1940* (Amherst, 1989); Joseph Ernst, *Weakness is a Crime: The Life of Bernarr McFadden* (Syracuse, NY, 1991), a fascinating biography of an arch–male chauvinist who was a founder of the physical fitness movement; and David L. Chapman, *Sandow The Magnificent: Edward Sandow and the Beginnings of Body Building* (Urbana, IL, 1994).

The seminal essay on the ideology of sport is John R. Betts, "Mind and Body in Early American Thought," *Journal of American History* 54 (1968): 787–805. See also his "Public Recreation, Public Parks, and Public Health Before the Civil War," in *The History of Physical Education and Sports*, ed. Bruce L. Bennett

(Chicago, 1972), 33–520. Also useful on the ideology of sport are Adelman, *A Sporting Time*; Hardy, *How Boston Played*; Roberta J. Park, "'Embodied Selves': The Rise and Development of Concern for Physical Education, Active Recreation for American Women, 1777–1865," *Journal of Sport History* 5 (1978): 5–41; and Linda J. Borish, "The Robust Woman and the Muscular Christian: Catharine Beecher, Thomas Higginson, and Their Vision of American Society, Health and Physical Activities," *International Journal of the History of Sport* 4 (1987): 139–53.

On the impact of technology on sport, see John R. Betts's article, "The Technological Revolution and the Rise of Sport, 1850–1900," *Mississippi Valley Historical Review* 40 (1953): 231–56, and his *America's Sporting Heritage*. For brief studies of the metropolitan press, see Bernard A. Weisberger, *The American Newspaperman* (Chicago, 1961); and Gunther Barth, *City People: The Rise of Modern City Culture in Nineteenth-Century America* (New York, 1980). On sports journalism, see Michael Oriard, *Reading Football: How the Popular Press Created an American Spectacle* (Chapel Hill, NC, 1993); John R. Betts, "Sporting Journalism in Nineteenth-Century America," *American Quarterly* 5 (1953): 39–56; and Norris W. Yates, *William T. Porter and the Spirit of the Times* (Baton Rouge, LA, 1957). On sport and public transportation, see e.g., Riess, *City Games*; Betts, *American Sporting Heritage*; and John B. Rae, *The American Automobile: A Brief History* (Chicago, 1975). On cycling, see Norman Dunham, "The Bicycle Era in American History" (Ph.D. diss., Harvard University, 1956); Robert A. Smith, *A Social History of the Bicycle* (New York, 1972); Hardy, *How Boston Played*; and George D. Bushnell, "When Chicago was Wheel Crazy," *Chicago History* 4 (1975): 172–75. For an excellent analysis of the social and symbolic functions of cycling in the late nineteenth century, see Richard Harmond, "Progress and Flight: An Interpretation of the American Cycling Craze of the 1890s," *Journal of Social History* 5 (1971): 235–57; and on touring, see Gary Allan Tobin, "The Bicycle Boom of the 1890s: The Development of Private Transportation and the Birth of the Modern Tourist," *Journal of Popular Culture* 7 (Spring 1974): 838–49.

Sport and Class

On the American elite, see Frederick C. Jaher, *The Urban Establishment: Upper Strata in Boston, New York, Charleston, Chicago, and Los Angeles* (Urbana, IL, 1982). On elite sport, see Thorstein Veblen's classic, *The Theory of the Leisure Class* (New York, 1899). Essential works include E. Digby Baltzell, *Philadelphia Gentlemen: The Making of a National Upper Class* (New York, 1958); Somers, *The Rise of Sports in New Orleans*; Hardy, *How Boston Played*; Frances G. Couvares, *The Remaking of Pittsburgh: Class and Culture in an Industrial City, 1877–1919* (Albany, NY, 1984); and Mrozek, *Sport and American Mentality*. Mrozek focuses on the eastern elite and their broad influence on Ivy League colleges, and on the military; he also examines ideas of manliness, regeneration, nationalism, and social efficiency. Mrozek points out that eastern elite sons were particularly prominent sportsmen who sought physical, psychological, and sexual regeneration through football and other strenuous activities to prove their manliness and secure the future of the race. On James G. Bennett, the leading elite sportsman, see Donald Seitz, *The James Gordon Bennetts* (Indianapolis, IN, 1928); and Richard O'Connor, *The Scandalous Mr. Bennett* (Garden City, NY, 1962).

Considerable attention has been devoted to elite sports. While there is no scholarly book-length study of racing, Adelman's *A Sporting Time* is essential for the mid-nineteenth century. See also William H. P. Robertson, *The History of Thoroughbred Racing in America* (Englewood Cliffs, NJ, 1964); and Dwight Akers, *Drivers Up! The Story of American Harness Racing* (New York, 1938). On elite track-and-field clubs, see Rader, *American Sports*; Frederick W. Janssen, *History of Amateur Athletics* (New York, 1885); Bob Considine and Fred B. Jarvis, *The First Hundred Years: A Portrait of NYAC* (London, 1969); and Joe D. Willis and Richard G. Wettan, "Social Stratification in New York City Athletic Clubs, 1865–1915," *Journal of Sport History* 3 (1975): 45–63. On the governance of amateur sport see Richard G. Wettan and Joe D. Willis, "Effect of New York Athletic Clubs on American Amateur Athletic Governance, 1870–1915," *Research Quarterly* 47 (1976): 499–505, and "Social Stratification in the New York Athletic Club: A Preliminary Analysis of the Impact of the Club on Amateur Sport in Late Nineteenth-Century America," *Canadian Journal of History of Sport and Physical Education* 7 (May 1976): 41–53. On cricket, see George B. Kirsch, *The Creation of American Team Sports: Baseball and Cricket, 1838–72* (Urbana, IL, 1989); and John A. Lester, ed., *A Century of Philadelphia Cricket* (Philadelphia, 1951). On hunting, see John F. Reiger, *American Sportsmen and the Origins of Conservation* (New York, 1975). An excellent treatment of the country club appears in Hardy, *How Boston Played*. On metropolitan men's clubs, see Baltzell, *Philadelphia Gentlemen*; Hardy, *How Boston Played*; and David Hammack, *Power and Society: Greater New York at the Turn of the Century* (New York, 1982).

Middle-class sport has received relatively less attention. On the formation of the urban middle class, see Stuart Blumin, *The Emergence of the Middle Class: Social Experience in the American City 1760–1900* (New York, 1989); Cindy Sondik Aron, *Ladies and Gentlemen of the Civil Service: Middle-Class Workers in Victorian America* (New York, 1987); John S. Gilkeson, Jr., *Middle-Class Providence, 1820–1940* (Princeton, NJ, 1986); and Burton J. Bledstein, *The Culture of Professionalism: The Middle Class and the Development of Higher Education in America* (New York, 1976). On middle-class manliness, see Steven A. Riess, "Sport and the Redefinition of American Middle-Class Masculinity," *International Journal of the History of Sport* 8 (1991): 5–27; E. Anthony Rotundo, *American Manhood: Transformations in Masculinity From the Revolution to the Modern Era* (New York, 1993); Peter Stearns, *Be A Man! Males in Modern Society* (New York, 1979); Joe L. Dubbert, *A Man's Place: Masculinity in Transition* (Englewood Cliffs, NJ, 1979); and Gerald F. Roberts, "The Strenuous Life: The Cult of Manliness in the Era of Theodore Roosevelt" (Ph.D. diss., Michigan State University, 1970). For a comparative Anglo-American analysis, see J. A. Mangan and James Walvin, eds., *Manliness and Morality* (London, 1987). On middle-class leisure, see also Grover, ed., *Hard at Play*.

For an introduction to working-class culture and recreation, see Herbert Gutman, *Work, Culture and Society in Industrializing America: Essays in Working-Class Culture* (New York, 1976); and on the work ethic, see Daniel Rodgers, *The Work Ethic in Industrial America, 1850–1920* (Chicago, 1978); and Daniel Nelson, *Managers and Workers: Origins of the New Factory System in the United States* (Madison, WI, 1975). Particularly valuable on all aspects of working-class leisure is Rosenzweig, *Eight Hours for What We Will.* For a comparative study of the quality of British and American working-class life, see Peter R. Shergold, *Working-Class Life: The "American Standard" in Comparative Perspective, 1899–1913* (Pittsburgh, 1982), who argues that British workers originally had more discretionary time.

The best place to begin on working-class sport is Elliott Gorn, *The Manly Art: Bare Knuckles Prize Fighting in Nineteenth Century America* (Ithaca, NY, 1986), an analysis of boxing from an American studies perspective that focuses on the subterranean working-class bachelor subculture. A masterful study of gender, folk history, and working-class culture, Gorn's work provides an excellent examination of some seedier sides of American history. He traces boxing's development from its Anglo-Irish origins, to its popularity with the antebellum subterranean working class, and finally to boxing's resurgence in the 1880s, which was encouraged by professional promotion, the charismatic heavyweight-champion John L. Sullivan, and the rise of gentlemen-amateur boxers. Gorn elegantly describes the nature of ring combat, its development into a more modern and civilized enterprise, and the cultural meaning of pugilism..Other works that focus on working-class sport include Riess, *City Games*; and Ted Vincent, *Mudville's Revenge: The Rise and Fall of American Sport* (New York, 1981), a largely overlooked book that examines blue-collar participation in major sports from the late nineteenth century to the 1940s. A lot of valuable information on industrial sport can be found in Betts, *America's Sporting Heritage*. For an excellent overview of British working-class sport, see Holt, *Sport and the British*, which argues that historians underestimated working-class agency of the development of their favorite pastimes.

On the debate over the congruence of baseball with working conditions see Steven Gelber, "Working at Playing: The Culture of the Workplace and the Rise of Baseball," *Journal of Social History* 16 (1983): 3–22; Steven Gelber, "'Their Hands Are All Out Playing': Business and American Baseball, 1845–1917," *Journal of Sport History* 11 (1984): 5–27; and Melvin L. Adelman, "Baseball, Business and the Work Place: Gelber's Thesis Reexamined," *Journal of Social History* 23 (1989): 285–301.

Information on workers' sports is scattered. See, e.g., Katherine A. Harvey, *The Best Dressed Miners: Life and Labor in the Maryland Coal Region, 1835–1910* (Ithaca, NY, 1969); Duane A. Smith, *Rocky Mountain Mining Camps: The Urban Frontier* (Bloomington, IN, 1967); John T. Cumbler, *Working-Class Community in Industrial America: Work, Leisure and Struggle in Two Industrial Cities, 1880–1930* (Westport, CT, 1979); David Walkowitz, *Worker City, Company Town: Iron and Cotton Worker Protest in Troy and Cohoes, New York, 1855–1884* (Urbana, IL, 1978); Couvares, *The Remaking of Pittsburgh*; and Steven J. Ross, *Workers on the Edge: Work, Leisure and Politics in Industrializing Cincinnati, 1788–1890* (New York, 1985). For sport in southern mill towns, see Nelson, *Managers and Workers*; Donald Gropman, *Say It Ain't So Joe: The True Story of Shoeless Joe Jackson and the 1919 World Series* (New York, 1988); and Thomas K. Perry, *Textile League Baseball: South Carolina's Mill Teams, 1880–1955* (Jefferson, NC, 1993).

On welfare capitalism see Stuart Brandes, *American Welfare Capitalism* (Chicago, 1970). On sport at Pullman, see Wilma Pesavento, "Sport and Recreation in the Pullman Experiment, 1880–1900," *Journal of Sport History* 9 (Summer 1982): 38–62; Pesavento and Lisa C. Raymond, "'Men Must Play: Men Will Play': Occupations of Pullman Athletes, 1880 to 1900," *Journal of Sport History* 11 (1985): 233–51; Stanley Buder, *Pullman: An Experiment in Industrial Order and Community Planning, 1880–1930* (Chicago, 1977); and Almont Lindsey, *The Pullman Strike: The Story of a Unique Experiment and of a Great Labor Upheaval* (New York, 1964). For other programs, see Gerald Zahavi, *Workers, Managers, and Welfare Capitalism: The Shoemakers and Tanners of Endicott Johnson, 1890–1950* (Urbana, IL, 1988); and

John Schleppi, "It Pays: John H. Paterson and Industrial Recreation at the National Cash Register Company," *Journal of Social History* 6 (1979): 20–28. See also such company histories as Alfred Lief, *The Firestone Story: A History of the Firestone Tire and Rubber Company* (New York, 1951).

Historians have given due consideration to saloons, the primary site of male working-class recreation, as sports centers. See Perry Duis, *The Saloon: Public Drinking in Chicago and Boston, 1880–1920* (Urbana, IL, 1983); Elliott West, *The Saloon on the Rocky Mountain Mining Frontier* (Lincoln, NE, 1979); Jon Kingsdale, "The 'Poor Man's Club': Social Functions of the Working-Class Saloon," *American Quarterly* 25 (1977): 472–89; and Mark Haller's seminal essay, "Organized Crime in Urban Society: Chicago in the Twentieth Century," *Journal of Social History* 5 (1971–72): 210–34. Still useful is Herbert Asbury, *Sucker's Progress: An Informal History of Gambling in America from the Colonies to Canfield* (New York, 1938). Otherwise, the secondary literature on popular indoor sports is sparse. On billiards see Ned Polsky's classic sociological study *Hustlers, Beats and Others* (Chicago, 1967); and John Grissim, *Billiards: Hustlers & Heroes, Legends & Lies, and the Search for a Higher Truth on the Green Felt* (New York, 1979), an informative, popular account. On early billiards, see Adelman, *A Sporting Time*, and on billiards at the turn of the century, see Riess, *City Games*. Rick Kogan, *Brunswick: The Story of an American Company from 1845 to 1985* (Skokie, IL, 1985) is a lavishly illustrated volume recounting the history of the foremost American manufacturer of table games. On bowling, see Herman Weiskopf, *The Perfect Game: The World of Bowling* (Englewood Cliffs, NJ, 1978); and Riess, *City Games*.

Sport and Women

The literature on sporting women, a rapidly growing topic, focuses on elite and upper-middle-class women. A good place to start is Allen Guttmann's *Women's Sports: A History* (New York, 1991), a prizewinning interpretive analysis of women's sport history from ancient times to the present. For a guide to the literature, see Mary Lou Remley's *Women in Sport: An Annotated Bibliography and Resource Guide, 1900–1990* (Boston, 1991). A growing number of monographs have recently been published that examine women's sport and fitness. Verbrugge's *Able Bodied Womanhood* focuses on the rise of well-being among middle-class nineteenth-century female Bostonians, examining various athletic training programs, particularly athletics at Wellesley and the establishment of the city's Normal School of Gymnastics, to demonstrate their growing awareness and understanding of health issues. She does not, however, point out how such knowledge was used to improve society. Patricia Vertinsky, *The Eternally Wounded Woman: Women, Exercise and Doctors in the Late Nineteenth Century* (Manchester, UK, 1990) examines the impact of mainstream physicians on limiting the athletic behavior of Anglo-American women. On physical fitness and health, see Frances B. Cogan, *All-American Girl: The Idea of Real Womanhood in Midnineteenth-Century America* (Athens, GA, 1989). On baseball, see Gai Berlage, *Women in Baseball: The Forgotten Story* (Westport, CT, 1994); and on cycling see Patricia Marks, *Bicycles, Bangs and Bloomers: The New Woman and the Popular Press* (Lexington, KY, 1990). See also the essays in Joan S. Hult and Marianna Trekell, eds., *A Century of Women's Basketball: From Frailty to Final Four* (Reston, VA, 1991); Reet Howell, ed., *Her Story in Sport: A Historical Anthology of Women in Sports* (West Point, NY, 1982); and Stephanie L. Twin, ed., *Out of the Bleachers: Writing on Women and Sport* (Old Westbury, NY, 1979). For excellent comparative studies on Anglo-American sport and gender, see Roberta J. Park and J. A. Mangan, eds., *From "Fair Sex" to Feminism: Sport and the Socialization of Women in the Industrial and Post-Industrial Eras* (London, 1987). Other valuable studies include Stephanie L. Twin, "Jock and Jill: Aspects of Women's Sports History in America, 1870–1940" (Ph.D. diss., Rutgers University, 1978); Cindy L. Himes, "The Female Athlete in American Society, 1860–1940," (Ph.D. diss., University of Pennsylvania, 1986); and Susan Cahn, *Coming on Strong: Gender and Sexuality in 20th Cen-*

tury Women (New York, 1994), which emphasizes the years following the 1920s. On working-class women's sport, see Monys Ann Hagen, "Industrial Harmony through Sports: The Industrial Recreation Movement and Women's Sports" (Ph.D. diss., University of Wisconsin, 1990).

Ethnic Sports

The place to begin on ethnic sports is Riess, *City Games*; and Rader, *American Sports*. On English Americans, see Rowland Berthoff, *British Immigrants in Industrial America, 1790–1950* (Cambridge, MA, 1958); and Adelman, *A Sporting Time*. For Scottish newcomers see Gerald Redmond, *The Caledonian Games in Nineteenth-Century America* (Rutherford, NJ, 1971); and Benjamin G. Rader, "The Quest for Subcommunities and the Rise of American Sport," *American Quarterly* 29 (1977): 355–69. On French Canadians, see Richard Sorrel, "Sports and the Franco-Americans in Woonsocket, 1870–1930," *Rhode Island History* 31 (1972): 117–26. There is a considerable literature on the turners. See Henry Metzner, *A Brief History of the American Turnerbund* (Pittsburgh, 1924), an informative insider's account, and the more scholarly Carl Wittke, *Refugees of Revolution: The German Forty-Eighters in America* (Philadelphia, 1952). See also Horst Ueberhorst, *Turner Unterm Sternenbanner: Der Kampf der Deutsch-Americanischen Turner für Einhelt, Freiheit, und Soziale Gerechtigkeit, 1848 bis 1918* (Munich, 1978); and *Turner und Sozialdemokraten in Milwaukee: Fünf Jahrzehnte der Kooperation, (1910–1960)* (Bonn, 1980), which examines the close ties between Milwaukee's turners and the Socialist party, and especially Ralf Wagner, "Turner Societies and the Socialist Tradition," in *German Workers' Culture in the United States, 1850 to 1920*, ed. Hartmut Keil (Washington, D.C., 1988), 221–39.

On the Irish, see Hardy, *How Boston Played*; Carl Wittke, *The Irish in America* (Baton Rouge, 1956); William V. Shannon, *The American Irish* (New York, 1963); Michael T. Isenberg, *John L. Sullivan and His America* (Urbana, IL, 1988). On Irish social and athletic clubs, see Frederick M. Thrasher's classic, *The Gang:*

A Study of 1,313 Gangs in Chicago (Chicago, 1928); William M. Tuttle, Jr., *Race Riot: Chicago in the Red Summer of 1919* (New York, 1974); and Chicago Commission on Race Relations, *The Negro in Chicago* (Chicago, 1922), a report written by sociologist Charles Johnson, who compiled considerable oral testimony about the behavior and image of the Ragen Colts.

There is limited scholarship on the sporting pastimes of the new immigrants. On Slavic-Americans, see, e.g., Gems, "Sport and Culture Formation in Chicago"; Vaclad Vesta, ed., *Panorama: A Historical Review of Czechs and Slovaks in the U.S.A.* (Cicero, IL, 1970); Casimir J. B. Wronski, "Early Days of Sport Among Polish Americans of Chicagoland," in *Poles of Chicago, 1837–1937* (Chicago, 1937); Donald E. Pienkos, *One Hundred Years Young: A History of the Polish Falcons of America* (Boulder, CO, 1987); Myron B. Kuropas, "Ukrainian Chicago: The Making of a Nationality Group in America," in Peter D. Jones and Melvin Holli, *Ethnic Chicago* (Grand Rapids, MI, 1981), 165–73; and Steven A. Riess, *Touching Base: Professional Baseball and American Culture in the Progressive Era* (Westport, CT, 1980). On Italians, see John H. Mariano, *The Italian Contribution to American Democracy* (Boston, 1921). On Jewish American sport, see Bernard Postal, Jesse Silver, and Roy Silver, *Encyclopedia of Jews in Sports* (New York, 1965) which has many interesting anecdotes, however a few of the subjects are incorrectly identified as Jewish. Peter Levine, *From Ellis Island to Ebbets Field: Sport and the American Jewish Experience* (New York, 1992) is excellent on Brooklyn, but the work mainly focuses on the post–1920s. See also Benjamin Rabinowitz, *The Young Men's Hebrew Association, 1854–1913* (New York, 1948); and Cary Goodman, *Choosing Sides: Playground and Street Life on the Lower East Side* (New York, 1979), for Jewish German-American attitudes. This book, however, is marred by ideological fallacies. The negative attitudes to sport of Russian immigrants are described in Irving Louis Howe, *World of Our Fathers* (New York, 1976). On boxing, see Steven A. Riess, "The Jewish American Boxing Experience, 1890–1940," *American-Jewish History* 56 (1985): 223–54; Levine, *From Ellis Island to*

Ebbets Field; and William B. Kramer and Norton B. Stern, "San Francisco's Fighting Jew," *California History* 53 (1974): 333–45, on Joe Choynski, the first great Jewish American heavyweight. The literature on African American sports is extensive and of high quality. A lot of information on black sports can be found in Arthur Ashe's encyclopedic *A Hard Road to Glory: A History of the Afro-American Athlete, 1619–1986*, 3 vols. (New York, 1988). For a survey of the literature, see David K. Wiggins, "From Plantation to Playing Field: Historical Writings on the Black Athlete in American Sport," *Research Quarterly* 57 (1986): 101–16. The fascinating history of black baseball was first explored in Robert Peterson, *Only the Ball Was White* (Englewood Cliffs, NJ, 1970), supplemented by John B. Holway, *Blackball Stars: Negro League Pioneers* (Westport, CT, 1988). For an early history by a contemporary, see Sol White, *Sol White's Official Baseball Guide* (1907; reprint, Philadelphia, 1984). For valuable interviews, see John B. Holway, *Voices From the Great Black Baseball Leagues* (New York, 1975). Most of the literature focuses on the post–1920s, including Donn Rogosin's *Invisible Men: Life in Baseball's Negro Leagues* (Boston, 1983). He emphasizes that Negro League teams were important community institutions and among the largest black businesses in the interwar era; and Janet Bruce's *The Kansas City Monarchs: Champions of Black Baseball* (Lawrence, KS, 1985).

On racism and professional African American athletics, see, e.g., David K. Wiggins, "Isaac Murphy: Black Hero in Nineteenth-Century American Sport, 1861–1896," *Canadian Journal of History of Sport and Physical Education* 10 (May 1979): 15–32, which examines the career of the outstanding nineteenth-century jockey; and David K. Wiggins, "Peter Jackson and the Elusive Heavyweight Championship: A Black Athlete's Struggle Against the Late-Nineteenth-Century Color Line," *Journal of Sport History* 12 (1985): 143–68, on a ranking contender who never got a title shot. Al-Tony Gilmore, *Bad Nigger! The National Impact of Jack Johnson* (Port Washington, NY, 1975), explores American fears of the black heavyweight champion. Some themes are largely derived from William H. Wiggins, Jr., "Jack

Johnson as Bad Nigger: The Folklore of His Life," *Black Scholar* 2 (1971): 35–41. For a more sophisticated treatment, see Randy Roberts, *Papa Jack: Jack Johnson and the Era of White Hopes* (New York, 1983), which makes extensive use of classified FBI files to give a complete and well-rounded picture of Johnson. On cyclist champion Marshall W. "Major" Taylor, see his autobiography, *The Fastest Bicycle Rider in the World* (1927; reprint, Battleboro, VT, 1972), and the fine biography by Andrew Ritchie, *Major Taylor: The Extraordinary Career of a Champion Bicycle Racer* (San Francisco, 1988). See also John Carroll, *Fritz Pollard: Pioneer in Racial Advancement* (Urbana, IL, 1992), a biography of one of the first black All-Americans, and the first African American National Football League head coach.

Sport in black communities is briefly discussed in such works as Somers, *The Rise of Sports in New Orleans*; Allan Spear, *Black Chicago* (Chicago, 1967); Kenneth L. Kusmer, *A Ghetto Takes Shape: Black Cleveland, 1870–1930* (Urbana, IL, 1976); and Howard Rabinowitz, *Race Relations in the Urban South, 1865–1890* (Urbana, IL, 1980). Rob Ruck, *Sandlot Seasons: Sport in Black Pittsburgh* (Urbana, IL, 1987) is a model local study that shows how sports helped Pittsburgh's black neighborhoods after the turn of the century to carve out their own arenas of creativity, expression, and organization. There is some information on the black YMCA movement in C. Howard Hopkins, *The History of the Y.M.C.A. in North America* (New York, 1951). On recreational facilities in southern cities, see James F. Murphy, "Egalitarianism and Separatism: A History of Approaches in the Provision of Public Recreation and Leisure Services for Blacks, 1906–1972" (Ph.D. diss., Ohio State University, 1972). On segregated southern parks see Rabinowitz, *Race Relations*; Somers, *Rise of Sports in New Orleans*; and Carl V. Harris, *Political Power in Birmingham, 1871–1921* (Knoxville, TN, 1977). For Chicago parks, see Chicago Commission on Race Relations, *Negro in Chicago*; Spear, *Black Chicago*; and Tuttle, *Race Riot*.

The impact of welfare capitalism on black sports is briefly examined in James Grossman, *Land of Hope: Chicago, Black Southerners and the Great Migration* (Chicago, 1989). On African American women, see Gwendolyn Captain, "Enter Ladies and Gentlemen of Color: Gender, Sport and the Ideal of African American Manhood and Womanhood During the Late Nineteenth and Early Twentieth Centuries," *Journal of Sport History* 18 (1991): 81–102.

Sport and the Educational Process

The relationship between sport and education has received considerable attention. A good place to begin on college sports is Ronald A. Smith, *Sports & Freedom: The Rise of Big-Time College Athletics* (New York, 1988). Smith focuses on Harvard and Yale from the beginnings of intercollegiate sport through 1906, when the National Collegiate Athletic Association was established. He argues that Oxford and Cambridge provided role models for elite American colleges, that the fundamental nature of modern college sport was achieved before the turn of the century, and, somewhat elliptically, that the development of intercollegiate sports was always connected to the idea of freedom. Students were originally free to develop their own extracurricular activities, but over time freedom in intercollegiate sports meant institutional autonomy to deal with athletics as administrators felt best. See also Robin D. Lester, *Stagg's University: The Rise, Decline and Fall of Big-Time Football* (Urbana, IL, 1995), which provides a fascinating narrative of Amos Alonzo Stagg's career. Lester also analyzes the purpose of establishing a high-profile sports program at a new research-oriented university, describes the life of the college star-athlete, and evaluates the impact of football on the college community. Oriard in *Reading Football* points out that the rise of football occurred in the late nineteenth century, simultaneously with the great boom in American newspapers and magazines. His thesis is that the daily press largely created football as a popular spectacle. He analyzes how football narratives developed often contradictory versions of what the sport meant. On the early days of Notre Dame football, see Murray Sperber, *Shake Down the Thunder: The Creation of Notre Dame Football* (New York, 1993). See also

Guy M. Lewis, "The American Intercollegiate Football Spectacle, 1869–1917" (Ph.D. diss., University of Maryland, 1963); and Patrick B. Miller, "Athletes in Academe: College Sports and American Culture, 1850–1920" (Ph.D. diss., University of California, Berkeley, 1987), a wide-ranging study of manly values and intercollegiate sports. More specialized studies include John H. Moore, "Football's Ugly Decades, 1893–1913," *Smithsonian Journal of History* 2 (1967): 49–68 (reprinted in Riess, ed., *American Sporting Experience*), and Roberta J. Park, "From Football to Rugby—and Back, 1906–1919: The University of California–Stanford Response to the Football Crisis of 1905," *Journal of Sport History* 11 (1984): 15–40. On the origins of crew, the first intercollegiate sport, see Guy M. Lewis, "The Beginning of Intercollegiate Sport," *American Quarterly* 22 (1970): 222–29; and "America's First Intercollegiate Sport: The Regattas from 1852 to 1875," *Research Quarterly* 38 (1967): 637–48.

On youth sport there is a lot of useful information in Gems, "Sport and Culture Formation in Chicago." The best study of elementary-school sport is J. Thomas Jable, "The Public Schools Athletic League of New York City: Organized Athletics for City School Children, 1903–1914," in Riess, ed., *American Sporting Experience*. On secondary schools, see Jeffrey Miral, "From State Control to Institutional Control of High School Athletics: Three Michigan Cities, 1883–1905," *Journal of Social History* 16 (1982): 82–99; Timothy O'Hanlon, "School Sports as Social Training: The Case of Athletics and the Crisis of World War I," *Journal of Sport History* 9 (1982): 1–14; Joel Spring, "Mass Culture and School Sports," *History of Education Quarterly* 14 (1974): 483–95; and Hardy, *How Boston Played*. On the development of physical education, see Wilma Pesavento, "A Historical Study of the Development of Physical Education in the Chicago Public Schools, 1860 to 1965" (Ph.D. diss., Northwestern University, 1966).

Historians have analyzed the acculturating function of adult-directed play and sports at playgrounds and such institutions as the YMCA, settlement houses, and youth sport leagues. The history of the play movement is summarized by Lee Rainwater, *The*

Play Movement in the United States (Chicago, 1922). On the municipal park movement in New York, see Richard Knapp, "Parks and Politics: The Rise of Municipal Responsibility for Playgrounds in New York City, 1887–1905" (M.A. Thesis, Duke University, 1968). For a study that emphasizes the role of elites, see Jerry A. Dickason, "The Development of the Playground Movement in the United States: A Historical Survey" (Ph.D. diss., New York University, 1979). The philosophical underpinnings of the play movement and structured play are examined in Donald J. Mrozek, "The Natural Limits of Unstructured Play, 1880–1914," in Grover, ed., *Hard at Play*, 18–46; Dominick Cavallo, *Muscles and Morals: Organized Playgrounds and Urban Reform, 1880–1920* (Philadelphia, 1981); Bernard Mergen, "The Discovery of Children's Play," *American Quarterly* 27 (1975): 399–420; and Mark Kadzielski, "'As a Flower Needs Sunshine': The Origins of Organized Children's Recreation in Philadelphia, 1886–1911," *Journal of Sport History* 4 (1977): 169–88.

There is an extensive literature on juvenile sports. A good place to begin is Rader, *American Sports*. For more specialized studies, see Hardy, *How Boston Played*; Paul Boyer, *Urban Masses and Moral Order in America, 1820–1920* (Cambridge, MA, 1978); David I. Macleod, *Building Character in the American Boy: The Boy Scouts, YMCA and Their Forerunners, 1870–1920* (Madison, WI, 1983); Cavallo, *Muscles and Morals*; Goodman, *Choosing Sides*; David Nasaw, *Children of the City: At Work and At Play* (New York, 1986); and Lawrence A. Finfer, "Leisure and Social Work in the Urban Community: The Progressive Recreation Movement, 1890–1920" (Ph.D. diss., Michigan State University, 1974). For a summary of contemporary studies of street youth activities, see Alan Havig, "The Commercial Amusement Audience in 20th Century American Cities," *Journal of American Culture* 5 (1982): 1–19.

On the Y movement, see Boyer, *Urban Masses*; Hardy, *How Boston Played*; Elmer L. Johnson, *The History of YMCA Physical Education* (Chicago, 1979); Hopkins, *History of the Y.M.C.A.*; Macleod, *Building Character*; Betts, *America's Sporting Heritage*; and Aaron Abell, *The Urban Impact of American Protestantism,*

1865–1900 (Cambridge, MA, 1943). Evangelical Protestants were very concerned about the problem of sexual awakening. See Adelman, *A Sporting Time*; and Charles E. Rosenberg, "Sexuality, Class, and Role in Nineteenth Century America," *American Quarterly* 25 (1973): 131–53. On the impact of muscular Christianity on the adult-directed boys' sport movement, see Rader, *American Sports*. On the attitudes of Luther Gulick, see his *A Philosophy of Play* (New York, 1920); Rader, *American Sports*; Jable, "Public Schools Athletic League"; and Stephanie Wallach, "Luther Halsey Gulick and the Salvation of the American Adolescent" (Ph.D. diss., Columbia University, 1989).

On the role of settlement houses in the youth sports movement, see Allen F. Davis, *Spearheads for Reform: The Social Settlement and the Progressive Movement, 1890–1914* (New York, 1967); and Cavallo, *Muscles and Morals*; and Boyer, *Urban Masses*. See also Jane Addams, *The Spirit of Youth and the City Streets* (New York, 1909); and *Twenty Years at Hull-House* (1910; reprint, New York, 1990).

Professional Sports

A lot of excellent work has been done on professional sports. On prizefighting, one should begin with Adelman, *A Sporting Time*, for information on midcentury New York pugilism, and Gorn, *The Manly Art*, an excellent analysis of the bare-knuckle era. For a detailed study of boxing in two of its major loci, see Somers, *The Rise of Sports in New Orleans*; William H. Adams, "New Orleans as the National Center of Boxing," *Louisiana Historical Quarterly* 39 (1956): 92–112; and Steven Riess, "In the Ring and Out: Professional Boxing in New York, 1896–1920," in *Sport in America*, ed. Donald Spivey (Westport, CT, 1985), which is especially valuable for its analysis of boxing's connections to urban political machines and organized crime. See also Thomas M. Croak, "The Professionalization of Prize-Fighting: Pittsburgh at the Turn of the Century," *Western Pennsylvania Historical Magazine* 62 (1979): 333–43; and James Chinello, "The Great Goldfield Foul," *Westways* 68 (September 1976): 27–30. On the impact of World War I on the legalization of boxing, see Guy M. Lewis, "World War I and the Emergence of Sport for the Masses," *The Maryland Historian* 4 (1973): 109–22. On Madison Square Garden, see Joseph Durso, *Madison Square Garden: 100 Years of History* (New York, 1979); and Riess, *City Games*.

Biographies are an important segment of the boxing literature. See Randy Roberts, *Jack Dempsey: The Manassa Mauler* (Baton Rouge, LA, 1979); and *Papa Jack*. See also Isenberg, *John L. Sullivan and His America*, a biography of the greatest nineteenth-century sports hero that also describes the male bachelor subculture that was abhorred by the respectable classes; and Robert Catwell, *The Real McCoy: The Life and Times of Norman Selby* (Princeton, NJ, 1971), an informative biography of a leading turn-of-the-century fighter. The autobiographies, John L. Sullivan, *I Can Lick Any Sonofabitch in the House!* (New York, 1980); and Jack Johnson, *In the Ring and Out* (Chicago, 1927) must be used with caution. On the early career of promoter Tex Rickard, see Mrs. Tex Rickard, *Everything Happened to Him: The Story of Tex Rickard* (New York, 1936).

For popular overviews of thoroughbred racing, see Robertson, *The History of Thoroughbred Racing in America*; C. B. Parmer, *For Gold and Glory: The History of Thoroughbred Racing in America* (New York, 1939); and William S. Vosburgh, *Racing in America, 1866–1921* (n.p., 1921). For the sport's ties with gambling, see Henry Chayfetz, *Play the Devil: A History of Gambling in the United States From 1492 to 1955* (New York, 1960); and Asbury, *Sucker's Progress*. For a more scholarly perspective, see David R. Johnson, "A Sinful Business: The Origins of Gambling Syndicates in the United States, 1840–1887," in *Police and Society*, ed. David H. Bayley (Beverly Hills, CA, 1977). Adelman's *A Sporting Time* is essential for an understanding of the modernization of harness racing and the mid-nineteenth-century development of thoroughbred racing in New York. See also his "Quantification and Sport: The American Jockey Club, 1866–1867, A Collective Biography," in Spivey, ed., *Sport in America*, 51–65. Considerable attention is given to the turf in Somers, *Rise of Sports in New Orleans*; and Riess, *City Games*, which analyzes the nexus that emerged between the turf, professional politics, and organized crime to facilitate illegal gambling. On the relationship between Chicago's horse racing and its levee district machine, see Herman Kogan and Lloyd Wendt, *Lords of the Levee: The Story of Bathhouse John and Hinky Dink* (Indianapolis, IN, 1943).

The literature on professional sports is richest on baseball, which was the first sport to get serious scholarly attention. The place to begin is Harold Seymour's *Baseball*, 3 vols. (New York, 1960–90), a beautifully written, painstakingly researched (albeit unfootnoted) trilogy. *Baseball: The Early Years* (vol. 1) and *Baseball: The Golden Age* (vol. 2) examines the emergence of baseball from a simple antebellum boys' game into a popular commercial spectator sport operated as a monopsony. Seymour regards baseball's development as a reflection of contemporary industrial capitalism. *The Golden Age* is a definitive study of major-league baseball in the period from 1900 to 1930. The third volume, *Baseball: The People's Game*, is a far-ranging study that examines all aspects of amateur baseball, including sandlots, colleges, and prisons, as well as women's participation and professional black baseball. Much of Seymour's work on the major leagues is paralleled by David Voigt's *American Baseball*, a three-volume work that brings the history of major-league baseball up to the 1980s (Norman, OK, 1966–71; University Park, PA, 1983). The three volumes are summarized by Voigt in *Baseball: An Illustrated History* (University Park, PA, 1987). For single-volume histories, see Charles A. Alexander, *Our Game: An American Baseball History* (New York, 1991), and especially Benjamin G. Rader, *Baseball: A History of America's National Game* (Urbana, IL, 1992).

Seymour's and Voigt's analyses of baseball's early days have been supplanted by Adelman, *A Sporting Time*; Kirsch, *The Creation of American Team Sports*; and Warren Goldstein, *Playing for Keeps: A History of Early Baseball* (Ithaca, NY, 1989). They demonstrate how a boys' game became a popular, modern, middle-class pastime, supplanting cricket as the leading team sport. Goldstein's slender work is less well researched than either Adelman or Kirsch, but he presents some interesting ideas. Goldstein points out that the game has both a linear and cyclical history. He also argues that in the 1860s baseball began to be played for keeps, stressing the spirit of work over the element of fun through the rise of championship seasons, scientific play, and greater demands for victory.

There are several specialized studies of baseball. For an examination of how baseball's ideology influenced public behavior at the turn of the century, when it was unchallenged as the national pastime, see Riess, *Touching Base*. On baseball and urban politics, see Riess, *Touching Base*; and Vincent, *Mudville's Revenge*. For additional studies of baseball and cultural values, see Richard Crepeau, *Baseball: America's Diamond Mind, 1919–1941* (Orlando, FL, 1980); and Leverett T. Smith, Jr., *The American Dream and the National Game* (Bowling Green, OH, 1975). On the composition of crowds, see Kirsch, *The Creation of American Team Sports*; and Riess, *City Games*, who argues that commercialized baseball sought and attracted a largely middle-class crowd, contradicting the conclusions Allen Guttmann draws in *Sports Spectators* (New York, 1986), asserting that spectators were mainly working class.

On the business history of baseball, see Robert F. Burk, *Never Just A Game: Players, Owners, & American Baseball to 1920* (Chapel Hill, NC, 1994), a study of labor-management conflict primarily based on secondary sources marred by questionable statistics, and Peter Levine, *A. G. Spalding and the Rise of Baseball: The Promise of American Sport* (New York, 1985), which analyzes Spalding's ownership of the Chicago National League club, his leadership in the National League, and his entrepreneurial activities in the sporting goods industry. Eugene C. Murdock, *Ban Johnson: Czar of Baseball* (Westport, CT, 1982), examines the life of the founding president of the American League and such issues as the war for recognition with the National League, Johnson's recruitment of magnates, and labor-management disputes. For a general analysis of sport and business, see three of Stephen Hardy's works: "Entrepreneurs, Organization and the Sport Marketplace," *Journal of Sport History* 13 (1986): 14–33; "Entrepreneurs, Structures, and the Sportgeist: Old Tensions in Modern Industry," in *Essays on Sport History and Sport Mythology*, ed. Donald G. Kyle and Gary Stark (College Station, TX, 1990), 83–117; and "Adopted by All the Leading Clubs: Sporting Goods and the Shaping of Leisure, 1860–1900," in *For Fun and Profit: The Transformation of Leisure into Consumption*, ed. Richard Butsch (Philadelphia, 1990), 71–101.

On major-league ballparks, see Riess, *City Games*; David John Kammer, "Take Me Out to the Ballgame: American Cultural Values as Reflected in the Architectural Evolution and Criticism of the Modern Baseball Stadium" (Ph.D. diss., University of New Mexico, 1982); and Michael Gershman, *Diamonds: The Evolution of the Ballpark* (Boston, 1993), an excellent illustrated history. For basic reference, see Philip J. Lowry, *Green Cathedrals* (Reading, MA, 1992); and Michael Benson, *Ballparks of North America: A Comprehensive Historical Reference to Baseball Grounds, Yards, and Stadiums, 1845 to the Present* (Jefferson, NC, 1989), which is largely derivative. On ballparks and their neighboring communities, see Bruce Kuklick, *To Every Thing a Season: Shibe Park and Urban Philadelphia, 1909–1976* (Princeton, NJ, 1991); and Riess, *City Games*. Gunther Barth's chapter, "Ballpark," in his *City People*, is a provocative discussion of baseball's role in promoting a homogeneous urban culture. He emphasizes the psychological impact of urbanization and the ways the park promoted a sense of shared identity among sports fans. His conclusions, however, based on dubious assumptions, erroneous inferences, and factual misstatements, are unreliable.

On labor relations, see Lee Lowenfish, *The Imperfect Diamond: A History of Baseball's Labor Wars*, rev. ed. (New York, 1992). Excellent interviews of early-twentieth-century ballplayers appear in Lawrence Ritter's *The Glory of Their Times* (New York, 1966). For biographies of two prominent players see Charles C.

Alexander's *Ty Cobb* (New York, 1984) and *John J. McGraw* (New York, 1988). On baseball and professional sports as an avenue of social mobility, see Riess, *City Games*; and "Sport and Social Mobility: American Myth or Reality," in Kyle and Stark, eds., *Essays on Sport History*, 83–117.

On early professional basketball, see Robert W. Peterson, *Cage to Jump Shots: Pro Basketball's Early Years* (New York, 1990); and Vincent's *Mudville's Revenge*. On early professional football, see Marc Maltby, "The Origin and Early Development of Professional Football, 1890–1920" (Ph.D. diss., Ohio State University, 1987); J. Thomas Jable, "The Birth of Professional Football: Pittsburgh Athletic Clubs Ring in Professionals in 1902," *Western Pennsylvania Historical Magazine* 62 (1979): 136–47; and Tom Bennett et al., *The NFL's Official Encyclopedic History of Professional Football* (New York, 1979). The literature on professional track is pretty sparse, but Vincent, *Mudville's Revenge*, is particularly good on nineteenth-century working-class track and field. Vincent reported some extraordinary professional records, but without attribution. See also John Cumming, *Runners & Walkers: A Nineteenth-Century Chronicle* (Chicago, 1981); and John A. Lucas, "Pedestrianism and the Struggle for the Sir John Astley Belt, 1878–1879," *Research Quarterly* 39 (1968): 587–95. On America at the Olympics, see Allen Guttmann, *The Olympics: A History of the Modern Games* (Urbana, IL, 1992); and Steven W. Pope, "American Muscles and Minds: Public Discourse and the Shaping of National Identity During Early Olympiads, 1896–1920," *Journal of American Culture* 15 (1992): 83–94.

INDEX

About the author: Steven A. Riess is professor of history at Northeastern Illinois University. His other books include *Society and the Rise of Sports* and *City Games: The Evolution of American Urban Society and the Rise of Sports.* He was recently a consultant for Ken Burns *Baseball* shown on PBS television stations.

Sport in Industrial America, 1850–1920 was copyedited by Claudia Lamm Wood and proofread by Andrew J. Davidson. Production editor was Lucy Herz. The text was set by Robin M. Stearns and printed and bound by BookCrafters, Inc.